CW01017631

15-95

MEDICAL AND SCIENTIFIC ASPECTS OF CYCLING

Edmund R. Burke, PhD
Spenco Medical Corporation

Mary M. Newsom, MLS
United States Olympic Committee

Editors

Human Kinetics Books
Champaign, Illinois

Library of Congress Cataloging-in-Publication Data

Medical and scientific aspects of cycling.

Bibliography: p.
1. Cycling—Physiological aspects. 2. Human mechanics.
I. Burke, Ed, 1949– . II. Newsom, Mary Margaret.
RC1220.C8M43   1988   612'.04   87-3321
ISBN 0-87322-126-5

Senior Editor: Gwen Steigelman, PhD
Production Director: Ernie Noa
Projects Manager: Lezli Harris
Assistant Editor: Phaedra Hise
Copy Editor: Laura E. Larson and Patrick Hayes
Proofreader: Laurie McGee
Typesetter: Sonnie Bowman
Text Design: Keith Blomberg
Text Layout: Cathy Romans
Cover Design: Jack Davis
Printed By: Braun-Brumfield

ISBN: 0-87322-126-5

Proceedings of the 1986 World Congress on the Medical and Scientific Aspects of Cycling held September 2-3, 1986 in Colorado Springs, CO.

Printed in the United States of America

10 9 8 7 6 5 4 3 2 1

Human Kinetics Books
A Division of Human Kinetics Publishers, Inc.
Box 5076, Champaign, IL 61820
1-800-DIAL-HKP
1-800-334-3665 (in Illinois)

Contents

Preface

The 1986 Congress on the Medical and Scientific Aspects of Cycling was conceived to provide a forum at the 1986 World Cycling Championships for an exchange of current information and ideas on cycling research, medical care, and training. The major objectives of the Congress were to analyze and communicate the current state of knowledge and to explore potentially fruitful lines of future communication. To this end, the Congress was a success.

Many of the renowned scientists, medical personnel, and coaches on the faculty prepared their papers so as to share their ideas in an applied and integrated way for use by individuals in all fields of cycling. Let us hope these papers not only give information summaries, but constitute another step in the development of studies on biomechanics, performance, training, and so forth, and in the promotion of future cycling research.

The Congress was planned and organized by the United States Cycling Federation and was funded by a generous grant from the Southland Corporation. Additional support was received from Spenco Medical Corporation and MAX Athletic Drink. Without the support of these sponsors, the Congress would not have been possible; their contributions to its success are gratefully acknowledged.

The Congress has ended and the publication of its proceedings is now complete, but that does not mean that the work is finished. It must continue. Close cooperation is a prerequisite if the plans initiated by the Congress are to be successfully implemented. We believe that this Congress, attended by representatives of many countries, professed the necessary attitude of cooperation, and we look to the future with bright hopes for the sport of cycling.

Edmund R. Burke, PhD
Mary Margaret Newsom

PART I

Biomechanics and Physiology

Pathomechanics of the Lower Extremity in Cycling

Peter R. Francis

For the greater part of the 20th century the bicycle has been an important form of transportation for millions of people all over the world. Indeed, in some countries the bicycle is still the only viable alternative to domesticated animals as a means of transporting both people and goods from one place to another. No doubt the success of this ingenious machine can be attributed to its cost-effectiveness in terms of both economics and human resources. In the former case, the bicycle is easy to maintain and its running costs are low. In the latter case, it has a remarkable record of safety.

The safety record of the bicycle is especially intriguing in view of the complexity of the skill involved. The rider is required to balance upon an unstable system while simultaneously providing motive forces and controlling both speed and direction. Perhaps the ease with which human beings accomplish this seemingly monumental task is due to the fact that it may require the use of simple and conditioned balancing reflexes that are utilized in both walking and running gait. In fact, Basmajian (1976) used the analogy of cycling to explain some of the kinematic characteristics of human walking gait. Another factor that contributes to the safety of the conventional bicycle is the comfortable seated posture that provides an unobstructed view of the environment. Therefore, on any reasonably flat surface where the rider is not subjected to competition for free passage from larger and faster vehicles, the rider can reasonably assume that the chance of becoming harmed is not much greater than if he or she chose to walk in the same location.

In countries where basic needs can be met in less than 24 hr in a day, bicycling has also become an extremely popular leisure and competitive sporting activity. Unfortunately in these endeavors the safety record of the bicycle is less auspicious. However, this is hardly surprising when one considers that many cyclists venture into hazardous environments such as urban highways, deserts, and mountains. Each of these environments subjects the machine and the rider to stresses that are absent during normal use of the bicycle. Furthermore, successful and highly motivated competitors repeatedly subject themselves to potentially dangerous situations involving close proximity to other competitors and extremely rapid descents on steep inclines. These same riders often progressively increase the intensity, frequency, and duration of training and competition to levels close to the limits of mechanical tolerance of the human body. Under these conditions the injury rate becomes a cause for some concern, but it remains remarkably low when all of these factors are taken into consideration.

An examination of the literature reveals a surprising paucity of information dealing with cycling injuries. However, cyclists can become injured in two distinctly different ways (Francis, 1986; Leadbetter & Schneider, 1982). The first involves instantaneous traumatic situations such as falls or collisions, and the second involves the repetitive stresses that are placed upon the body of the cyclist during prolonged training and competition. These latter injuries can be classified as *overuse injuries*. For the purpose of background information the former will be mentioned briefly here, but the main focus of this chapter is on overuse injuries.

Instantaneous Trauma Injuries

In many cases instantaneous trauma injuries are superficial and go without medical attention; therefore, determining the frequency with which they occur is impossible. However, during the time that the National Electronic Injury Surveillance System was used to collect injury data in the United States, almost 20,000 bicycle accidents were reported to medical facilities in a single year (1978). On the basis of available data, it was estimated that about 448,000 bicycle accidents actually occurred in the United States during the same year.

On the basis of a newspaper questionnaire together with personal interviews and observations of competitive cyclists, Bohlmann (1981) concluded that most injuries occur to the left-hand side of the body of the cyclist and take the form of abrasions. The most common causes of injuries appeared to be flat tires and collisions with other cyclists, but "98% of injured cyclists returned to cycling in less than a week and to competition within a month, including 18 of the 23 riders who sustained fractures" (p. 117).

Overuse Injuries

By definition, overuse injuries occur when the cumulative effects of repetitive stress exceed the tolerance limits of specific anatomical structures. In common with all mechanical systems, the human body is subject to failure if excessive mechanical stress in the forms of compression, tension, bending, torsion, and shear forces are exerted upon its various components (Frankel & Nordin, 1980). If the stresses are the results of participation in gross motor activities such as vigorous sports, failures usually occur in the structures that are responsible for maintaining the mechanical integrity of the body, that is, in the musculoskeletal system. This system includes muscles, tendons, bones, ligaments, and joints. Tendons are flexible cords that transmit muscle forces to the bones. Ligaments are flexible bands that connect bones to adjacent bones and restrict the motions of joints. The site of any mechanical failure depends on both the specific stresses to which the body is subjected and the mechanical resiliency of the various components.

Specifically, bone can withstand considerable compressive loads, but it fails relatively easily under bending stress. In the latter case bone will fracture soon after exceeding its elastic limits. In addition, high frequency shock waves produced by repetitive impact forces can produce stress fractures that are remarkably similar to those observed in nonorganic materials such as metals and ceramics.

Connective tissues such as ligament and tendon are viscoelastic in nature. That is, when they are subjected to tension they will initially behave like an elastic spring that returns to its resting length when tension is removed. If the tension stress exceeds the elastic limit of the material, the tissue will become plastic and it will continue to elongate with no further increase in the tensile loading. If the tension is within certain tolerance limits the tissue will subsequently "creep" back to its original length over a period of time following removal of the stress. If the tension stress is excessive, or if the same tension stress is applied before the original length is resumed, these tissues may be irreversibly lengthened. Finally, extremely high levels of tension can completely rupture tendons and ligaments. Ruptures of these tissues are especially serious because, unlike bones and muscles, which have rich blood supplies, these important structures are incapable of self-repair. They must therefore be reconnected by surgical procedures.

The actual tolerance of biological tissues depends upon both genetic and environmental factors. For example, it has been shown that the density of bone is determined by the degree of mineralization. This, in turn, determines the mechanical strength of the bone (Smith, 1981). Some individuals are born with relatively high bone density, whereas others tend to possess rather low bone density. However, diet and activity patterns can both affect density. Specifically, calcium deficiency has been linked to low density, especially among females, and prolonged inactivity is associated with a decrease in bone mineralization. Similarly, it has been demonstrated that mechanical stress produced by vigorous exercise can result in a compensatory increase in the tensile strength of ligaments and tendons (Booth & Gould, 1975). However, it would appear that dramatic increases in the intensity, frequency, or duration of training can create stresses that exceed the current mechanical tolerance limits of the body. It has therefore been recommended that training levels be gradually increased over a period of time so that compensatory improvements in the resiliency of the musculoskeletal system can keep pace with the additional mechanical stresses imposed by an increasingly demanding training regimen (American College of Sports Medicine, 1986).

The factors discussed above illustrate that the ability to withstand mechanical stress depends on the individual. It is also apparent that if training-induced stress increases gradually over time, the compensatory increase in the resiliency of the musculoskeletal system will permit progressively greater stress to be tolerated by the system. Over the short term the likelihood of failure will always increase as the total amount of stress is increased. These facts explain why some individuals can remain injury-free despite fairly high levels of training and competitive stress, whereas other riders are often injured at relatively modest levels of training. On the other hand, these factors also explain the observed tendency for greater pain and discomfort as both mileage and cycling intensity are increased, especially if any such changes take place within a relatively short period of time.

Typically, the adverse effects of mechanical stresses gradually create changes in the anatomical tissue involved, and the nervous system begins to provide feedback by registering discomfort. As the mechanical damage to the tissues becomes progressively more severe over time, the feedback will take the form of pain. If the mechanical stresses producing the damage are continued, in spite of the pain, the damage will inevitably progress until it creates a significant injury. In other words, overuse injuries do not rehabilitate themselves; they simply continue to become worse over time. Unfortunately, athletes tend to tolerate overuse injuries even though they readily seek medical attention for less serious instantaneous trauma injuries caused by falls or collisions. There do not appear to be any available data to indicate the extent of the consequences of ignoring overuse injuries, but it has been reported that the average length of time between the onset of overuse symptoms and seeking specialized medical advice for people engaged in exercise classes is 4.8 months (Vetter, Helfet, Spear, & Mathews, 1985). Medical experts have indicated that rehabilitation after prolonged overuse is inevitably slower and more complicated than in cases where treatment is sought during the initial stages of the development of an overuse injury. Furthermore, these same experts have indicated that certain individuals are predictably more prone to injuries of this kind. This leads to a consideration of pathomechanical injuries.

Pathomechanical Injuries

Pathomechanical cycling injuries can be defined as overuse injuries that result from incompatibilities between the cyclist and the bicycle. Incompatibilities result from differences between the fixed motion patterns of the drive mechanism of a bicycle and the complex anatomical motion patterns of the individual cyclist. Shortcomings in the anatomy of a cyclist may prevent him or her from maintaining the undersurface of the ball of the foot in a fixed position with respect to the top of the pedal while it is moving in a perfect circle. Therefore, when the foot and pedal are firmly attached together with a cleat and toe clip, the foot will try to force the pedal to deviate from its circular motion pattern. At the same time, the pedal will try to force the foot to deviate from its complex motion pattern. Unfortunately, the strength of the pedal and crank greatly exceeds the strength of the foot and leg's anatomical structures, and so the foot and leg are forced to perform motions that can place dangerous stresses upon the bones and joints of the cyclist.

A cyclist who suffers from the early signs of a pathomechanical overuse injury has only three roads to recovery. The first option is to remove the repetitive damaging stress by becoming inactive. The second alternative is to make anatomically acceptable changes in the human body so that the cyclist can conform to the motion pattern of the bicycle. The final alternative is to make mechanically feasible changes in the bicycle so that the machine will function within the constraints of the rider's anatomy. The first alternative, that of rest, is unacceptable to many enthusiastic riders, so the remainder of this chapter will consist of a review of anatomical factors that appear to predispose cyclists to pathomechanical injuries. Experience has shown that it is frequently possible to predict the mechanical relationships between anatomical shortcomings and specific injuries. An understanding of the mechanical factors involved can often be used to prescribe corrective measures that may alleviate symptoms of overuse stresses.

The following descriptions of cycling pathomechanics are based upon clinical observations and preliminary research investigations. However, the limited data available are consistent with our knowledge of anatomy and with the laws of mechanics. As more detailed research is completed the relationship between anatomical structure and mechanical function will become more precisely established. At this time the prudent clinician will utilize the information with discretion and will keep abreast of future developments in this relatively new area of investigation.

Conditions Predisposing the Cyclist to Pathomechanical Injuries

Excessive Pronation

The human foot possesses an ingenious shock-absorbing mechanism. When weight is suddenly placed on the sole of the foot the longitudinal arch that runs along the inner border becomes flattened like a leaf spring. At the same time the front of the shank (the section of the lower leg between the ankle and the knee) pivots a few degrees inward so that the kneecap tends to rotate toward the midline of the body, as shown in Figure 1. When weight is removed from the foot, the elastic properties of the muscles and ligaments cause the arch to recoil back to its original elevated position. Simultaneously, the front of the shank pivots outward so that the kneecap once again faces forward.

These three-dimensional motions are created by the complex anatomy of the foot and ankle joint. The imaginary axis about which the ankle joint pivots is inclined downward and rearward toward the outer side of the foot. The ankle joint thereby constrains the foot to pivot in three planes of space. Similarly, two important joints in the foot that are involved in this motion (the subtalar and midtarsal joints) also have three-dimensional orientations. The two simultaneous motions consisting of a flattening of the arch and inward pivoting of the shank, together with a tendency to move the shin toward the top of the foot, comprise a complex three-dimensional motion known as *pronation*. The mechanism has been described in an earlier paper (Francis, 1986).

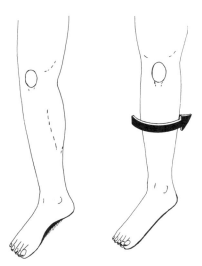

Figure 1   Inward twisting of the shank accompanying the flattening of the longitudinal arch of the foot.

High-speed videos and films of healthy cyclists confirm that the front of the shank tends to twist inward toward the midline of the body during the time that the foot is bearing heavy loads. This, of course, occurs when the foot is applying the most effective propulsion to the bicycle—on the downstroke. A great deal of the propulsive force can be attributed to powerful contractions of the quadriceps muscle group (Jorge & Hull, 1984). These muscles, which are situated on the front of the thigh, extend the knee joint by pulling upward on the kneecap. During the alternating extension and flexion of the knee that occur during the pedaling action, the kneecap slides smoothly up and down in a groove in the distal end of the thighbone (the femur).

Potential stress upon the cyclist's knee joint produced by the inward twisting motion of the shank tends to be alleviated by a simultaneous motion about the hip joint (adduction) that causes the cyclist's knee to move toward the midline of the body. Therefore the inward twisting motion of the shank appears to be quite normal; any stresses that result from the complex motion appear to fall within tolerance limits that are acceptable to the musculoskeletal system of the healthy cyclist. However, similar video and film examinations of cyclists who have had a history of recurrent knee pain have shown that some of them (but not all of them) have a tendency to show a more pronounced inward twisting of the shank during the propulsive phase of cycling. In other words, these latter individuals appear to pronate excessively. The excessive inward pivoting of the shank that occurs when there is a great deal of force pulling upward on the kneecap assumably causes the kneecap to be forced toward the outer wall of the groove of the femur. Surgical procedures have revealed that a recurrent rubbing of the kneecap on the outer wall of the groove can wear away the protective cartilage and eventually create an erosion of the bone itself. This can produce the painful condition known as *chondromalacia patella*, which is undoubtedly one of the commonest of those injuries often referred to collectively as *cyclist's knee*.

There are three corrective clinical procedures that may effectively reduce the inward twisting of the shank, and the moderately high success rate of the procedures tends to support the above description of the pathomechanical cause of this condition. The three procedures involve careful adjustments to mechanical devices, whereas a fourth approach to the problem involves an attempt to change the mechanics of muscles acting on the feet and knee joint.

In-shoe orthotics. Several cyclists who have been fitted with in-shoe pronation-control devices have shown both a reduction in the extent of inward twisting of the knees and a reduction in pain and discomfort of the knees. These in-shoe devices, known as orthotics, are designed as custom-fitted arch support mechanisms. In effect, they realign the various structures in the foot so that it behaves dynamically like a "desirable" or "neutral" foot, which is not subjected to excessive arch flattening.

Cleat adjustments. In an effort to alleviate knee pain, some cyclists have found temporary relief by trial-and-error adjustments of the position of their cleats so that the foot assumes an in-toed position (sometimes referred to as a pigeon-toed position) on the pedal. The mechanism by which this relieves stress on the knee is as follows. When the toes are turned inward to a pigeon-toed position the shank is effectively twisted outward with respect to the foot. This produces the opposite motion to that of pronation, a motion known as *supination*. Due to the three-dimensional orientations of the joints described earlier, the outward twisting of the shank is inevitably accompanied by a raising of the arch of the foot. Consequently, when the foot is loaded the elevated arch tends to prevent further inward twisting of the kneecap.

The procedure described above appears to have worked effectively for a number of fortunate cyclists. However, the fact that some riders who have tried the technique have later developed pain in other areas of the knee suggests that the pigeon-toed alignment of the feet may in fact twist the shank with respect to the thigh at the knee joint. The knee joint itself is a hinge joint rather than a ball-and-socket joint like the hip joint, and as such it is placed under potentially damaging stress if the articular surfaces are not "mated" with precision. Therefore, it is unwise to expect drastic pigeon-toed cleat adjustment to produce a long-term solution to cyclist's knee. If the technique is utilized, any adjustments should be made in very small increments and care should be taken to monitor any new discomfort.

Wedges. A third method of attempting to overcome stresses caused by excessive pronation involves various kinds of devices that elevate the inner border of the foot on the surface of the pedal. This tends to produce an outward twisting of the shank that ensures that the knee remains in its desirable tracking alignment in the groove of the head of the femur. The simplest device that can be used for this purpose is a wedge attached to either the top surface of the pedal or the sole or cleat of the shoe. Alternatively, the commercially available "Biopedal" permits precise adjustments to the "wedge angle" and, if necessary, simultaneous adjustments to the degree of in-toeing.

Anatomical intervention.   Finally, a number of therapists have advocated anatomical solutions to the problems associated with excessive pronation. Strengthening exercises for specific intrinsic and extrinsic muscles of the feet are often used to improve the muscular support for the arch mechanism of the foot (Francis, 1986). Some have reasoned that the increased tonus of these muscles will reduce the extent to which the arch mechanism is flattened when the foot is loaded, and the reduction in arch flattening will be accompanied by a reduction in the extent of inward twisting of the shank. Positive effects have been reported using this procedure, but some therapists believe that strengthening exercises of this kind are most effective for *maintaining* good arch mechanics, but may have limited effectiveness for actually *reducing* a condition that involves existing excessive pronation.

Another strengthening procedure that has been successfully used to reduce the severity of knee dysfunction involves the strengthening of the vastus medialis muscle. This is one of the four quadricep muscles that create powerful extensions of the knee joint (Figure 2). However, vastus medialis also has another vital function. Due to its oblique angle of pull it also tends to resist any tendency for the kneecap to be forced outward, away from the midline of the groove in the femur, and so it ensures that the kneecap glides smoothly up and down in its "track" in the knee joint. If this muscle is selectively strengthened, it will tend to overcome the tendency for the kneecap to be forced against the outer wall of the track during the time that pronation is excessive. Therapists have advocated a number of progressive resistance exercises for strengthening vastus medialis. Exercises using the last 15° of knee extension against resistance are often recommended, but there is some disagreement as to whether this actually strengthens vastus medialis any more effectively than the three other quadriceps muscles. Alternatively, it has been proposed that half-squatting exercises while balancing on one foot and knee extension exercises with the foot turned slightly outward ("duck-footed") may provide effective alternatives. Clearly, the problem needs further study.

In summary, there are a number of alternative ways of attempting to overcome the problem associated with excessive pronation in cyclists. Because of the precision necessary for effective orthotic control it would appear to be prudent to rely upon the expertise of a qualified professional such as an orthopedic surgeon or podiatrist for the prescription of custom-made orthotics. Furthermore, the cyclist should seek the assistance of an expert who is prepared to follow up on the effectiveness of the orthotics over a period of time. The cyclist may find in-shoe orthotics to be uncomfortable during initial usage. Often this can be relieved with minor adjustments, and in some cases they may require redesigning before they become effective. Unfortunately, a number of cyclists who have been fitted with orthotics have chosen to stop using them rather than endure discomfort. Because the problems associated with excessive pronation can only become worse in the absence of treatment, it is wise to continue to seek further assistance in order to determine the best possible corrective procedure.

The fitting of wedges and adjustments to the degree of in-toeing has been effective in some cases, but because of the potential danger of creating new injuries these techniques should be used with care. The technique that relies upon the strengthening of the vastus medialis muscle appears to be an intelligent approach for appropriate cyclists. However, advice should be sought from someone who has some academic knowledge of kinesiology. Although there are many well-informed people involved with strength training, the area is also associated with a certain amount of folklore and misconceptions.

Presently, there is no single clinical technique that is 100% effective in the treatment of knee problems caused by excessive pronation. As knee pain can be the result of factors other than excessive pronation, a careful diagnosis is a prerequisite to any form of treatment.

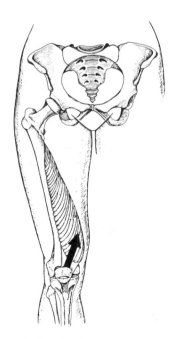

Figure 2 Vastus medialis muscle showing its approximate angle of pull on the kneecap.

Misalignments of the Foot, Shank, and Thigh

If the human foot, shank, and thigh were connected by simple parallel pin joints that permitted the cyclist's leg and foot to rotate in a single vertical plane, the motion of the cyclist would conform precisely to the motion of a bicycle pedal. However, as has already been discussed, the ankle, subtalar, and midtarsal joints create a three-dimensional motion pattern that can subject the cyclist to harmful stresses if pronation becomes excessive. Similarly, undesirable alignments of the knee joint can also predispose the cyclist to injuries in many ways.

Bowlegs and knock-knees.   In both of these cases the imaginary axis about which the knee joint pivots can actually be inclined at some angle from the horizontal when the cyclist is standing upright. If this is the case, there will be a tendency for the shank to pivot either to the outside or to the inside of a vertical plane when the cyclist rotates the pedals of the bicycle. If the foot is attached to a cleat and toe clip, the shank will be prevented from moving in this way by the pedal so that stresses will be placed upon the knee joint itself. However, the fact that a number of bowlegged and knock-kneed cyclists are injury-free indicates either that the stresses fall within the tolerance limits of the knee joint or that in some cases the imaginary axis of rotation of the knee joint can still be aligned like a normal knee joint, in spite of a bowlegged or knock-kneed condition.

There are logical treatments that may be effective for the relief of overuse injuries caused by these conditions. For example, it has been reported that a bowlegged condition inevitably creates a tendency for the inner side of the foot to raise up from the floor. In order to compensate for this tendency, the foot must assume a pronated position when it is placed upon a horizontal surface (Hlavac, 1979). A wedge on the inner side of the pedal or shoe will tend to correct the necessity for excessive pronation but will unfortunately not be effective in protecting the knee if its axis is unfavorably located.

Tibial torsion.   Some individuals have a condition in which the shank appears to be twisted along its length so that the foot is rotated either inward or outward when the thigh and kneecap are aligned in the normal fashion. In these cases the imaginary axis of the ankle joint will not be parallel to the imaginary axis of the knee joint. Any attempt to rotate the pedals of a bicycle while the foot is firmly attached to the pedals will subject the ankle and knee joints to a great deal of mechanical stress.

Abnormal angle of gait.   Although the average person tends to walk with the feet turned outward at about a 10° angle from the walking direction, there is a wide variation in the actual angle from person to person. Severely pigeon-toed individuals can have the feet turned inward several degrees, and severely duck-footed individuals may have the feet turned outward greatly in excess of the normal 10° angle. Many clinicians have reported that pigeon-toed individuals tend to have a sound arch mechanism of the foot, whereas duck-footed individuals frequently tend to pronate excessively. Consequently, cyclist's knee may occur more often among duck-footed individuals.

There are a number of causative factors for abnormal angles of gait. These may be congenital in nature or the result of injury or long-term stresses on the musculoskeletal system. Unfortunately, such problems can rarely be corrected without surgical intervention. In addition, any attempts to force the feet into a normal alignment will undoubtedly place damaging stress upon the feet or legs. For this reason it is important to avoid constraining the feet in cleats and toe clips that are aligned at an angle that is different from the angle naturally assumed by the foot.

It should be emphasized that all serious misalignments of the feet and legs are likely to predispose a cyclist to overuse injuries. At this time no logical adjustments can make complex three-dimensional motion patterns of the feet and legs conform to the fixed motion pattern of the drive mechanism of a conventional bicycle. Constraining the feet with toe clips and cleats inevitably makes matters worse, and so people who suffer from significant misalignments would be wise to restrict themselves to cycling without toe clips or cleats or to find alternative forms of sport, recreation, and transportation.

Leg-Length Discrepancies

Clinical examinations have revealed that a significant number of individuals appear to have one leg longer than the other. An asymmetry of this kind may be a "true" leg-length discrepancy caused by a measurable difference in the lengths of either the shanks or the thighs. Conversely, the asymmetry may be an "apparent" leg-length discrepancy caused by such things as an abnormal curvature of the spine (scoliosis), abnormal side-to-side tilt of the pelvis, or differences in the angles of the right and left necks that join the thighbones to their respective ball-and-socket joints. Quite clearly, apparent discrepancies involve serious structural shortcomings that should be identified and treated by highly competent medical specialists.

The adverse effects of true leg-length discrepancies appear to be proportional to the degree of the discrepancy. For example, podiatrists have indicated that a discrepancy of 1/4 in. or less is unlikely to cause serious problems in runners. On the basis of preliminary observations, the same would appear to be true for cyclists. In other words, any stress resulting from minor leg-length differences appears to fall within the tolerance limits of the musculoskeletal system. However, a number of cyclists who have significant leg-length discrepancies appear to suffer from overuse injuries. The cause of the injuries may simply be a function of the inability of the cyclist to adjust the dimensions of the bicycle so that stress is minimized on the feet and legs on both sides of the body. For example, many healthy cyclists have found by trial and error that there is an optimum seat height and crank length that minimizes overuse stress on the knees. In the case of a cyclist with a leg-length discrepancy, only one leg at a time can achieve this optimum position for any combination of seat height and crank length. Fortunately, it may be possible to compromise and find a position that creates mechanically acceptable stress on each side of the body.

In many cases cyclists have effectively compensated for a shank-length discrepancy by placing a lift between the pedal and the foot, which can be constructed from any rigid material that will build up the height of the top surface of the pedal. Some authorities have suggested that a lift does not have to completely compensate for the difference in length between the legs, and that a partial compensation can reduce stress to a mechanically acceptable level while simultaneously allowing for any long-term structural compensations that may have taken place in the musculo-skeletal system itself.

In addition to problems created directly by leg-length discrepancies, there are a number of problems that can be indirectly attributed to these conditions. In effect, a leg-length discrepancy creates stresses upon the musculoskeletal system that can in turn create structural changes that predispose the cyclist to overuse injuries. Clinicians have identified a number of such structural changes.

In some cases compensations take the form of changes in the structure of the feet. For example, the longer leg may be subjected to greater loads than the shorter leg, and so the arch of the longer leg collapses into a pronated position during normal stance. The cyclist is then predisposed to problems associated with excessive pronation on the side of the longer leg. The opposite form of compensation, consisting of a permanent supination on the shorter side is occasionally diagnosed. In these cases the absence of adequate pronation during walking and running can adversely affect the shock-absorbing qualities of the foot; this in turn can predispose the individual to painful disorders of the hip joint and lower back.

Compensations have also been observed at the knee joint. The longer leg can eventually assume either a knock-kneed or bowlegged alignment that effectively lowers the hip joint of the longer leg to the same level as the shorter leg. This of course predisposes cyclists to the problems associated with misalignments of the shank and thigh. In other cases the knee of the longer leg becomes hyperextended, that is, pushed backward, from its vertical alignment with the hip and ankle joints. Perhaps the major threats posed by this abnormality are the tendency for the knee joint to become vulnerable due to lack of stability and the likelihood that the condition will progressively worsen over time.

Finally, compensations can take place in the vicinity of the hip joint and the lower back. Asymmetrical loading of the legs can eventually change the angle at which the neck of the thighbone is aligned with respect to the hip joint. This can lead to a painful condition eventually requiring surgical correction. Similarly, a compensation that involves a change in the side-to-side alignment of the pelvis will usually produce a compensatory side-to-side curvature of the spine. The latter condition places an abnormal loading on the shock-absorbing discs of the spine and can eventually cause debilitating pain in the low back.

Summary and Conclusions

Due to the complex structure and function of the legs and feet, the human body is somewhat incompatible with the rigidly constraining motion of the conventional bicycle. This mechanical incompatibility creates stresses upon the musculoskeletal system, and the stresses appear to be proportional to the degree of incompatibility. For mechanically sound, healthy cyclists the stresses do not exceed the limits of mechanical tolerance of the musculoskeletal system. However, clinicians are beginning to recognize that many cyclists have anatomical shortcomings that make them especially incompatible with the bicycle, and these individuals seem to be at relatively high risk of sustaining overuse injuries. On the basis of the preceding observations, individuals who are aware of anatomical discrepancies or are experiencing ongoing pain or discomfort should be examined by a competent professional. Indeed, it would be desirable for any young person who intends to become a competitive cyclist to be given preliminary biomechanical screening. The information provided by the screening could be used as a guide for equipment adjustments and for the design of individual exercise programs.

It should also be apparent that a great deal of careful research needs to be done before confident predictions can be made about optimal corrective procedures for cyclists who suffer from pathomechanical injuries. When this is possible, it should also be feasible to recognize the potential for these injuries on the basis of biomechanical screening procedures. Specifically, the clinician should someday to able to employ precise measuring techniques that will assess anatomical risk factors of young cyclists and to utilize objective criteria for the design of the bicycle and its components.

Unfortunately, the potential benefits of current and future research programs do not help today's injured cyclists. They must therefore rely upon the expertise of medical and athletic training communities for the treatment of pathomechanical injuries rather than for precise guidelines for preventing those same injuries. For many years there has been a "cottage industry" consisting of experienced cyclists, usually associated with clubs and bicycle stores, who have offered their services to help inexperienced cyclists make equipment adjustments. In the near absence of qualified professionals many cyclists are grateful for this kind of expertise. Many cyclists have expressed frustration at their inability to locate an accredited professional who is knowledgeable in the area of cycling mechanics. Ongoing work in this area will possibly motivate an increasing number of medical experts and researchers to take a professional interest in the problems of cyclists.

References

American College of Sports Medicine. (1986). *Guidelines for exercise testing and prescription*. Philadelphia: Lea & Febiger.

Basmajian, J.V. (1975). The human cycle. In P.V. Komi (Ed.), *Biomechanics V-A* (pp. 297-302). Baltimore: University Park Press.

Bohlmann, J.T. (1981). Injuries in competitive cycling. *The Physician and Sportsmedicine*, **9**, 5.

Booth, F.W., & Gould, E.W. (1975). Effects of training and disuse on connective tissue. *Exercise and Sport Science Reviews*, **3**, 83-112.

Francis, P.R. (1986). Injury prevention for cyclists: A biomechanical approach. In E.R. Burke (Ed.), *Science of cycling* (pp. 145-184). Champaign, IL: Human Kinetics.

Frankel, V.H., & Nordin, M. (1980). *Basic biomechanics of the skeletal system*. Philadelphia: Lea & Febiger.

Hlavac, H.F. (1980). *The foot book*. Mountain View, CA: World Publications.

Jorge, M., & Hull, M.L. (1984). Biomechanics of bicycle pedalling. In J. Terauds, K. Barthels, E. Kreighbaum, R. Mann, & J. Crakes (Eds.), *Sports biomechanics* (pp. 233-246). Del Mar, CA: Academic Publishers.

Leadbetter, W.B., & Schneider, M.J. (1982). Orthopedics. In J. Krausz & V. van der Reis (Eds.), *The bicycling book* (pp. 195-214). New York: Dial Press.

Smith, E.L. (1981). Bone changes in exercising older adults. In E.L. Smith & R.C. Serfass (Eds.), *Exercise and aging: The scientific bases* (pp. 179-186). Hillsdale, NJ: Enslow.

Vetter, W.L., Helfet, D.L., Spear, K., & Matthews, L.S. (1985). Aerobic dance injuries. *The Physician and Sportsmedicine*, **13**, 2.

The Cyclist's Knee: Anatomical and Biomechanical Considerations

Andrew L. Pruitt

Bicycling at any level is a marriage of two machines, the bicycle and the human. The bike is composed of rigid components; although adjustable, the bicycle is not adaptable. The human is composed of a mixture of rigid levers (i.e., bones) held together by strong flexible connective tissue and moved by soft tissue with contractile abilities. This combination of tissues makes the human machine very adaptable and able to perform work under extreme conditions. If the goal is maximum success without injury, and if the marriage between the two machines is to be one of total harmony, much thought and design is necessary.

As stated above, the bicycle is adjustable and the human is adaptable, but if the human machine is made to adapt to the adjustments of the bicycle, success and comfort will be short-lived.

Skeletal Anatomy

Anatomy is a very individual matter. The anatomical variants are too numerous to mention, but the basics of function remain fairly constant. Few anatomical structures bear the sole responsibility of a particular function. Instead they synergistically work with other structures.

The knee joint actually consists of two joints or articulations (see Figure 1): the *tibiofemoral joint* (tibia = shin and femur = thigh) and the *patellofemoral* joint (patella = kneecap). The *femoral condyles* are the two rounded prominences on the end of the femur; the groove between them anteriorly is the *patellofemoral groove* that accepts the patella. The femoral condyles sit on top of the tibial plateau. The femur and the tibia are separated and cushioned by the *meniscus,* or fibrocartilaginous discs. These meniscus also create a dish to accept the femoral condyles.

The *patella* is a rounded triangular bone with the peak of the triangle being the inferior pole of the patella. On the back side of the kneecap, or patella, is a vertical ridge that works in the femoral groove mentioned earlier.

The stability of the knee is provided by four major bands of connective tissue plus secondary supports such as capsule and musculotendinous units. The medial and lateral supports are the *medial and lateral collateral*

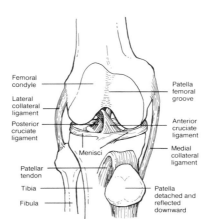

Figure 1   Anterior anatomy of right knee.

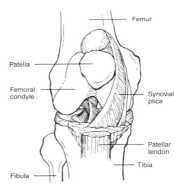

Figure 2   Anterior right knee with plica.

ligaments. These fairly strong connective tissue structures provide the ability of the knee joint to act as a hinge. The anteroposterior (front to back) stability is provided by the *anterior and posterior cruciate ligaments,* which both attach to the femur and the tibia but cross in the middle of the joint to control excess movement fore and aft. Their crossed position also controls excess rotation of the tibia on the femur, as the knees' primary movements are flexion and extension, not rotation.

The ends of the femurs and the back of the patella are covered with an *articular cartilage* that should not be confused with the meniscus. The articular cartilages can be compared to the nonstick surface of some modern cookware; it has been said that the articular surface of a healthy patella is five times slicker than wet ice on wet ice. The joint is filled with *synovial fluid*, a nutrient-loaded lubricating fluid that in combination with the articular cartilage makes for a well-oiled joint.

A capsular sac surrounds the entire joint. The capsule has several primary duties. It acts as a secondary stabilizer, and it secretes the synovial fluid from its lining. The lining of the capsule sometimes has an excess wrinkle known as a *plica* (see Figure 2). The synovial plica is a non-functional embryological remnant found in about 6 out of 10 knees in various locations.

Movements of the Knee

Simply stated, the knee is a hinge joint; in reality, a combination of movements occurs with each extension and flexion of the knee (see Figure 3). These movements include a rocking action, a gliding action, and rotational movements. For this text we will consider full extension to be 0° and full flexion 135°. In full extension (0°) the knee is locked with the tibia slightly externally rotated on the femur. From 0 to 20° of flexion the femur rocks on the tibia and the tibia begins to rotate internally on the femur. From 0 to 20° the tibial rotation is minimal compared to the femur rocking on the tibia. From 20 to 135° the femur glides on the tibia. When extending the knee from the flexed position, the opposite occurs. At 90° of flexion, up to 40° of tibial rotation is possible.

The patella femoral articulation is a gliding joint, with the patella moving in the patellofemoral groove between the femoral condyles while acting as the fulcrum in the lever system that actively moves the knee (see Figure 3).

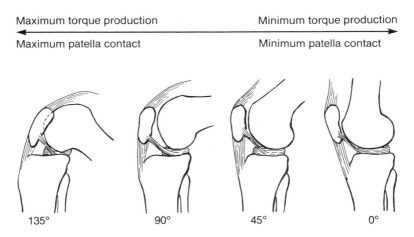

Maximum torque production ← → Minimum torque production

Maximum patella contact   Minimum patella contact

135°   90°   45°   0°

Figure 3 Schematic representation of knee from side view through range of motion.

Muscular Anatomy

Briefly mentioned earlier was some complex soft tissue with contractile capabilities. This tissue is muscle. The knee is controlled by several large groups of muscles as well as several large, more independent ones.

The *quadriceps* is a group of muscles that makes up the front of the thigh and is the main muscular stabilizer of the knee (see Figure 4). Just above the patella the quadriceps converge in the quadriceps tendon, which in turn inserts into the patella. The patella is then attached to the tibia via the patella tendon. The patella/patella tendon/tibial attachment is a fairly static connection for the quadriceps and is very strong. The quadriceps group consists of four muscles: the vastus medialis, the vastus lateralis, the vastus intermedialis (buried deep), and the rectus femoris. The primary function of the quadriceps is to extend the knee, but they also help in hip flexion (raising the leg at the hip).

The *hamstrings* make up the back of the thigh and are nearly as important as the quadriceps in both stabilizing and moving the knee. The primary action of the hamstrings is to flex or bend the knee, but they also help extend the hip (drop the leg at the hip: see Figure 5). The hamstrings are made up of three muscles: the semitendinosus, the semimembranosus, and the biceps femoris. The hamstrings are attached at the back of the tibia by two strong tendons, one on each side of the knee.

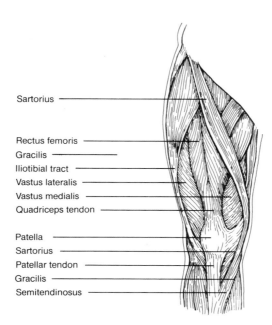

Sartorius

Rectus femoris
Gracilis
Iliotibial tract
Vastus lateralis
Vastus medialis
Quadriceps tendon

Patella
Sartorius
Patellar tendon
Gracilis
Semitendinosus

Figure 4 Muscles of the thigh, anterior view.

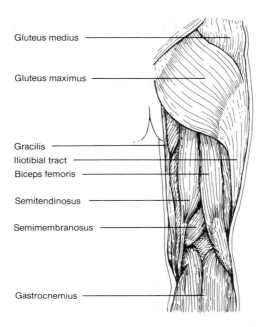

Gluteus medius

Gluteus maximus

Gracilis
Iliotibial tract
Biceps femoris

Semitendinosus

Semimembranosus

Gastrocnemius

Figure 5 Muscles of the thigh, posterior view.

The *iliotibial tract* sweeps down the entire length of the lateral thigh and attaches just below the outside of the knee. Its primary function is to abduct the leg (take the leg away from the midline), but it also helps stabilize the knee laterally during active extension and flexion. It may also be a flexor or extensor of the knee depending on the knee position.

The *gracilis* runs from the pubis to the inside of the tibia just below the knee. Its primary function is to adduct (pull in) the leg, but it also helps stabilize the knee medially during active extension and flexion.

The *gastrocnemius* or calf muscle is a primary plantar flexor (pointing the toes) of the ankle, but because it crosses behind the knee and attaches above on the femur it helps flex the knee.

Kinesiology

The constant coordinated flexion and extension of the knee pedaling a bicycle is where the marriage between the bicycle and human is either won or lost. Many factors are involved, some of which are totally out of our control, such as hereditary anatomical makeup. The analysis of muscle activity while pedaling the bicycle has been a topic of interest to scientists for decades. I find the easiest way to understand it is diagrammatically (Houtz, Whatley, & Dodelin, 1959; Hull & Jorge, 1983). What follows is an interpretation of many electromyogram studies in diagram form (see Figure 6).

Several electromyogram studies indicate that when toe clips are used, the muscles fire in the same use patterns, but each firing tends to last 20% longer than when pedaling without toe clips. When work load is increased in these studies, the muscle use patterns remain unchanged, and only the intensity of contraction rises, even when the resistance is so hard that the subject needs assistance in beginning the work bout.

Standing out of the saddle, on the other hand, does cause a change in muscle use pattern. The change of position results in increased muscle activity and intensity from 160 to 0° and a cessation of activity from 0 to 100°. The large muscle groups around the hip come into action to help the powerful hip extension while standing.

All of these facts and interpretations assume that the biomechanical marriage of human and bike are correct because a mismarriage can and does cause a reduction in comfort and production, and eventually can cause injury.

Many things must be considered when fitting a person on a bike; the focus of this text is the knee. As already mentioned, there are as many anatomical variants as there are people. There are also many cookbook formulas, and even measuring devices, on how to fit bikes. The main point that should be remembered is that the adaptable human should not be forced onto an adjustable machine. This can be assured at the knee by making sure that the relaxed anatomical position of the knee is reflected in the on-bike position. To meet this goal, have the cyclist sit on the edge of a table where the feet can hang relaxed from the knee. The knees should be positioned shoulder-width apart. Make note of patella and tibial positions. The best way to note tibial position is to view the feet; because the cycling shoe cleat stabilizes the foot, it also controls tibial rotation. It is extremely important to knee health for the relaxed foot posture to be noted while sitting on the edge of the table; the position of knees shoulder-width apart is reflected on the bike when the foot/cleat combination is secured. One ride with an incorrect cleat position can induce a painful knee injury. In cases of extreme external tibial rotation some modifications may need to be made to the bicycle cranks or pedals.

The other area of greatest concern and controversy is saddle height and its effect on the knee as well as on performance. In 10 years of riding and racing bicycles and caring for serious cyclists at all levels I have seen saddle height fads swing full circle. Again, it should be remembered that anatomy and bike fit are very individual and should not be controlled by some study that states where maximum power or strength are produced, when it takes at least 100° of knee joint movement to pedal one stroke.

I believe that the saddle should be as high as comfortably possible. It is too high if the pelvis is caused to rock or the leg must reach at the bottom of the stroke. The fore and aft saddle adjustment depends more on upper body anatomy but affects the saddle height knee flexion adjustments.

The extreme importance of saddle position is due to the fact that (a) the patella (kneecap) acts as a fulcrum in the lever system that moves

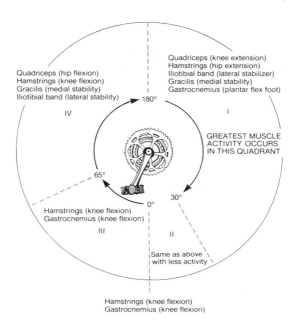

Quadriceps (hip flexion)
Hamstrings (knee flexion)
Gracilis (medial stability)
Iliotibial band (lateral stability)

Quadriceps (knee extension)
Hamstrings (hip extension)
Iliotibial band (lateral stabilizer)
Gracilis (medial stability)
Gastrocnemius (plantar flex foot)

180°

IV

GREATEST MUSCLE
ACTIVITY OCCURS
IN THIS QUADRANT

65°

30°

0°

Hamstrings (knee flexion)
Gastrocnemius (knee flexion)

III

II

Same as above
with less activity

Hamstrings (knee flexion)
Gastrocnemius (knee flexion)

Figure 6 Diagrammatic interpretation of EMG studies of pedal stroke with toe clips in seated position.

the knee and (b) there is a direct relationship between how far one flexes the knee and how much pressure is on the patella (see Figure 3). The more flexion there is, the greater the patella pressure. This pressure is then multiplied by the load or force of work being produced. The connective tissue of the quadriceps and patella tendons is also under its greatest stress during flexion.

Injuries

There are several specific ailments of the knee common to cyclists. These ailments can stem directly from either overuse or biomechanics; typically, the problems result from a combination of both. The three most common cycling knee ailments are chondromalacia, tendinitis, and inflammation of the synovial plica. It is beyond the scope of this presentation to delve into each ailment in detail, but each will be discussed briefly.

Chondromalacia

Chondromalacia is the end result of excessive wear and tear on the slick articular surface of the patella. It is manifested in subpatellar pain and crepitus (noise and grinding). The pain can have many patterns but usually follows hilly rides, time trial workouts (big gear, slow cadence), or riding with a group that is one gear too strong for you. The etiology of the wear and tear on the patella can be from several sources or a combination. A saddle that is too low, a gear too big, or a cadence too slow are all factors that can result in chondromalacia. In addition, several anatomical variants can aggravate the knees and contribute to chondromalacia. These include valgus knee (knocked knee), varus knee (bowlegs), or tibial/femoral/ patella malalignment. Incorrect off-season weight programs can also be a factor.

Tendinitis

Tendons provide the static attachment of muscle to bone. Their inflamed state—*tendinitis*—includes swelling, pain, squeaking, and localized fever. Microscopically, it can involve microtears in the tendon or just rubbing of the tendon on its sheath. In cycling the most common spot of affliction is the patella tendon (kneecap to tibia), but the quadriceps tendon (quadriceps muscle to patella) can also be affected. The causes of inflammation are similar to those of chondromalacia.

Synovial Plica Inflammation

As mentioned earlier, the synovial plica is a nonfunctional embryological remnant appearing as a fibrous band in the knee that can become clinically significant (see Figure 2). Most plica begin on the medial wall of the knee lining and proceed obliquely downward through the knee. Most are soft and pliable but can become thickened and inflamed. If the latter occurs the plica can begin to rub over the femoral condyle with every knee movement. There may be medial joint pain increasing with activity and clearing with rest, only to return again with the resumption of activity. There may also be a rhythmical popping feeling. The only etiology is one of overuse to the plica, in cycling usually due to the number of revolutions the cyclist's knee encounters during a career. All other anatomical and biomechanical factors may be perfect except that the athlete is cursed with a plica that has become inflamed and hardened. Excision through arthroscopic surgery is usually necessary although some have had results with noninvasive methods.

References

Houtz, J.C., Whatley, G.S., & Dodelin, R.A. (1959). An analysis of muscle action and joint excursion during exercise on a stationary bicycle. *The Journal of Bone and Joint Surgery*, **41-A**(1), 123-131.

Hull, M.L., & Jorge, M. (1983). *Preliminary results of EMG measurements during bicycle pedaling*. Unpublished manuscript, University of California, Department of Mechanical Engineering, Davis.

Nutrition for Sports Performance

David L. Costill

Aside from the limits imposed by heredity and the physical improvements associated with training, no single factor can play a greater role in optimizing performance than diet. Despite the wealth of published information dealing with proper nutrition, few efforts have been made to describe the nutritional needs and best dietary regimen for the competitive cyclist. Most cyclists have at one time searched for the "magic food" that would improve their performance. Unfortunately, most efforts to manipulate diet have been prompted by suggestions from more successful performers, poorly designed research studies, invalid commercial advertising claims, and the misinterpretation of nutritional information. The following discussion will take an objective look at the energy needs of the cyclist, with special attention given to the role of dietary carbohydrates on exercise performance.

Energy Exchange in Athletes

Training for competitive sports may increase one's daily energy expenditure by 25 to 50%. Long-distance runners, for example, commonly run 15 to 40 km/day at an average expenditure of 55 to 65 kcal/km. Thus, distance runners may expend 900 to 2,400 kcal/day during training. Skilled competitive cyclists, on the other hand, may cycle 50 to 400 km/day.

The energy expenditure in cycling increases approximately as the square of the speed, not as the cube of speed as expected. This is because of the varying contribution of rolling resistance and air resistance to the overall resistance of the cyclist and bicycle at various speeds. An example of the energy cost of racing may be taken from an example of riding a 100-mi road race in 4 hr at an average speed of 25 mph. The energy cost for such an effort is approximately 19.5 kcal/min, or 1,170 kcal/hr, a total energy cost of 4,680 kcal. This also suggests that cyclists in hard training may average more than 26,000 kJ per day.

Carbohydrates

It is generally agreed that endogenous carbohydrates (CHO) serve as the primary fuel during intense muscular activity (Gollnick, 1985). In long-term exercise bouts, limited muscle and liver glycogen supplies may be unable to sustain the rates of energy production associated with 2 hr or more of activity. CHO consumption before and during such activity has been used to enhance muscle and liver glycogen storage and to maintain blood glucose. The following discussion will focus on the impact of various CHO feeding patterns on exercise performance and their effects on energy metabolism.

Several factors other than muscular activity, however, must be considered when examining the influence of CHO feedings on exercise metabolism and performance. Endurance-trained subjects, for example, generally demonstrate a lesser hyperglycemia and a lower insulin response to a given oral glucose load than do normally active men and women (Costill & Miller, 1980; Jang, 1986; Lohmann, Liebdd, Heilmann, Singer, & Pohl, 1978). As illustrated in Figure 1, endurance training alters the tissue sensitivity to insulin and the controls on blood insulin and glucose. Thus, the responses to sugar feedings before, during, and after exercise will, to some extent, depend on the training status of the subject. Likewise, muscular activity has a bearing on the glycemic and insulin responses to CHO feedings. Studies of glucose uptake during 60 min of exercise and at rest demonstrate a marked reduction in blood glucose and insulin when the subjects ingested 70 g of glucose immediately before exercise (Costill, Bennett, Branam, & Eddy, 1973; Figure 2). In light of these interactions between exercise and the hormone responses to CHO feedings, it is not surprising that the metabolic responses to sugar ingestion are dramatically different when taken at varied times before and during exercise.

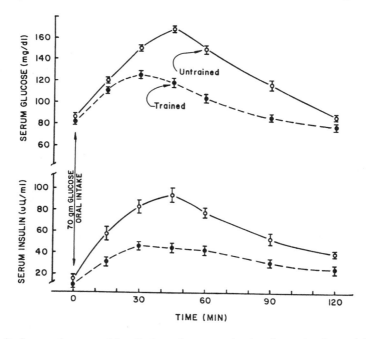

Figure 1 Serum glucose and insulin in endurance trained and untrained men following the ingestion of 70 g of glucose.

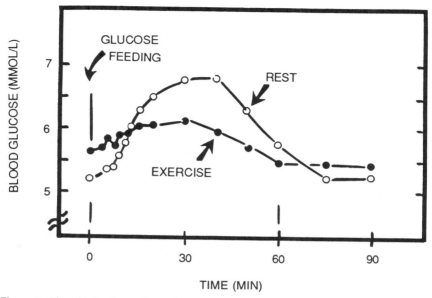

Figure 2   The effects of exercise on blood glucose concentrations following the ingestion of 70 g of glucose. In one trial the subjects remained inactive (REST), whereas in a second trial they ran on a treadmill at a speed that required 65 to 70% $\dot{V}O_2$max (EXERCISE).

The absorption and ultimate assimilation of oral CHO feedings depends, in part, on the rate of gastric emptying. Hunt and Pathak (1960) have shown that gastric motility and emptying are determined to some extent by the composition of the stomach's contents. The volume of fluid remaining in the stomach 15 min after the ingestion of selected glucose solutions increases in proportion to the glucose concentration of the solution (Costill & Saltin, 1974). Regardless of whether the drinks contain glucose, fructose, or sucrose, all solutions with sugar concentrations greater than 150 mM will be delayed in the stomach. In addition, the intensity of exercise has a retarding influence on gastric emptying when the intensity exceeds 70 to 75% of the subject's maximal oxygen uptake (Costill & Saltin, 1974; Fordtran & Saltin, 1967).

Although exercise intensities above 70% $\dot{V}O_2$max tend to slow gastric emptying, running at a lower effort tends to accelerate the rate of emptying (Sherman & Costill, in press). Fordtran and Saltin (1967) noted that exercise (71% $\dot{V}O_2$max) had a slight inhibitory effect on gastric emptying and no effect on intestinal absorption of glucose or xylose. These studies suggest that at least 50 g of glucose can be emptied from the stomach during 1 hr of heavy exercise (75% $\dot{V}O_2$max), an amount that would supply 25 to 50% of the glucose required by the body during that period (Saltin & Hermansen, 1967).

CHO Intake Before Exercise

CHO intake in the days, hours, and minutes before exercise has a significant effect on substrate utilization and performance (Ahlborg & Felig, 1977; Foster, Costill, & Fink, 1979; Jacobs, 1981). Feeding CHO-rich diets to subjects for 3 to 5 days results in elevated liver and muscle glycogen storage provided this regimen is preceded by prolonged, severe exercise (Hultman, 1978). In contrast to mixed and CHO-poor diets, subjects tend to oxidize more CHO at rest and during exercise after days of CHO intake (Hultman, 1978; Jansson, 1980). Evidence by Jansson (1980) suggests that the reduced rate of CHO metabolism observed after the high fat-protein diet is the result of increased intramuscular citrate production, which results in an inhibition of the prosphofructokinase reaction. Although this response tends to spare the limited muscle glycogen reserves, it does not diminish the demands on liver glycogen depots that are expectedly low as a consequence of the low-CHO diet. Thus the diet rich in CHO suffices to keep muscle and liver glycogen normalized and results in high blood glucose levels during exercise. Hultman (1978) has shown that when liver glycogen stores are high, such as after a CHO-rich diet, hepatic glucose production is derived principally from glycogenolysis. When liver glycogen is low, as the result of a low-CHO diet, the availability of blood glucose depends on gluconeogenesis, a relatively slow process that generally cannot match the rate of glucose uptake by the exercising muscles (Hultman, 1978).

Evidence to date has clearly shown that performance in prolonged, severe exercise is improved by eating a CHO-rich diet. Bergstrom, Hermansen, Hultman, and Saltin (1967) and Åstrand (1967) proposed that an optimal plan to maximize muscle glycogen storage should involve exhaustive exercise followed by 3 days of low dietary CHO consumption, with 3 additional days of high CHO intake. This regimen was reported to increase leg muscle glycogen by roughly twofold, from 100 to 220 mmol/kg wet muscle. More recent studies by Sherman, Costill, Fink, and Miller (1981) have tested the effectiveness of different dietary regimens on muscle glycogen storage. This research demonstrated that it was unnecessary to introduce a high fat-protein diet for 3 days to attain very high muscle glycogen depots. To the contrary, after exhaustive exercise similar muscle glycogen values were achieved when 3 days of either a mixed (353 g CHO/day) or a low-CHO diet (104 g CHO/day) was followed by 3 days of rich CHO intake (542 g CHO/day).

Diet also plays an important role in preparing the liver for the demands of endurance exercise. Hultman and Nilsson (1977) have shown that when subjects are deprived of CHO for only 24 hr the glycogen stores of the liver will decrease rapidly to values below 10 g/kg wet tissue. As a result of strenuous exercise lasting 60 min, liver glycogen was reported to decrease from a mean of 44 g/kg tissue to 20 g/kg. In combination with a low-CHO diet, hard physical activity will likely empty the liver glycogen stores. It is interesting to note, however, that when the period of CHO starvation was followed by 2 days of a normal caloric, carbohydrate-rich diet (400 g CHO/day), liver glycogen content increased rapidly to 78 to 102 g/kg tissue. Thus, the inclusion of CHO in the diet and rest during the days preceding prolonged (more than 2 hr), severe (more than 70% $\dot{V}O_2max$) exercise will maximize liver and muscle glycogen reserves and minimize the threat of premature exhaustion associated with exertional hypoglycemia and/or glycogen depletion.

Although the ingestion of carbohydrates in the days before exercise has demonstrated a positive influence on performance, the intake of sugar solutions in the last 30 to 60 min before the activity may reduce the subject's exercise tolerance (Costill et al., 1977; Foster et al., 1979). Ingesting glucose and/or sucrose before exercise elevates blood glucose and insulin and stimulates CHO oxidation. Ahlborg and Felig (1977) have demonstrated that glucose ingestion 50 min before exercise increased arterial glucose levels by 30 to 40%, whereas glucose uptake by the exercising legs was 40 to 100% greater than when no CHO was taken before the activity. Under these conditions, blood-borne glucose accounted for 48 to 58% of the total oxidative fuel consumption compared with 27 to 41% in the control treatment. Although such CHO feedings result in elevated blood glucose (6.5 to 7.0 mmol/l) at the initiation of the exercise, in some individuals a rapid decline occurs in the first 10 to 15 min of activity, reaching levels of less than 2.5 mmol/l (Bonen, Malcolm, Kilgour, MacIntyre, & Belcastro, 1981; Costill et al., 1977; Foster et al., 1979). Despite their state of hypoglycemia, the subjects experienced no greater fatigue than during the exercise when their blood glucose averaged 4.6 to 5.8 mmol/l. This suggests that hypoglycemia per se may not be responsible for the sensation of fatigue associated with long-term activity. It is interesting to note, however, that two of the subjects who were found to have the lowest blood glucose values after the glucose-exercise regimen also utilized 72 to 100% more muscle glycogen than when no sugar was ingested before the exercise (Costill et al., 1977). This would suggest that when blood glucose concentrations are very low, the exercising muscles may adjust their rate of glycogen utilization to compensate for the lack of available glucose, provided muscle glycogen stores are high. Ahlborg and Felig (1977) suggest that the hyperinsulinemia accompanying the glucose feeding is responsible for the increased muscle glucose utilization during exercise. The greater dependence on muscle glycogen results in a more rapid depletion of these reserves and an earlier onset of exhaustion (Costill et al., 1977).

Recent research with preexercise (45 min before) feedings of glucose, fructose, or water (control) show that the blood glucose and insulin levels are related to the rate of CHO metabolism and glycogen utilization during subsequent exercise (Hargreaves, Costill, Coggan, Fink, & Nishibata, 1984). When fed 50 g of glucose, the blood glucose of 8 resting subjects in this study increased from 4.4 to 6.2 mmol/l in 45 min. A similar fructose feeding (i.e., 50 g) resulted in a rise from 4.3 to 5.0 mmol/l in the same time period. After 20 min of exercise blood glucose declined to 3.8,

3.1, and 4.0 mmol/l in the fructose, glucose, and control trials, respectively. The blood insulin levels at the start of exercise averaged 8.8 (control), 13.4 (fructose), and 17.9 μU/ml (glucose). As a result of 30 min of cycling at approximately 75% of $\dot{V}O_2$max, glycogen concentration in the vastus lateralis muscle decreased 42.8 mmol/kg in the control trial, and 45.6 and 55.4 mmol/kg in the fructose and sucrose trials, respectively. Similar patterns of total CHO oxidation were calculated from the respiratory exchange data. That is, 64.1, 65.3, and 79.1 g of CHO were metabolized during the 30 min of exercise in the control, fructose, and sucrose trials, respectively. Thus it appears that fructose consumption before exercise will not induce the same order of stimulation for carbohydrate oxidation and glycogen use observed after the intake of glucose and/or sucrose.

CHO Intake During Exercise

The occurrence of frank hypoglycemia during long-distance running and cycling was noted early in this century and has been considered one of the factors responsible for fatigue in long-term exercise (Christensen & Hansen, 1939; Levine, Gordon, & Drick, 1924). On the other hand, Felig, Cherif, Minagawa, and Wahren (1982) have recently concluded that hypoglycemia during prolonged exercise failed to affect endurance, because its prevention did not consistently delay exhaustion. Although they observed that prolonged exercise to exhaustion (mean $\pm$ SEM, 142 $\pm$ 15 min) precipitated hypoglycemia (less than 2.5 mmol/l) in 30 to 40% of the subjects, the ingestion of glucose during the exercise did not consistently delay exhaustion or alter the subjective sensations of exertion.

In contrast, Ivy, Costill, Fink, and Lower (1979) reported a significant increase in work output over the final 30 to 40 min of a 2-hr cycling bout when the subjects were given sugar feedings at 15-min intervals during the exercise. During control trials blood glucose and insulin fell steadily throughout the exercise, reaching respective mean values of 3.9 mmol/l and 5.1 μU/ml), remaining elevated throughout the activity. As in the study by Felig et al. (1982), the effect of the sugar feeding on the subjects' perception of effort and general fatigue was inconsistent among the subjects.

Inasmuch as blood-borne glucose serves as only one source of CHO for muscle metabolism during exercise, hypoglycemia and exhaustion likely coincide only when other endogenous CHO sources are also depleted. Under those circumstances sugar feedings might contribute more to the total energy pool, thereby reducing the rate of muscle glycogen depletion and the onset of exhaustion. There are, however, no published data to support the concept that CHO feedings during exercise will reduce the muscle's reliance on its glycogen stores. On the other hand, several studies have shown that exogenous glucose (31.8 to 172 g) taken during 2 to 4 hr of exercise increases the rate of CHO oxidation, with the CHO intake contributing from 5 to 55% of the CHO metabolized (Costill et al., 1973; Pirnay et al., 1982; Van Handel, Fink, Branam, & Costill, 1980). It has been noted that at relatively low work intensities (22 to 51% $\dot{V}O_2$max), the oxidation of exogenous glucose was linearly correlated with the exercise intensity (Pirnay et al., 1982). At higher intensities, however, more demand was placed on the endogenous CHO sources than on ingested glucose.

Hargreaves, Costill, Coggan, Fink, and Nishibata (1984) observed that sugar feedings before and at 1 hr-intervals during 4 hr of cycling (50% $\dot{V}O_2$max) resulted in less glycogen utilization than under conditions when no sugar was ingested. In one trial 10 men were fed 43 g of sucrose immediately before and at 1, 2, and 3 hr of cycling. A second trial was performed with the subjects receiving an artificially sweetened drink at the same time intervals. Blood glucose and CHO metabolism were significantly higher throughout the trials when sucrose was fed than during the control trial. Glycogen used from the vastus lateralis muscle averaged 126 (SE $\pm$ 6) mmol/kg tissue during the control trial and 101 (SE $\pm$ 8) during the exercise when the men were fed sucrose (Figure 3). At the end of the 4-hr cycling trial each man performed an exercise bout at 100% $\dot{V}O_2$max until exhaustion. As a result of the sucrose feedings the men were able to cycle 39.6 s (+ 45%) longer ($p < .05$) than at the end of the control trial. Although drawing a relationship between muscle glycogen content and exercise performance in these short sprint bouts (80 to 130 s) is difficult, it appeared that the sugar feeding altered the muscle's source of CHO for oxidation, thereby sparing glycogen stores that serve as a critical fuel in sprint exercise. This concept is supported by recent evidence

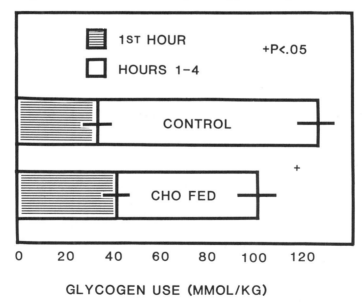

Figure 3 Muscle glycogen use during 4 hr of cycling at 50% $\dot{V}O_2$max. In one trial the subjects were given an artificially sweetened drink (Control) at 1-hr intervals during the exercise. In a second treatment they were fed a solid snack food containing 47.5 g of carbohydrate each hour. Note that there was significantly less glycogen used during the CHO-fed trial than during the Control trial.

demonstrating that reduced intramuscular glycogen levels may impair performance during anaerobic exercise (Jacobs, 1981; Maughan & Poole, 1981). This is not to say that CHO feedings during exercise will enhance performance when muscle glycogen stores are already normal or above.

One final point concerning the value of CHO feedings during long-term exercise must be made. That is, repeated studies using varied levels of CHO intake (20 to 60 g/hr) during 1 to 4-hr of cycling have shown that there were no significant improvements in performance when the CHO intake was less than 45 g/hr. Nor were there detectable improvements when the amount of CHO exceeded 45 to 50 g/hr, suggesting that endurance performance is enhanced with hourly feedings of liquids and/or solid foods containing 45 to 50 g of CHO.

CHO Intake After Exercise

Exertional depletion of muscle glycogen results in a marked elevation of glycogen synthetase activity, the enzyme complex critical to muscle glycogen storage. The rate of muscle glycogen resynthesis after exhaustive exercise appears to be related to the muscle's glycogen synthetase after exhaustive exercise and the CHO content of the diet (Piehl, 1974). Without first activating this enzymatic step, little or no glycogen storage appears to occur. That is, a high-CHO diet will not increase muscle glycogen storage above normal (80 to 120 mmol/kg tissue) unless the diet is preceded by a depletion of muscle glycogen and a concomitant increase in synthetase activity.

When muscle glycogen is depleted by less than 50 to 55 mmol/kg tissue, a CHO-rich diet will restore the glycogen to its preexercise levels within 24 hr (Bergstrom & Hultman, 1966; Costill, Sherman, et al., 1981; Kochan et al., 1979). On the other hand, when glycogen use is greater than 70 to 80 mmol/kg muscle, glycogen resynthesis is generally incomplete after 24 hr on a high-CHO diet (Costill, Blom, & Hermansen, 1981; Costill, Bowers, Branam, & Sparks, 1971; Costill, Sherman, et al., 1981). Although it appears that the rate of muscle glycogen resynthesis is proportional to the CHO content of the diet, glycogen synthetase activity, elevated by exertional glycogen depletion, returns to normal within the first 12 to 24 hr when the subjects are fed large quantities of carbohydrates (more than 400 g/24 hr; Costill, Blom, et al., 1981). After a marathon race, for example, muscle glycogen may be decreased by more than 150 mmol/kg tissue, and subjects may regain only 50 to 60 mmol/kg of glycogen within the following 24 to 48 hr of recovery despite an intake of 400 g of CHO per day (Costill, Blom, et al., 1981). Under those conditions, glycogen synthetase returned to normally low levels within this period of time (Figure 4). In spite of continued CHO feedings over the next 5 days, muscle glycogen failed to increase and remained at less than 50% of the premarathon concentration (200 mmol/kg wet tissue).

During repeated days of endurance training, we have noted a small restoration of muscle glycogen when the subjects were fed a mixed diet

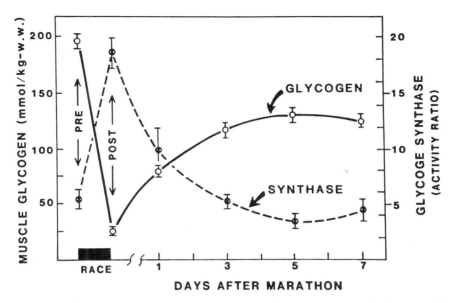

Figure 4 Muscle glycogen and synthase activity ratio for distance runners before, immediately after, and for 7 days after a marathon race. Note the inverse relationship between these two variables.

containing 250 g of CHO/day (Costill et al., 1971). These subjects showed a steady decline in muscle glycogen content with successive days of training. A diet rich in CHO (550 to 600 g/day), on the other hand, effectively restored muscle glycogen in the 22 hr between the training sessions. It has been observed that the high-CHO diet (more than 500 g/day) often required the subjects to eat more food than they desired to satisfy their hunger (Costill & Miller, 1980). Consequently, when the subjects were allowed to eat *ad libitum*, they often underestimated their caloric needs and entered into a negative caloric balance with too little CHO for full muscle glycogen restorage. From a practical point of view, it appears that individuals who perform prolonged, intense exercise on repeated days must consume a diet rich in CHO to minimize the accumulative effects of glycogen depletion and chronic fatigue.

Despite variations in the digestion and assimilation of different forms of CHO (i.e., starch, glucose, fructose, etc.), there seems to be only a small difference in their influence on muscle glycogen resynthesis (Costill, Craig, Fink, & Katz, 1983; Costill, Sherman, et al., 1981). Subjects fed diets composed principally of either simple sugars (glucose and fructose) or starches for 2 days after exhaustive exercise showed similar rates of glycogen resynthesis, although there was a trend ($p > .05$) toward greater glycogen storage on the 2nd day when the subjects consumed the starch diet. Recent studies with rats have shown that glucose or fructose feedings (1.56 mg/g body weight) given immediately after exhaustive exercise result in similar glycogen storage in the liver and muscle, although the mechanisms responsible for this resynthesis were different (Costill et al., 1983). The two sugars were uniformly labeled with ^{14}C, which allowed for measurements of the glucose and fructose carbon distribution in body tissues. It was noted that 3 hr after the feeding, greater ^{14}C activity was found in the liver glycogen of the fructose-fed rats than after the glucose treatment. The ^{14}C activity in muscle, on the other hand, was greater in the glucose-fed animals than in those given fructose. Despite this difference in carbon distribution, absolute glycogen storage in liver and muscle was not different 3 hr after the glucose and fructose feedings.

Summary

The preceding discussion has attempted to describe the large energy expenditure experienced by competitive cyclists during training. Our studies have shown that, on the average, these athletes are able to achieve a dietary energy balance despite caloric demands in excess of 4,000 kcal/day. Previous research has made it clear that carbohydrate is the primary fuel for muscular energy during sports competition and training. The ingestion of carbohydrates before, during, and after prolonged, heavy exercise has been shown to enhance performance and to reduce the risk of premature exhaustion caused by the depletion of muscle glycogen.

References

Ahlborg, G., & Felig, P. (1977). Substrate utilization during prolonged exercise by ingestion of glucose. *American Journal of Physiology, 233,* E188–E194.

Åstrand, P.O. (1967). Diet and athletic performance. *Federation Proceedings,* **26,** 1772–1777.

Bergstrom, J., Hermansen, L., Hultman, E., & Saltin, B. (1967). Diet, muscle glycogen and physical performance. *Acta Physiologica Scandinavica,* **71,** 140–150.

Bergstrom, J., & Hultman, E. (1966). Muscle glycogen synthesis after exercise: An enhancing factor localized to the muscle cells in man. *Nature* (London), **210,** 309–310.

Bonen, A., Malcolm, S.A., Kilgour, R.D., MacIntyre, K.P., & Belcastro, A.N. (1981). Glucose ingestion before and during intense exercise. *Journal of Applied Physiology: Respiratory, Environmental, and Exercise Physiology,* **50,** 766–771.

Christensen, E.H., & Hansen, O., III. (1939). Arbeitsfahigkeit und Ernahrung [Fitness for work and nutrition]. *Skandinavisches Archiv fur Physiologie,* **81,** 160–171.

Costill, D.L., Bennett, A., Branam, G., & Eddy, D.O. (1973). Glucose ingestion at rest and during prolonged exercise. *Journal of Applied Physiology*, **34**, 764–769.

Costill, D.L., Blom, P., & Hermansen, L. (1981). Influence of acute exercise and endurance training on muscle glycogen storage. *Medicine and Science in Sports and Exercise* (abstract), **13**, 90.

Costill, D.L., Bowers, R., Branam, G., & Sparks, K. (1971). Muscle glycogen utilization during prolonged exercise on successive days. *Journal of Applied Physiology*, **31**, 834–838.

Costill, D.L., Coyle, E., Dalsky, G., Evans, W., Fink, W., & Hoopes, D. (1977). Effects of elevated plasma FFA and insulin on muscle glycogen usage during exercise. *Journal of Applied Physiology*, **43**, 696–699.

Costill, D.L., Craig, B., Fink, W.J., & Katz, A. (1983). Muscle and liver glycogen resynthesis following oral glucose and fructose feedings in rats. In H.G. Knuttgen, J.A. Vogel, & J. Poortmans (Eds.), *Biochemistry of exercise* (pp. 281–285). Champaign, IL: Human Kinetics.

Costill, D.L., & Miller, J.M. (1980). Nutrition for endurance sports: Carbohydrate and fluid balance. *International Journal of Sports Medicine*, **1**, 2–14.

Costill, D.L., & Saltin, B. (1974). Factors limiting gastric emptying during rest and exercise. *Journal of Applied Physiology*, **37**, 679–683.

Costill, D.L., Sherman, W.M., Fink, W.J., Maresh, C., Witten, M., & Miller, J.M. (1981). The role of dietary carbohydrates in muscle glycogen resynthesis after strenuous running. *American Journal of Clinical Nutrition*, **34**, 1831–1836.

Felig, P., Cherif, A., Minagawa, A., & Wahren, J. (1982). Hypoglycemia during prolonged exercise in normal men. *New England Journal of Medicine*, **306**, 895–900.

Fordtran, J.S., & Saltin, B. (1967). Gastric emptying and intestinal absorption during prolonged severe exercise. *Journal of Applied Physiology*, **23**, 331–335.

Foster, C., Costill, D.L., & Fink, W.J. (1979). Effects of preexercise feedings on endurance performance. *Medicine and Science in Sports*, **11**, 1–5.

Gollnick, P.D. (1985). Metabolism of substrates: Energy substrate metabolism during exercise and as modified by training. *Federation Proceedings*, **44**, 353–357.

Hargreaves, M., Costill, D.L., Coggan, A., Fink, W.J., & Nishibata, I. (1984). Effect of carbohydrate feedings on muscle glycogen utilization and exercise performance. *Medicine and Science in Sports and Exercise*, **16**, 219–222.

Hargreaves, M., Costill, D.L., Katz, A., & Fink, W.J. (1985). Effect of fructose ingestion on muscle glycogen usage during exercise. *Medicine and Science in Sports and Exercise*, **17**, 360–363.

Hultman, E. (1978). Liver as glucose supplying source during rest and exercise, with special reference to diet. In J. Parizkova & V.A. Rogzkin (Eds.), *Nutrition, physical fitness, and health* (pp. 9–30). Baltimore: University Park Press.

Hultman, E., & Nilsson, L.H. (1971). Liver glycogen in man: Effect of different diets and muscular exercise. In B. Pernow & B. Saltin (Eds.), *Muscle metabolism during exercise* (pp. 143–151). New York: Plenum.

Hunt, J.N., & Pathak, J.D. (1960). The osmotic effects of some simple molecules and ions on gastric emptying. *Journal of Physiology* (London), **154**, 254–269.

Ivy, J.L., Costill, D.L., Fink, W.J., & Lower, R.W. (1979). Influence of caffeine and carbohydrate feedings on endurance performance. *Medicine and Science in Sports,* **11**, 6–11.

Jacobs, I. (1981). Lactate concentrations after short, maximal exercise at various glycogen levels. *Acta Physiologica Scandinavica,* **111**, 465–469.

Jang, K.T. (1986). *Energy balance in swimmers and runners.* Unpublished master's thesis, Ball State University, Muncie, IN.

Jansson, E. (1980). Diet and muscle metabolism in man. *Acta Physiologica Scandinavica* (Suppl.), **487**, 24.

Kochan, R.G., Lamb, D.R., Lutz, S.A., Perill, C.V., Reimann, E.M., & Schlender, R.R. (1979). Glycogen synthetase activation in human skeletal muscle: Effects of diet and exercise. *American Journal of Physiology,* **236**, E660–E666.

Levine, S.A., Gordon, B., & Drick, C.L. (1924). Some changes in the chemical constituents of the blood following a marathon race. *Journal of the American Medical Association,* **82**, 1778–1779.

Lohmann, D., Liebdd, F., Heilmann, W., Singer, H., & Pohl, A. (1978). Diminished insulin response in highly trained athletes. *Metabolism,* **27**, 521–524.

Maughan, R.J., & Poole, D.C. (1981). The effects of a glycogen-loading regimen on the capacity to perform anaerobic exercise. *European Journal of Applied Physiology,* **46**, 211–219.

Piehl, K. (1974). Time course for refilling of glycogen stores in human muscle fibers following exercise-induced glycogen depletion. *Acta Physiologica Scandinavica,* **90**, 297–302.

Pirnay, F., Crielaard, J.M., Pallikarakis, N., Lacroix, M., Mosora, F., Drzentowski, G., Luyckx, A.S., & Lefebvre, P.J. (1982). Fate of exogenous glucose during exercise of different intensities in humans. *Journal of Applied Physiology: Respiratory, Environmental, and Exercise Physiology,* **53**, 1620–1624.

Saltin, B., & Hermansen, L. (1967). Glycogen stores and prolonged severe exercise. In G. Blix (Ed.), *Nutrition and physical activity* (Vol. 5, pp. 15–20). Uppsala, Sweden: Almquist and Wicksell.

Sherman, W.M., & Costill, D.L. (in press). The marathon: fuel utilization and dietary manipulation to optimize performance. *American Journal of Sports Medicine.*

Sherman, W.M., Costill, D.L., Fink, W.J., & Miller, J.M. (1981). Effects of exercise-diet manipulation on muscle glycogen and its subsequent utilization during performance. *International Journal of Sports Medicine, 2*, 1–15.

Van Handel, P.J., Fink, W.J., Branam, G., & Costill, D.L. (1980). Fate of ^{14}C glucose ingested during prolonged exercise. *International Journal of Sports Medicine, 1*, 127–131.

Is There an Optimum Body Size for Competitive Bicycling?

David P. Swain

J. Richard Coast

Martin C. Milliken

Philip S. Clifford

Robert Vaughan

James Stray-Gundersen

Competitive bicycling is a very complex sport that takes place under a variety of conditions in which strategy and technique can often play as great a role as the physical conditioning of the athletes. The outcome of a cycling race is influenced by such diverse factors as the presence or absence of hills on the course, the use of drafting as a means of reducing the energy requirement of cycling, and the use of the most modern aerodynamic equipment. One potentially important factor that has received little scientific attention is the body size of the athletes themselves. There exists in many sports an optimum size for competitive success, for example, lightweight distance runners and tall high jumpers (Åstrand, 1986). In the following, we examine the theoretical influence of body size on the energy requirements of bicycling, and we present data that was obtained in an attempt to verify this influence. We chose to use the limiting condition of bicycling on level ground in relatively still air as a first approach to the problem.

The energy requirement of steady-state work production can be approximated by the oxygen consumption ($\dot{V}O_2$) and has been theoretically defined for bicycling by a number of workers (Di Prampero, Cortili, Mognoni, & Saibene, 1979; Kyle, Crawford, & Nadeau, 1973; Whitt & Wilson, 1982). In bicycling, energy is expended to overcome both rolling resistance and air resistance. The rolling resistance component is directly proportional to the combined weight of the cyclist and bicycle, and thus a larger cyclist must perform more work than a smaller rider to travel at the same speed. However, the larger cyclist has more muscle mass with which to perform the work. Because the ratio of combined weight to body weight (BW) is similar between large and small cyclists, little difference in oxygen consumption normalized to body weight ($\dot{V}O_2$/BW in ml/min/kg) would be expected in overcoming rolling resistance.

Air resistance is directly proportional to the combined frontal drag of the cyclist and bicycle, of which the cyclist's contribution is of greatest importance. Di Prampero et al. (1979) made the assumption that frontal drag is directly proportional to the cyclist's total surface area (SA), as similar portions of each cyclist's SA are likely exposed to the air flow while bicycling. The large cyclist must perform more work than the small cyclist to overcome his or her greater SA. However, as SA increases only as the two-thirds power of BW, the SA/BW ratio decreases with increasing size. Thus, if work output is expressed relative to body weight, or if $\dot{V}O_2$ is measured in ml/min/kg, the large cyclist should be at a marked advantage over the smaller cyclist in overcoming air resistance.

To the competitive cyclist operating at high rates of speed, air resistance is of far greater concern than rolling resistance. This is because air resistance increases as the square of speed while rolling resistance is approximately constant, and of low magnitude, at any speed. Accordingly, the work of competitive cycling is primarily dependent on SA, and we would expect, as predicted by Di Prampero et al. (1979), that the $\dot{V}O_2$/BW of large cyclists is less than that of small cyclists when traveling at the same speed on level ground.

To test for the effect of body size on the $\dot{V}O_2$ of cycling, we measured the oxygen consumption of 5 large and 5 small cyclists while they bicycled on a level road at various speeds.

Methods

Ten experienced cyclists were recruited from local touring and racing clubs and participated in the study after informed, written consent was obtained.

The subjects were divided on the basis of weight into large (81 to 89 kg) and small (53 to 63 kg) groups. Their characteristics are listed in Table 1.

Percent body fat was determined by underwater weighing, using predicted residual volumes. Maximal oxygen consumption was measured during incremental cycling tests.

Table 1 Characteristics of Subjects ($M \pm SD$)

Trait	Small ($n = 5$)	Large ($n = 5$)
Body weight (kg)	59.4 ± 4.1	84.4 ± 3.2*
Height (cm)	169 ± 7	190 ± 7*
Age (years)	28 ± 8	33 ± 8
$\dot{V}O_2$ max (L/min)	3.78 ± 0.30	4.71 ± 0.51*
$\dot{V}O_2$/BW max (ml/min/kg)	63.8 ± 5.5	55.8 ± 6.3
Body fat (%)	8.4 ± 3.3	13.4 ± 3.4*
Bicycle weight (kg)	9.7 ± 0.6	10.7 ± 0.7*

*$p < .05$.

Road tests were performed to measure steady state oxygen consumption while bicycling at 16.1, 24.1, and 32.2 kmh (10, 15, and 20 mph). Each cyclist rode his own bicycle in a racing position with hands on the lower section of the handlebars. All cyclists had modern, lightweight (Table 1), and well-maintained bicycles, with tire pressures of 100 psi (6.80 atm). To minimize variability in oxygen consumption as a function of pedaling rate, subjects pedaled at approximately 60 rpm at 16.1 kmh, and at 75 to 80 rpm at 24.1 and 32.2 kmh. These rates have been shown to be optimal at these power outputs (Coast & Welch, 1985).

During road tests, each subject bicycled alongside a motor vehicle at a distance of 1 to 1.5 m, with the front of the bicycle slightly leading the motor vehicle. Each subject breathed through a mouthpiece and valve (Hans-Rudolph #2000) that was connected on the expiratory side by a flexible hose to Douglas bags in the test vehicle. The hose was suspended from a boom to prevent tension from being exerted on the subject.

At each speed, every subject made four runs over a straight, relatively flat (0.9-m total elevation change), 1,100-m long course, two runs in each direction. Immediately prior to each set of runs, each subject warmed up for 4 to 5 min at the test speed. The subjects utilized computerized bicycle speedometers as feedback to control their speed across the entire 1,100 m. In addition, they were timed independently over a 300-m section of the course to determine their actual speed. Runs that varied by more than 0.5 mph from the nominal test speed were discarded. The results of the four runs were averaged to account for the minor elevation changes of the road and the presence of light winds (less than 5 mph). Expired air was analyzed for the calculation of oxygen consumption with a Perkin-Elmer 1100A mass spectrometer and a Tissot spirometer.

The SA for each subject was computed as $0.007184 \cdot BW^{0.425} \cdot H^{0.725}$, where BW is in kilograms and height (H) is in centimeters (DuBois & DuBois, 1916). To assess the assumption that frontal drag is a constant fraction of total SA, both SA and frontal area (FA) were determined. The subjects' FA was determined by taking a frontal photograph of each subject in a racing position on his own bicycle in the laboratory. The outlines of the subject and of a rectangle of known surface area placed next to the subject were traced, cut out, and weighed. By comparing the weights of the pictures of the subject and of the rectangle, the subject's frontal area was calculated.

Results from each group are presented as mean ± standard deviation. Comparisons between the two groups were made with unpaired Student's t tests. Significance was judged at the .05 level.

Results

As illustrated in Figure 1, absolute $\dot{V}O_2$ (in L/min) was approximately 10% greater in the large cyclists at all three speeds, although the difference was statistically significant only at 20 mph.

As illustrated in Figure 2, $\dot{V}O_2$ normalized to body weight was approximately 22% less in the large than in the small cyclists at all three speeds, giving a marked advantage to the large cyclists.

The total SA of the large cyclists averaged 2.12 ± 0.09 m², whereas that of the small cyclists averaged 1.68 ± 0.09 m². If $\dot{V}O_2$ is normalized to the cyclists' total SA, we would expect no differences between the two groups

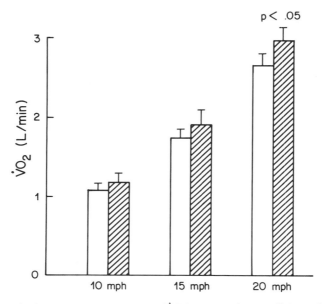

Figure 1 Absolute oxygen consumption ($\dot{V}O_2$) measured in small (open bars) and large (hatched bars) cyclists while cycling on the road.

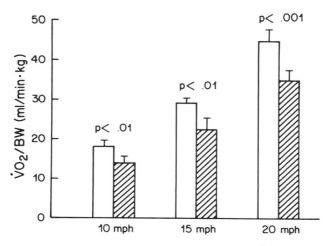

Figure 2 Oxygen consumption normalized to body weight ($\dot{V}O_2$/BW) of small (open bars) and large (hatched bars) cyclists while cycling on the road.

based on the theoretical considerations discussed earlier. However, as illustrated in Figure 3, there was a 13% difference in $\dot{V}O_2/SA$ between the groups.

The frontal surface area of the large cyclists averaged 0.378 ± 0.021 m², whereas that of the small cyclists averaged 0.318 ± 0.028 m². When $\dot{V}O_2$ was normalized to FA, as illustrated in Figure 4, there were no statistically

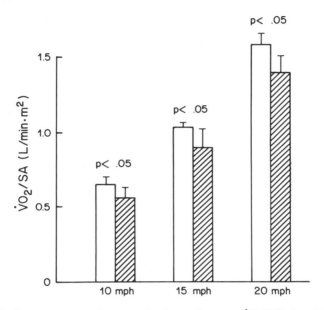

Figure 3 Oxygen consumption normalized to surface area ($\dot{V}O_2/SA$) of small (open bars) and large (hatched bars) cyclists while cycling on the road.

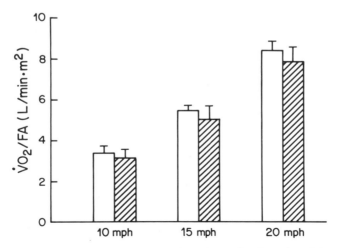

Figure 4 Oxygen consumption normalized to frontal area ($\dot{V}O_2/FA$) of small (open bars) and large (hatched bars) cyclists while cycling on the road.

significant differences between the two groups at any speed, although the value for the large cyclists averaged 7% less than that of the small.

Discussion

We have demonstrated that large cyclists are at a distinct advantage, in terms of lower oxygen consumption expressed per unit body weight, over small cyclists while bicycling at any given speed on level ground. Surprisingly, this advantage is greater than would be expected on the basis of surface area considerations. The SA/BW ratio of the large cyclists was 11% less than that of the small cyclists, and the difference in $\dot{V}O_2$/BW was twice as great.

However, the large cyclists exhibited a 16% lower FA/BW ratio than the small cyclists, and when oxygen consumption was normalized to our measure of the cyclists' frontal area, no statistical difference between the groups was observed. The fact that a nonsignificant difference of 7% was still present may simply reflect limitations in the accuracy of the measurement systems. Alternatively, our photographic characterization of the cyclists' FAs may not provide a true reflection of frontal drag. However, the nonsignificant differences in $\dot{V}O_2$/FAs between the two groups implies that this technique is adequate. The fact that the difference in FA/BW between our two groups was greater than the difference in SA/BW implies that large cyclists are inherently better at reducing their drag when adopting a racing position. Wind tunnel data from Nonweiler (1957) supports this finding.

Although we have demonstrated that large cyclists have a lower $\dot{V}O_2$/BW than small cyclists traveling at the same speed on level ground, does this imply that large size is in fact optimum for competitive cycling? If the large and small cyclist have the same maximal $\dot{V}O_2$/BW, then clearly the large cyclist would benefit on flat courses (providing drafting behind another rider is not allowed). However, in idealized, highly trained athletes it is unlikely that maximal $\dot{V}O_2$/BW would be constant across a large size range. Such a constancy would imply that absolute $\dot{V}O_2$ (in L/min) is scaled in direct linear proportion to BW, that is, $\dot{V}O_2$max α BW$^{1.0}$. However, Taylor et al. (1981) demonstrated that maximal $\dot{V}O_2$ across a large size range of mammals is scaled only as BW$^{0.81}$. Åstrand (1986) reports that elite Norwegian athletes studied by Vaage and Hermansen demonstrated a $\dot{V}O_2$max that scales as BW$^{2/3}$; that is, as body size decreases there is an increase in maximal oxygen consumption measured in ml/min/kg.

These findings imply that small athletes should excel at endurance sports that are BW-dependent, such as running. However, as we have noted, cycling is BW-dependent only at slow speeds but is largely dependent on frontal area at higher speeds. Across the range of our 10 cyclists, FA was proportional to BW$^{0.55}$, with $r = .91$. Thus, a well-trained large cyclist would have a considerable advantage over a well-trained small cyclist, because the large cyclist's deficit in maximal $\dot{V}O_2$/BW is made up by his or her greater advantage in FA/BW. To compare the abilities of cyclists on level ground properly, one should express their maximal oxygen consumption in terms of $\dot{V}O_2$/FA, which may be approximated as $\dot{V}O_2$/BW$^{1/2}$.

Although the large cyclist is at an advantage on level ground (provided drafting is disallowed), cycling on hills is a different matter. The energy required for the vertical component of ascending a hill is dependent on the total weight of bicycle and rider, not on frontal drag (Di Prampero et al., 1979). Furthermore, as the cyclist's speed is reduced during an ascent, the energy required to overcome air resistance is decreased markedly. Thus, hill climbing is a BW-dependent activity and not an FA-dependent activity, and smaller cyclists should excel due to their greater maximal $\dot{V}O_2$/BW. When descending the hill, the situation is reversed and large riders should excel. The ratio of their velocities going up and then down hills of equal grade should be similar though reversed. Given equal distances up and down these grades, the ascent will require a much greater time period than the descent. Accordingly, the time gained by the small cyclist on the ascent will exceed the time subsequently gained by the large cyclist and the small rider should prove dominant on hilly courses.

Conclusion

We have shown that large cyclists have a distinctly lower $\dot{V}O_2$/BW than small cyclists while bicycling on level ground, due to the large cyclists' lower FA/BW ratio. Furthermore, the advantage of the large cyclists in FA/BW is greater than the idealized advantage of the small cyclists in maximal $\dot{V}O_2$/BW, and therefore we would expect large cyclists to excel in level cycling. This finding does not imply, however, that large cyclists will excel at all forms of competitive cycling because of such factors as hills and drafting.

Acknowledgments

We thank Paul Stricker for his technical assistance, and Pamela Maass, Cindy Lawson, and Janet Wright for their help in preparing the manuscript. We also thank our subjects for their generous cooperation.

References

Åstrand, P.O. (1986). *Textbook of work physiology* (3rd ed.). New York: McGraw-Hill.

Coast, J.R., & Welch, H.G. (1985). Linear increases in optimal pedal rate with increased power output in cycle ergometry. *European Journal of Applied Physiology, 53*, 339–342.

Di Prampero, P.E., Cortili, G., Mognoni, P., & Saibene, F. (1979). Equation of motion of a cyclist. *Journal of Applied Physiology*, **47**, 201–206.

DuBois, D., & DuBois, E.F. (1916). A formula to estimate the approximate surface area if height and weight be known. *Archives of Internal Medicine*, **17**, 863–871.

Kyle, C.R., Crawford, C., & Nadeau, D. (1973). *Factors affecting the speed of a bicycle*. Engineering Report 73-1, California State University, Long Beach.

Nonweiler, T. (1957). Power output of racing cyclists—Wind tunnel tests at Cranfield. *Engineering*, **183**, 586.

Taylor, C.R., Maloiy, G.M.O., Weibel, E.R., Langman, V.A., Kamau, J.M.Z., Secherman, H.J., & Heglund, N.C. (1981). Design of the mammalian respiratory system III. *Respiration Physiology*, **44**, 25–37.

Whitt, F.R., & Wilson, D.G. (1982). *Bicycling science* (2nd ed.). Cambridge: MIT Press.

Measurement and Interpretation of Physiological Parameters Associated With Cycling Performance

Peter J. Van Handel

Camille Baldwin

Jackie Puhl

Andrea Katz

Shelley Dantine

Patrick W. Bradley

Laboratory and field tests are designed to evaluate physiological, mechanical, psychological, and nutritional variables important for athletic training and competition. Physiological factors often included in evaluation of capacity for cycling are those associated with cellular energy production, nutrient status of the muscle or blood, oxygen intake, delivery and use, and muscular production of chemical wastes and their removal.

Several basic concepts form the basis of this laboratory's approach to evaluation of competitive cyclists. These include (a) the mode of testing should be as specific as possible to the manner in which the athlete trains and competes; (b) repeated testing is necessary to evaluate both the current status of the athlete and the extent to which appropriate adaptations are taking place; and (c) a variety of maximal and submaximal variables should be included since there is ample evidence that competitive success can be attained in spite of an apparently mediocre test response on a single physiological measure.

Work and Test Variables

Factors associated with energy production, oxygen use, and waste accumulation all increase linearly or as some exponential function in response to work stress. Determination of maximal capacity on the one hand requires protocols that get progressively more difficult in small increments and in a relatively short period of time. Recent studies, however, have demonstrated that submaximal responses such as fractional utilization of aerobic capacity or economy of effort may be as important as

$\dot{V}O_2$max for competitive success. Observation of these factors requires different types of protocols.

The most notable feature of the latter is that they require more time and consist of a series of steady-state work levels. They can be either continuous and progressive (work gets more difficult with no rest interval) or can be discontinuous (a brief rest period is allowed between work sessions). Our objective has been to combine the best features of maximal and submaximal protocols into one, providing the athlete with the same information, but saving time. This is an important consideration when testing is requested for large numbers of athletes. Initially a series of submaximal, steady-state loads are applied. Measures of blood lactic acid, heart rate, oxygen use, and ventilatory equivalent for oxygen are monitored in real time. When it appears that the subject is past an anaerobic threshold, work is rapidly and continuously increased to the point of voluntary exhaustion. Typical criteria for describing maximal capacities are used.

U.S. Cycling Points Test

U.S. Cycling administered a special test protocol to all athletes in its program. To consolidate testing and ensure accuracy, the Physiology Laboratory began to administer this test, and at one point it served as the protocol for determining $\dot{V}O_2$max, a measure used by cycling for athlete selection. Details regarding this protocol are provided in Table 1.

The purpose of this cycling test is to quantify capacity of the individual. This is accomplished by awarding points for performance. Basic features of this test are (a) work load is initially set, then remains constant for 6 min; (b) at the end of 6 min and every 5 min thereafter, work is increased; (c) a work score is accumulated every 10 s of riding time; and (d) final total work accumulated is multiplied by a percentage and then divided by the sum of heart rates taken at 1, 2, and 3 min of recovery. The result is a points score awarded to the athlete. A relative points score is also calculated, which is total work accumulated divided by body mass in kilograms. We have been unable to determine how or where this test was developed or why certain features are included.

As noted above, we have conducted this test for cycling and, at the same time, measured $\dot{V}O_2$max. Both points and $\dot{V}O_2$max are used by the coaching staff for ranking and selection of athletes for U.S. Cycling-sponsored programs.

Several comments should be made about this test. First, the assigned work loads do not account for differences in body size. Smaller, lighter individuals are immediately penalized as the amount of muscle mass available is related to how much absolute work can be accomplished. All other things being equal and regardless of talent for cycling, bigger individuals will ride longer. If only body size were the criterion factor for team selection, then this aspect of the protocol would be adequate.

Second, the amount of work completed each 10 s is multiplied by a percentage in the equation for points (Table 1). One hundred percent or

Table 1   U.S. Cycling Ergometer Protocol

Time	Work (Watts) Men	Women	RPM
0– 6	180	120	60
6–11	280	210	70
11–16	400	320	80
16–21	450	360	90

Recovery Heart Rates

min 1 _____
2 _____
3 _____

Total   _____

Accumulated Work and Percents

	Men	Women
min 1	1,080 (4)	720 (3.6)
2	2,160 (8)	1,440 (7.1)
3	3,240 (12)	2,160 (10.7)
4	4,320 (16)	2,880 (14.2)
5	5,400 (20)	3,600 (17.8)
6	6,480 (24)	4,320 (21.4)
7	8,160 (30)	5,580 (27.6)
8	9,840 (37)	6,840 (33.8)
9	11,520 (43)	8,100 (40.0)
10	13,200 (49)	9,360 (46.3)
11	14,880 (55)	10,620 (52.5)
12	17,280 (64)	12,540 (62.0)
13	19,680 (73)	14,460 (71.5)
14	22,080 (82)	16,380 (81.0)
15	24,480 (91)	18,300 (90.5)
16	26,880 (100)	20,220 (100.0)
17	29,580 (110)	22,380 (110.7)
18	32,280 (120)	24,540 (121.4)
19	34,980 (130)	26,700 (132.0)
20	37,680 (140)	28,860 (142.7)
21	40,380 (150)	31,020 (153.4)
22	43,080 (160)	33,180 (164.1)

$$\text{Points} = \frac{\text{Work} \times \text{Percent}}{\text{Total hr}}$$

$$\text{Relative points} = \frac{\text{Work}}{\text{Kg Weight}}$$

10 Sec Fraction

Time	Men Points	%	Women Points	%
0– 6	180	0.6	120	0.6
7–11	280	1.0	210	1.0
12–16	400	1.3	320	1.6
17–22	450	1.6	360	1.8

Note.   Protocol awards a progressively increasing number of points for length of time to exhaustion. A rider must go 16 min to be given credit for all the actual work accumulated.

a multiplication factor of 1.00 is awarded at 16 min ride time. For each 10 s less, or longer than 16 min, the percentage is correspondingly lower or greater than 1.00 (also shown in Table 1).

Observations

For nearly 1,500 cyclists we have tested with this protocol, the range of ride time to exhaustion is approximately 11 to 18 min, with different means and standard deviations for men and women and senior (SR) and junior (JR) athletes (Tables 3 & 4, for example). Thus there is no rational explanation for how (or why) the percentage calculation is made in total work and why 16.0 min is 100%.

The data presented in Figure 1 show that the points test can distinguish between JR and SR level athletes and between men and women. Seniors of either sex ride longer than juniors, thus completing more work and accumulating more points. That is about all that can be said for the test

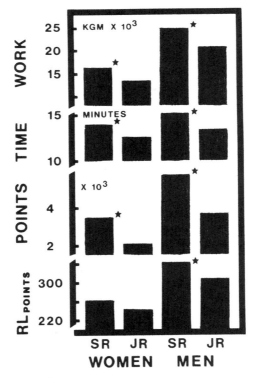

Figure 1 Comparison of junior (JR) and senior (SR) level men and women cyclists for total work (kgm × 10³), ride time to exhaustion (minutes) and points or relative points. Men are different from women, and SRs better than JRs, for performance on this U.S. Cycling devised test.

and we have recommended that cycling no longer use these data for evaluating athlete capability or potential.

This recommendation is based upon the following observations. First, not only are points significantly different between competitive levels (JR vs. SR), but so are variables such as age, body weight, and cycling experience. While age and experience probably have little effect upon ability to ride a cycle ergometer to exhaustion, body mass (weight) definitely does. This effect can be seen in Figure 1. While work values are significantly different between SR and JR women, relative points are not different. Relative points are work divided by weight.

Statistical analysis of data, however, provides greater insight into the effects of body weight on this test. As can be seen in Table 2, weight is significantly correlated to total work completed $(r = .758)$. Any given work level is physiologically easier for the bigger individual and as a consequence there is a tendency for lower heart rates and blood lactic acid levels. The test is biased in favor of larger cyclists and definitely discriminates against small athletes.

Other observations based upon statistical analysis of data are important to mention. As noted, work related variables are different *between* groups and sexes. But the importance of a test should be to discriminate within a given group, especially if team selection is a consideration. The following observations are based upon analysis of data on 103 JR men but are representative of the other groups as well. Age of the athlete was unrelated to any other variable, but height was significantly correlated to nearly everything in a fashion that also suggests that body size is an extremely important variable for success on the ergometer test.

Total work was not related to heart rate $(r = .004)$ or relative oxygen uptake (ml/kg • min^{-1}) at maximum, but was correlated to oxygen uptake in liters/minute. This again points out the importance of size as the greater the muscle mass, the greater the O_2 intake in absolute terms. As weight

Table 2 Correlational Analysis Describing the Relationship of Body Weight to Physiological Variables

	Body weight	Total work (watts)	Submaximal heart rate 1	Submaximal heart rate 2	Submaximal blood lactic acid > anaerobic threshold	Points	Relative points	Physiology score
r		.758	− .440	− .551	− .280	.762	.212	.480
p^*		<.001	<.001	<.001	.002	<.001	.016	<.001

Note. The points test is biased for larger individuals and is inappropriate for describing differences within a homogenous group of cyclists.

$^*p < .05$ is generally required for significance.

is supported on the bicycle, greater weight is not a disadvantage, at least in level cycling. Maximal heart rate was also unrelated to other variables except total recovery heart rate (3-min total); in other words, the higher the maximum, the greater the total recovery heart rate. In a sense, having a high maximal heart rate then penalizes the subject because the recovery total is a denominator in the calculation of points (Table 1). Heart rate at maximum effort has also been used by U.S. Cycling staff as a criterion measure. From the correlational analysis, however, neither the maximal heart rate nor the recovery total seems to provide information of value. In contrast, the submaximal heart rates that were obtained at 180 and 280 W do appear to be related to other variables in a fashion that describes the physiological abilities of the subject. The higher the heart rate at these loads, the worse was everything else (lower points, poor maximal oxygen consumption, etc.).

These data make a practical and important point. Simple total work done on the ergometer and points are basically the same thing ($r = .96$; $p < .001$) and larger athletes will get higher values. There is no need to go through the calculations required to derive points or relative points.

Submaximal and Maximal Values

While manipulation of the work/heart rate/weight information to obtain a quantitative performance score (points or relative points as used by U.S. Cycling) does not appear to be appropriate, maximal physiological values can be obtained from the test when conducted in the laboratory. Tables 3, 4, and 5 present oxygen uptake, heart rate, and blood lactic acid values for JR and SR men and women tested in 1986. Significant level (JR vs. SR) differences exist not only for work output, ride time to exhaustion,

Table 3   Maximal Characteristics of Junior and Senior Level Women Tested in 1986

	Age (yr)	Wt (kg)	Ht (cm)	$\dot{V}O_2$max (ml/kg•m^{-1})	HRmax (bpm)	HLamax (mM)	Work (Kg•m)	Ride time (min)
SR (15)								
X̄	24.2	62.4	163.5	51.0	181	8.7	16,306	14.0
SD	3.3	6.3	15.5	4.9	10	3.2	3,081	1.5
Range	18.0	50.4	132.8	43.2	154	3.6	11,250	11.5
	29.0	72.4	177.8	58.9	199	14.1	22,380	17.0
JR (20)								
X̄	16.1	56.7	164.1	44.6	196	10.1	13,852	12.6
SD	0.9	3.4	6.0	2.7	7	1.9	1,345	0.6
Range	15.0	52.4	152.4	38.7	181	5.7	10,620	11.0
	18.0	66.6	175.3	49.5	209	14.2	17,020	14.3

and body weight, but also for maximal oxygen consumption expressed per unit body mass (ml/kg • min^{-1}). Maximal heart rate and blood lactic acid levels are less likely to be different. There is a substantial range for these values, with the lows close to those seen for relatively sedentary, age-matched controls. The highs are comparable to those obtained on trained endurance athletes in other high energy demand sports such as Nordic skiing, distance running, and rowing, for example.

Numerous studies have shown that within a homogeneous group of athletes, $\dot{V}O_2$max alone fails to describe competitive success (Bradley,

Table 4 Maximal Characteristics of Junior and Senior Level Men Tested in 1986

	Age (yr)	Wt (kg)	Ht (cm)	$\dot{V}O_2$max (ml/kg•m^{-1})	HRmax (bpm)	HLamax (mM)	Work (Kg•m)	Ride time (min)
SR (75)								
$\overline{X}$	21.2	72.1	177.7	61.6	189	10.8	24,901	15.2
SD	2.5	6.7	9.5	5.4	8	2.2	4,020	1.6
Range	16.0	58.6	152.4	49.1	168	5.1	16,280	11.6
	28.0	86.7	193.0	76.4	207	15.0	33,000	18.3
JR (103)								
$\overline{X}$	16.4	66.7	177.7	54.7	192	11.1	20,722	13.4
SD	0.6	6.3	8.2	4.4	7	2.3	3,199	0.9
Range	15.0	53.1	147.3	43.8	176	6.0	14,600	10.8
	17.0	82.9	194.3	66.9	208	18.0	29,580	17.1

Table 5 Maximal and Anaerobic Threshold Data for Senior Cyclists Tested in 1986

	Age (yr)	Wt (kg)	Ht (cm)	$\dot{V}O_2$max (ml/kg•m^{-1})	HRmax (bpm)	HLamax (mM)	ATHR	$\dot{V}O_2$AT %$\dot{V}O_2$max
Men (70)								
$\overline{X}$	22.1	71.4	178.9	60.9	189	10.2	176	88.6
SD	3.2	6.0	7.5	5.0	8	2.3	8	4.9
Range	17.0	56.8	152.4	50.3	168	5.7	159	76.0
	37.0	85.7	193.0	73.1	209	16.8	191	97.0
Women (14)								
$\overline{X}$	24.2	57.1	163.4	51.6	184	8.0	174	88.8
SD	3.1	3.9	6.6	2.7	8	1.6	7	5.1
Range	20.0	51.7	142.2	44.0	170	3.6	158	76.0
	32.0	63.0	170.2	57.8	203	12.0	189	95.0

Daniels, Baldwin, Scardina, & Morrow, 1986; Pollock, Jackson, & Pate, 1980; Sjodin & Svedenhag, 1985; Van Handel, Katz, Morrow et al., in press). A similar situation exists for cycling as well. Table 6 presents maximal capacity values obtained on U.S. medalists in the 1986 World Cycling Championships and several 1986 U.S. National Champions. These values are little different from those obtained on less competitively successful cyclists. Again, the use of measures such as $\dot{V}O_2$max for selection purposes may be ill advised. Other variables such as the anaerobic threshold, the fractional utilization of oxygen, or the economy of effort may be equally important.

Oxygen cost, heart rate, and blood lactic acid are plotted in Figure 2 for two submaximal work loads. Data on both JR and SR men and women are shown. At each work level, the JRs demonstrate slightly higher blood lactic acid values than the SR athletes (lower panel). This is likely due to the relatively greater stress imposed on the former, as alluded to earlier, and which is illustrated by the heart rate and oxygen cost data also shown in Figure 2.

Although the absolute oxygen cost at 180 and 280 W are nearly equivalent for JR and SR men (approximately 28 and 45 ml O_2, upper panel), as a percentage of maximal capacity (maximal data in Table 4) they are markedly different, 51% and 47% and 83% and 73%, respectively. A similar pattern exists for the women as well. These data demonstrate that fractional utilization of maximal capacity in ergometer cycling is affected by both competitive level (SR vs. JR) and by sex (male vs. female). Similar observations have been made for other sports (Baldwin et al., 1986; Costill et al., 1985; Van Handel et al., 1988a, b).

There are also JR-SR level differences in the submaximal heart rate responses with SR < JR at any work load (middle panel Fig. 2). As the JR and SR men have equivalent maximal values for heart rate, this again emphasizes the differences in relative stress between groups. Interestingly, the females had markedly different maximal heart rates (SR = 181, JR = 196). The steady-state submaximal heart rate values expressed as

Table 6   Maximal Physiological Data on 1986 World Championship and U.S. National Medalists

	VO₂max ($ml \cdot kg \cdot m^{-1}$)	HRmax (bpm)	HLamax (mM)
M	59.9	202	17.4
M	58.8	179	18.6
F	59.0	188	15.6
F[a]	59.6	178	4.9

Note.   Values are well within the ranges seen for all athletes tested at the Olympic Complex.
[a]Olympic medalist also.

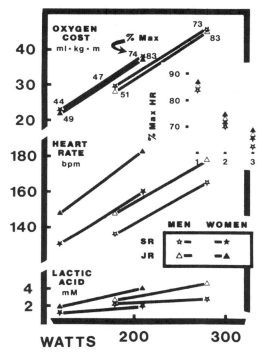

Figure 2 Submaximal oxygen cost (ml/kg • min⁻¹), heart rate, and blood lactic acid (mm) are shown for JR and SR men and women cyclists. The inset shows recovery heart rates expressed as percent of maximal heart rate for each group. SR level riders have lower heart rate and blood HLa values than JR athletes at the same work loads. While the oxygen costs are similar between groups, expressed as a percent of maximal aerobic capacity, there are JR-SR level differences.

percentages of maximum are approximately 72% and 88% SR and 75% and 93% JR. For men the values were 72% and 87% SR and 76% and 93% JR. That the same absolute oxygen costs exist (upper panel) suggests both training level and sex differences in the distribution of cardiac output and/or in the extraction of oxygen at these submaximal exercise loads. This is possibly related to the amount of muscle mass involved during ergometer cycling.

The inset of Figure 2 illustrates the recovery heart rate response for these same athletes. As noted previously, there is a strong relationship between the maximal heart rate and the 3-min recovery total. For this reason we have chosen to express these values as percent of maximum. As might be expected, this reduces considerably the range of values as absolute maximums were anywhere from 154 to 209 bpm. As an average, each athlete group is below 70% of the maximum heart rate by the 3rd min of recovery. Senior athletes recovered faster than JRs and men faster than women (SR men < SR women < JR men < JR women).

Although it is possible to obtain data on at least one submaximal work load, and possibly two, using the U.S. Cycling points protocol, neither the anaerobic threshold nor true measures of economy or efficiency of effort can be determined. In terms of adaptations to training, this would seem to be an important consideration since (a) a large number of competitive events are conducted at intensities requiring less than $\dot{V}O_2$max; (b) the pattern of submaximal physiological responses may change with training while maximums may not, especially in highly trained athletes; and (c) both the point at which the anaerobic threshold occurs and economy of effort have been related to performance in elite groups. The last may be especially important since aerobic maximum is not highly related to competitive success.

In summary, the U.S. Cycling points test does not appear to be one that adequately describes the physiological capacity of the athlete. Response is, in part, dependent upon the size of the individual. As submaximal responses are important, a protocol that ascribes work on a relative basis as well as allows for steady-state measurements should be considered.

Economy and Fractional Oxygen Use

The measurement of economy and/or the anaerobic threshold requires exercise protocols that provide a minimum of three to four submaximal, steady-state work loads. Typically we have used six to eight work levels, with heart rate, oxygen use, and blood lactic acid measurements at each. Table 5 and Figure 3 present some of these data on senior athletes tested in the spring of 1986. Steady-state work levels were 3 min in duration and were increased by 25 W beginning at 125 W for women and 175 W for men. Subjects rode until voluntary exhaustion.

Mean values for oxygen uptake, heart rate, and blood lactic acid maximums are typical for cyclists tested in the laboratory in Colorado Springs. Anaerobic threshold was calculated from the submaximal lactic acid curve with the threshold defined as the point where the sharp inflection in values occurs.

Heart rate (ATHR) and oxygen cost for this work level were calculated off their respective regression curves. Interestingly, for these senior athletes, the heart rate expressed as percent of maximum was essentially the same for both men and women. This is also true for the oxygen cost at the anaerobic threshold expressed as percent of $\dot{V}O_2$max. Values for the latter were 88.6% and 88.8% for men and women, respectively. Although this suggests, in part, no sex differences in trainability, it is important to note that maximal aerobic capacity, whether relative (ml/kg • min^{-1}) or in absolute liters, is markedly different. Males averaged 4.35 l/min^{-1} and females 2.95 l/min^{-1}. Therefore even though heart rate or $\dot{V}O_2$ as percent of maximum at the anaerobic threshold are the same, the actual work load or velocity at which this occurs is considerably less for the women. The measurement and practical use of anaerobic threshold data for training is discussed later in this chapter.

Our studies on several other sports have shown that efficiency or economy of effort can be related to competitive success. These terms define the individual athlete's energy utilization relative to some standard, usually the average cost for a group of athletes in the same sport. Obviously, the average is made up of some number of individual responses. These observations have clearly shown that any given individual may have a response considerably different from the group average, either better or worse (Bradley et al., 1986; Van Handel, Katz, Morrow, et al., 1988). This is also illustrated in Figure 3, which presents the regressions for oxygen cost on work for the male and female cyclists whose maximal data is included in the inset of the figure.

Several points can be made regarding these data. First, the relative oxygen use (ml/kg • min⁻¹) at any given workload is similar for men and women; neither the slope nor the intercept of the respective regression lines are different. Therefore, the energy cost per unit mass is the same

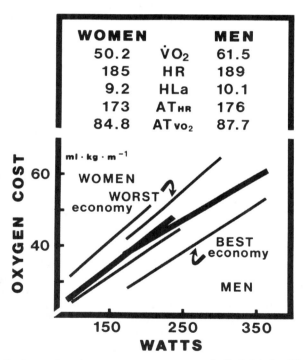

Figure 3 Best, worst, and group average economy of effort data for SR men and women tested in 1986. Maximal and anaerobic threshold data are shown in the inset. Relative oxygen costs are similar for men and women and there is a considerable range in efficiency, similar to that observed for elite runners and swimmers. While relative O_2 cost, and both percent max $\dot{V}O_2$ or absolute heart rate at anaerobic threshold, are similar for the two sexes, because maximal capacities are markedly different, so too is the work level or cycling speed at which AT occurs and the fractional utilization of oxygen at any intensity of effort.

regardless of sex. This observation is consistent with our previous studies on elite runners and swimmers. As noted earlier, however, the gross oxygen costs are in fact different as men are typically heavier than women. This is a consideration in cycling as we would expect that the weight of the bicycle is nearly similar between the sexes. Also, the body weight is supported against gravity. The more mass available to move the bike, the easier it is at any given speed (or ergometer setting). This was demonstrated earlier by the strong relationship between body weight and performance on the U.S. Cycling points test.

A second point is that while the relative oxygen costs are similar as described by the common regression lines, the fractional utilization (or percent of $\dot{V}O_2$max) for any given work level is lower for men compared to women (and for SRs compared to JRs; Figure 2, Tables 3 & 4). These differences are important in that it is the fractional utilization that determines the perception of stress and the extent to which anaerobic metabolism contributes to the total energy demand. The latter, for example, dictates the pace that can be sustained for endurance races (Conconi, Ferrari, Ziglio, Droghetti, & Codeca, 1982), the ability to go with a breakaway, the speed at which carbohydrate stores of the body are used, and, ultimately, the capacity to generate and maintain a final sprint. The lower the fractional utilization at any time point, the greater the reserve capacity for the rest of the race.

The third point to note from these data is that there is considerable individual variability in the oxygen cost at any work load. Individual values may range approximately ± 10 ml O_2/kg on either side of the regression line. At 250 W for example, the submaximal cost for men is anywhere from about 37 ml to 55 ml O_2. The "best" and "worst" individual curves for this group of athletes are also shown in the figure.

The individual variation in this example appears to be typical of any given athlete group as the range is similar to what we have observed for male and female athletes in running and swimming at submaximal levels (Baldwin et al., 1986; Bradley et al., 1986; Van Handel, Katz, Morrow, et al., 1988). Better economy or efficiency may be a mechanism by which the athlete is able to compensate for a lower maximal aerobic capacity. While correlations between $\dot{V}O_2$max and economy are not high (rs may be .40 or so), they are statistically significant suggesting that individuals with lower maximal capacity tend to be more economical in what they do.

An example of the importance of economy of effort is illustrated in Figure 4. Data on the energy cost of cycling at submaximal and maximal speeds are shown for two competitive athletes, both of whom have a $\dot{V}O_2$max of 70 ml O_2/kg weight. The cyclist whose data are illustrated by the triangles (▲), however, is approximately 9% more efficient than his colleague, meaning that at any cycling speed, he uses less oxygen to accomplish the same work.

The practical effect of this difference in oxygen cost is made clear by the following examples drawn from the data shown in Figure 4. Let us assume that the anaerobic threshold occurs at 80% of maximal capacity for both athletes. This is a reasonable assumption as the data in Figure

3 and Table 5 have shown. As noted above, both athletes have 70 ml aerobic maximums, so 80% of this is an oxygen uptake of 56 ml. Extrapolating from 56 ml to each of the oxygen cost curves shows that while their maximal capacities are the same and the percent where the anaerobic threshold occurs is the same, the actual cycling speed where this occurs is different. Studies in a variety of sports have shown that in races of an endurance nature, the average speed or pace that athletes can sustain in competition is very close to that where the anaerobic threshold occurs (Conconi et al., 1982). Clearly, all other things being equal as illustrated, the more economical cyclist will be riding at a faster average speed.

The converse of this situation also should be mentioned. Assume that a breakaway occurs during a race. The speed or pace is 755 m/min (Figure 4). Both cyclists in our example go with this group. Even though their maximal capacities are the same, the relative stress (fractional utilization) on the two athletes is different. The more economical cyclist is now riding at 84% of maximum while the less economical athlete is at 93% of maximum. As lactic acid accumulates rapidly above the anaerobic threshold, it is likely that the less economical cyclist is not only building up more of this waste product but also at a faster rate. It is not unreasonable to assume that this rider will not be able to sustain the breakaway or will fall off this pace earlier.

Most sport scientists would indicate that these differences in economy are due to better application of muscle forces in the task, that is, better stroke mechanics in swimming or less wasted motion in running, and so

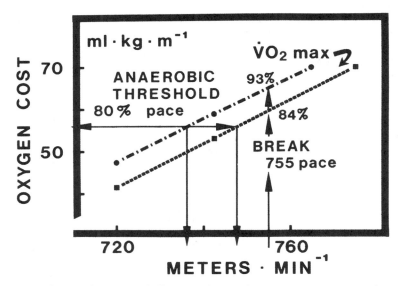

Figure 4 Influence of economy of effort on cycling performance. Assuming equivalent maximal aerobic capacity, the more economical cyclist is riding at a lower percent of maximum for any speed or at a faster pace at the same percent of maximum.

on. Our limited observations tend to support this contention though the picture is far from clear. It is also possible that there may be differences in metabolic efficiency as well, in part related to genotype for key metabolic regulating enzymes (Mitton & Grant, 1984; Mitton, Carey, & Kocher, in press).

In cycling there is another important factor that can contribute to the efficiency of effort. That is the use of aerodynamic equipment including helmet, frame, and even clothing. These can markedly reduce air resistance. Certainly, use of aerodynamic rims and tires with proper pressure is as important as is basic position on the bike in reducing drag. Consideration of all these factors can reduce considerably the energy cost of moving at any given speed (Kyle, 1988).

Figures 3 and 4 depict economy of effort. Basically this is the position of an athlete's oxygen cost curve relative to either a group average cost for the same work levels or compared to another individual's data (Bradley et al., 1986; Van Handel, Katz, Morrow, et al., 1988). On a group basis, we do not see major differences in economy of effort between JR and SR level cyclists tested in our facility (Figure 2). As noted, however, there are large individual variations around the group average cost curves, which can be shown by also plotting the "best" and "worst" individual curves on either side of the group regression (Figure 3).

Visualization of an athlete's economy curve, however, does not allow one to quantify the position nor statistically relate this data to other important variables such as $\dot{V}O_2$max, performance time, or even ride time to exhaustion. To make this possible, we have developed the equation presented below. Essentially this equation sums the total distance each individual O_2 cost value is above (a positive number and "uneconomical") or below (a negative value and "economical") the regression line. The total is the economy score for that individual compared to that particular group. The equation is:

$$(y^1 - \hat{y}^1) + (y^2 - \hat{y}^2) + (y^3 - \hat{y}^3) \ldots (y^n - \hat{y}^n)$$

where:

$$y^1, y^2, y^3 \ldots y^n = ml\ O_2 \cdot Kg \cdot min^{-1}$$

$$\hat{y}^1, \hat{y}^2, \hat{y}^3 \ldots \hat{y}^n = a + bx$$

$$x = velocity\ for\ 1,\ 2,\ 3 \ldots n$$

Data on economy of effort and fractional utilization are extremely important. They clearly indicate that factors other than aerobic or anaerobic maximum contribute to success in sport. In our experience, many athletes and coaches are overly concerned with the latter, failing to understand the complexity of the mechanisms of energy production. Implications of athlete differences in maximal capacity, economy, and fractional utilization for training are discussed later in this paper.

Collectively, the data described to this point indicate that use of single test measures, for example the points system of U.S. Cycling or even $\dot{V}O_2$max values, does not discriminate between individuals within a homogeneous athletic group. More importantly, the physiological status of the athlete is not described, especially as related to training adaptations.

Physiology Score

As noted, individual responses to submaximal and/or maximal exercise tasks may vary widely. Even within a relatively homogenous group there can be a considerable range for any test measure, and relationships to competitive performance criteria may be low. Ranking individuals on the basis of $\dot{V}O_2$max, for example, may result in passing over the highly economical athlete who, in fact, has better potential for certain events in spite of the low maximum capacity.

On the other hand, interpretation and use of a large number of test scores are even more difficult, for example $\dot{V}O_2$, heart rate, and lactic acid maximums; submaximal responses such as economy and anaerobic threshold, and lactic acid and heart rate responses to standard training sets may comprise a typical physiological test battery conducted in this laboratory or in the field during training.

It is possible to generate a composite test score using these or any other combination of results. Essentially this is accomplished by the use of standard scores (Games & Klare, 1967). They are unaffected (i.e., independent of) the original scale units such as ml Oxygen/kg/minute, millimolar, or beats/minute. The contribution for any given variable can be weighted relative to the others in the equation, for example $\dot{V}O_2$max may be given twice the importance of other scores, or three submaximal lactate values may each contribute one third. The relative position or ranking of an athlete for the total score can be compared to any other group of athletes for the same variables. For example, the score on a battery of tests for a promising JR cyclist can be compared to those obtained for SR level athletes.

The general equation for development of a composite score is shown in Figure 5. The group mean ($\bar{X}$) for any set of values is subtracted from

$$S = 50 + \frac{10}{SD}(x - \bar{X})$$

$$S\dot{V}O_2 \text{ max} = 50 + \frac{10}{SD}(ml\ O_2 \cdot kg \cdot m - \bar{X})$$

$$SHLaSubmax = 50 - \frac{10}{SD}(mM - \bar{X})$$

$$\text{TOTAL SCORE} = S_1 + S_2 + S_3 + \ldots S_n$$

Figure 5 Equation for generating a composite physiology score from any number of different test results. The score is independent of units of the values and can be used to compare any athlete to data available on any other group. Calculation of individual scores for maximal aerobic capacity and submaximal blood lactic acid are shown.

the individual score in question and this quantity is multiplied by the result of 10 divided by the standard deviation. In turn this value is either added to, or subtracted from, 50. The value is added if having a high score is desirable, for example $\dot{V}O_2$max. On the other hand, the result is subtracted from 50 if having a low score is advantageous, for example submaximal blood lactic acid. The total score is merely the sum of any number of individual values all of which have been converted to a standard basis. To compare an individual to another group, use the latter's mean and standard deviation.

As an example, we have provided U.S. Cycling with a composite physiology score for each of 103 JR men tested in early 1986. This score included values for maximal aerobic capacity, the blood lactic acid concentration at maximum, submaximal blood lactic acid levels, body weight, total work accomplished in the maximal test, and recovery heart rates. Ranking on the basis of this score (or any portion of it) can be used in relation to any other objective performance measure such as race time. Promising JRs can be individually compared to the SRs, the National Team, or any other group for which data is available.

Practical Use of Test Data

Laboratory test data can be used for a variety of purposes. These may include (a) identification of talent or potential, including specific strengths and weaknesses, and (b) monitoring adaptations to training, including prescription of training loads.

Unfortunately, results of tests are often misused or the information is misinterpreted. We have already alluded to the situation concerning points in the U.S. Cycling ergometer test. Another example concerns the use of maximal aerobic capacity data. $\dot{V}O_2$max is often considered to be the best single indicator of fitness and capacity for success in high energy demand sports, as the value represents optimal functioning of the respiratory, cardiovascular, and neuromuscular systems.

Identifying Talent or Potential

Studies have demonstrated that as a group, elite level swimmers, cyclists, rowers, Nordic skiers, and distance runners have higher $\dot{V}O_2$maxes than less successful competitive athletes. These observations have led to the conclusion that the athlete must have a high value to be successful. The data on cyclists presented in this paper and those obtained for other sports clearly indicate that this is not the case. Submaximal responses for both oxygen uptake and lactate production or even the maximal anaerobic capacity can be equally important. Noted earlier was the test data available on several cycling medalists from the 1984 Olympics or the 1986 World Championships (Tables 6 and 7). Comparison of these measures of maximal aerobic capacity to those presented in Tables 3, 4, and 5 and Figure 3 clearly shows that the medalists are not super physiological specimens. Moreover, intense training over several years may not cause dramatic changes in these measures (Table 7). Rather, there may be subtle shifts in economy or anaerobic responses or changes in power output. Thus it is clear that single time (or use of single variable) results provides little, if any, information that can be used practically. At best this testing merely characterizes the athlete relative to what is known about his peers in that sport.

Related to use of data for talent identification is the concept of identifying strengths and/or weaknesses. Certainly having an extremely low aerobic maximum may be an ultimate deterrent to success in endurance activities. Training in certain phases of the annual cycle should be geared to working on the weakness, and interpretation of test data should be made in relation to the overall goals of the training program (Figure 6; Van Handel, 1987). Does this period represent off- or preseason conditioning? Or is this taper prior to major competition? Studies have demonstrated that physiological responses to work cycle in a general pattern coordinated to intensity, frequency, and duration of training (Costill, King, Thomas, & Hargreaves, 1985; Hickson, Foster, Pollock, Galassi, & Rich, 1985; Van Handel, Katz, Troup, Daniels, & Bradley, 1988). Long-term planning and coordination are essential in order to prevent a haphazard approach to training, which invariably leads to overstress and reduced performance capacity.

Figure 7 illustrates how test data can be used to work specifically on physiological weaknesses. Oxygen cost versus cycling speed is plotted for two individual athletes and the average for a group of elites. The athlete with the high aerobic maximum but poor economy would work specifically to improve the latter. Athlete B with the low maximum would train to improve this capacity. This is especially important when one considers

Table 7   Adaptations to Training by Two 1986 World Championship Medalists

	Date (mo•yr)	$\dot{V}O_2$max (m•kg•m^{-1})	HRmax (bpm)	HLamax (mM)
M	6.85	53.3	172	12.0
	12.85	53.7	178	10.8
	7.86	58.8	179	18.6
F	2.83	51.2	188	—
	1.84	56.8	188	8.1
	1.85	54.4	184	15.6
	8.86	59.0	188	15.6

Note. Data represent changes in maximal capacity over several years for two U.S. medalists at the 1986 World Championships.

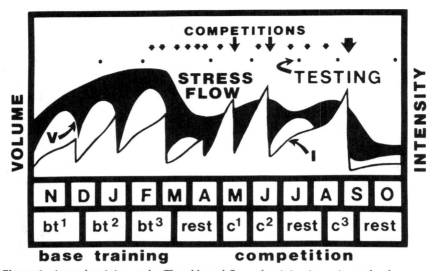

Figure 6 Annual training cycle. The ebb and flow of training intensity and volume are shown in coordination with testing dates and important competitions. Each meso cycle forms a portion of a training phase designed to improve some particular physiological function or provide for rest and recovery.

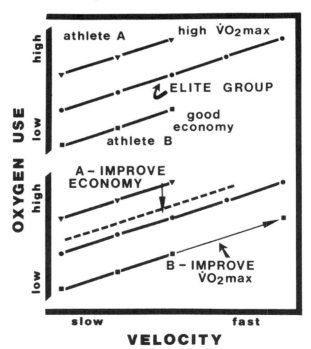

Figure 7 Example of test data being used to specify appropriate training. Weaknesses identified in testing are the focus of specific workouts in certain segments of the annual training cycle.

the basic differences in energy demand between competitive events such as the 1-km sprint, 4000-m pursuit, or 100-km road race.

Use of test data to monitor physiological adaptations and for the prescription of appropriate training work loads is illustrated in Figures 8 and 9. The basic feature of the test protocol is that it incorporates a series of submaximal, steady-state efforts at least through a point estimated to be around 90% of the individual's maximal capacity. In the laboratory, oxygen uptake, blood lactic acid, and heart rate are monitored (Figure 8). In the field (velodrome or road), heart rate is obtained by radio telemetry. Blood lactic acid is also obtained and it is possible, but more difficult, to monitor oxygen use.

Figure 8 illustrates use of such data for identifying training paces. The first is at the cycling velocity or work load at which $\dot{V}O_2$max occurs. Interval repeats of short duration are completed at this intensity, the purpose of which is to improve maximal aerobic and anaerobic capacities. Note that working at a greater intensity ("supramaximal") will result in a considerably greater accumulation of lactic acid (dashed line), but oxygen use is not higher. Neither is heart rate likely to be higher. The second training pace is for improving the anaerobic threshold (also see Figure 9), that is, shifting the lactate profile to the right. There are indications that the pace at which the anaerobic threshold occurs is the same as the average pace that can be sustained for an endurance race (Conconi et al., 1982). Independent of other physiological adaptations, shifting this point

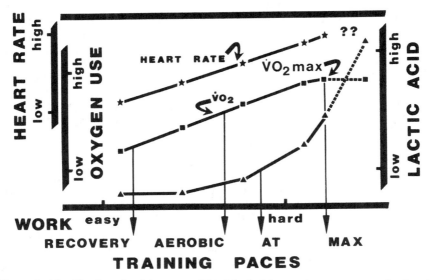

Figure 8 Identification of training paces. Physiological data such as oxygen uptake, heart rate, and blood lactate responses to work are used to identify very specific training paces. Interval repeats at the speed that induces $\dot{V}O_2$max, for example, are used specifically to improve maximal capacity. Tempo rides are completed at the pace associated with the anaerobic threshold. The aerobic pace is for long (several hours) efforts and recovery paces are more properly defined as active rest from more intense efforts.

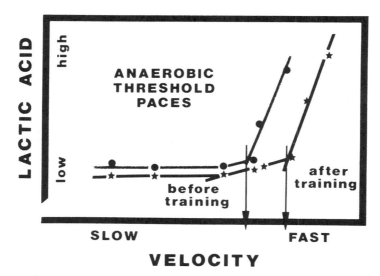

Figure 9 Anaerobic threshold data. The point at which blood lactic acid begins to rapidly accumulate is known as the anaerobic threshold. The work intensity at which this occurs shifts left or right at various times in a training cycle.

to the right (Figure 9) results in better race performance. The third training pace we define as aerobic referring to the fact that it is used for long, endurance-type efforts of one or more hours duration. Depending upon the level of training, this pace may be at an intensity requiring anywhere from 50% to 75–80% of maximal aerobic capacity. As an example, this pace is held for the once-a-week long endurance run. Note that this pace is below the anaerobic threshold and is *not* associated with increasing aerobic maximal capacity. The fourth training pace that can be recommended is a very low intensity work load, which, for all practical purposes, is best used as recovery from more intense training sessions or after competition. In cycling, this is often referred to as spinning, but it is actually active recovery. The work intensity and heart rate are very low and this workout typically follows highly intense training bouts.

This information is used to optimize training time as well as to prevent overtraining or overstress. For example, if the specific objective is to ultimately increase maximal aerobic capacity, why would interval repeats be completed at intensities *above* that which induces $\dot{V}O_2max$? Chance of injury is greater and less total work can be accomplished. Or for the same training objective, why would the training meso cycle (Figure 6) consist primarily of long aerobic workouts, since the latter do not induce physiological processes demanding $\dot{V}O_2$ max?

Unfortunately, most athletes do not have access to the sophisticated testing like that conducted in our laboratories and they must rely upon more simple estimates of training intensity.

Monitoring Training—Heart Rate and Anaerobic Threshold

Data such as that presented in Figure 8 illustrate that a number of physiological markers can be used to describe work intensity. On a day-to-day basis, however, it is impractical if not impossible to monitor oxygen use. Even blood lactic acid, while easily obtained from finger puncture samples, requires use of expensive and technically sophisticated equipment.

Heart rate, on the other hand, is easily obtained by palpation. There are also a number of simple and relatively inexpensive monitors that detect either pulse pressure or electrical changes with each heart beat. These are either worn by the athlete or placed on or near their person when the heart rate is desired. The monitor's digital display shows the rate.

As can be seen in Figures 2 and 8, heart rate is directly (linearly) related to work intensity. It should be theoretically possible then to relate the heart rate at any cycling speed or work intensity or to any other physiological measure if the appropriate testing is conducted (example Figure 8) and the measurements are accurate. Most athletes, however, do not have access to such testing. As a consequence, simpler ways of estimating physiological capacity and associated training paces have received considerable attention, in particular the Conconi Test. This test has been described in numerous publications (*Velo News* and *Bicycling Magazine*, for example) and is based upon data first published by Dr. Conconi and co-workers in 1982 (Conconi et al., 1982).

Dr. Conconi states that a highly significant and predictable relationship exists between the work intensity where a "break," or deflection, in the linear response of heart rate to work occurs and the point where lactic acid begins to accumulate in the blood. At the Cycling Congress, Dr. Conconi reported that heart rate data have been obtained on over 300 cyclists and lactate data on approximately 20 of these athletes. Apparently all of these athletes demonstrate a deflection in heart rate response to work. The suggestion is that by using the Conconi Test, one can know the work intensity or pace for training at the anaerobic threshold.

Several observations regarding this concept need to be mentioned, however. First and perhaps most important is the fact that this pace is only one of several that are required in a well-designed training program (Figures 6 & 8). Indeed, workouts at this intensity may actually comprise only a small percentage of the total in any given micro or meso cycle of the annual program (Van Handel, 1987). Second, while shifts in the anaerobic threshold occur with training, detraining, and taper (Figure 9), there is no evidence or indication that parallel changes in the heart rate response also occur. In fact, there is some indication that there may be a dissociation of these responses during taper for competition (Costill, Kovaleski, et al., 1985; Hickson et al., 1985; Van Handel, Katz, Troup, et al., 1988). Third, while heart rate response has been observed for a large number of athletes in Dr. Conconi's studies, considerably fewer (< 10%) have undergone blood lactic acid monitoring. None have had lactic acid measured simultaneously during the session during which heart rate deflections are detected. Lactic acid monitoring is completed on a separate day and with different testing protocols.

In contrast, we have conducted both laboratory and field (velodrome) tests on nearly 600 competitive cyclists during which both lactic acid and steady-state heart rate are simultaneously obtained. A variety of protocols have been used that alter either or both the length of the steady-state period and the magnitude of the work increment. Data from these observations are presented in Figures 10 to 12 and Table 8. In all cases, group statistics show that both lactic acid and ventilatory equivalent for oxygen are curvilinear functions of work ($r > .94$; $p < .001$). Submaximal heart rate is linearly related to work at the same levels of significance. Adding even maximal heart rate to the regression does not affect the slope of the response curve; that is, it remains linear as long as supramaximal efforts are excluded.

Randomly selected individual response curves have been independently inspected (example Figure 11). Data in Figure 11 were obtained with work increased 25 W every 2 min. Blood samples were obtained in the last 15 s of each work period and heart rate averaged over this same time interval. We would be hard pressed to suggest that a deflection in heart rate occurs at the same point where the rapid increase in blood lactate occurs.

Laboratory ergometry and velodrome tests were also conducted within 4 to 5 days of each other. Data from 4 subjects are presented in Figure 12. Two of these athletes medaled in the 1986 World Cycling Championships. Comparison of laboratory and velodrome results clearly indicates that (a) individuals may respond differently to the same testing or experimental mode, and (b) if deflections in heart rate occur at all, they may be very

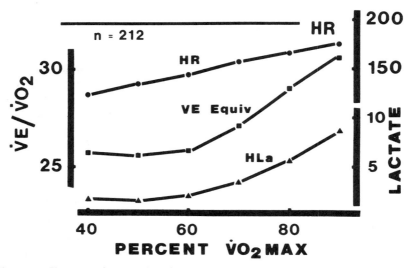

Figure 10 Heart rate, lactic acid, and ventilatory equivalent plotted versus work on a cycle ergometer. Group statistics define a linear relationship for heart rate, not curvilinear as suggested by Conconi.

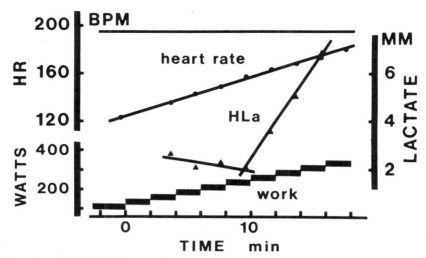

Figure 11   An individual heart rate/lactic acid response curve. Inspection of individual data does not support the Conconi Test data. There is no deflection or "break" in the heart rate curve.

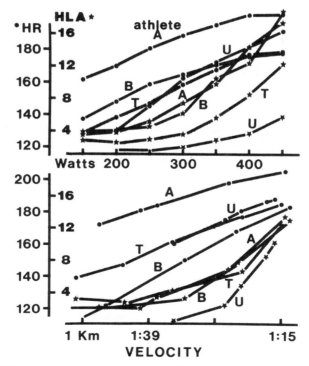

Figure 12   Laboratory and velodrome studies of four cyclists. Responses vary with conditions and between athletes. Overall the data on nearly 600 cyclists suggests that heart rate alone cannot be used to identify an anaerobic threshold.

Table 8 Multiple Linear Regression Analysis of Cyclists' (N = 212) Heart Rate, Ventilatory, and Oxygen Uptake Data

	Multiple r	F	Significance of change
HR			
1	.945	8901	.000
2	.945	4452	.298
HLa			
1	.759	1456	*
2	.872	1701	*
VE/$\dot{V}O_2$			
1	.516	312	*
2	.698	408	*

Note. Significance of the heart rate versus work relationship is not improved by curvilinear functions.
*Values less than .001.

close to the point of maximal aerobic capacity and/or they are not associated with the sudden accumulation of lactate in the blood.

Since wind resistance, drag, drafting, and body position all contribute to the metabolic response to cycling, heart rate-lactate relationships may vary considerably with testing or training conditions. Moreover, with anaerobic thresholds occurring very close to $\dot{V}O_2$max in highly trained athletes, it is possible to identify maximum heart rate as a leveling in submaximal response. As the lactate versus velocity curve is extremely steep under these conditions, small changes in the latter result in large increases in the former. Even a small error in one of the variables can result in greatly over- or underestimating the anaerobic response.

Based upon our observations on cyclists as well as heart rate/lactic acid profiles conducted on runners and swimmers, we are convinced that estimates of anaerobic contributions to energy production must be directly quantified. The use of heart rate alone to identify a specific training pace should be viewed with caution.

Summary

It is clear that acute and chronic responses to training are complex, especially at elite levels. Measurement of a single or even several physiological variables may not present a complete picture of the current status of the athlete. It is necessary to correlate both maximal and submaximal responses, preferably measured in the field, to cycling performance. Most important is the need to monitor training. Close cooperation between coaches, athletes, and sports science personnel is required if the best interests of the athlete are to be met.

References

Baldwin, C., Bradley, P.W., Daniels, J., Daniels, N., Katz, A., & Morrow, J. (1986). Comparison of submaximal oxygen cost of running between elite male and female distance runners. *Medicine and Science in Sports and Exercise*, **18**, (Suppl.), S 37.

Bradley, P., Daniels, J., Baldwin, C., Scardina, N., & Morrow, J. (1986). Running economy: Quantification and relationship with physiological determinants of performance. *Medicine and Science in Sports and Exercise*, **18**, (Suppl.), S 37.

Conconi, F., Ferrari, M., Ziglio, P.G., Droghetti, P., & Codeca, L. (1982). Determination of the anaerobic threshold by a noninvasive field test in runners. *Journal of Applied Physiology: Respiratory, Environmental, and Exercise Physiology*, **52**(4), 869–873.

Costill, D.L., King, D.S., Thomas, R., & Hargreaves, M. (1985). Effects of reduced training on muscular power in swimmers. *Physician in Sports Medicine*, **13**, 94–101.

Costill, D.L., Kovaleski, J., Porter, D., Kirwan, J., Fielding, R., & King, D. (1985). Energy expenditure during front crawl swimming: Predicting success in middle-distance events. *International Journal of Sports Medicine*, **6**, 266–270.

Games, P.A., & Klare, G.R. (1967). *Elementary statistics: Data analysis for the behavioral sciences*. New York: McGraw-Hill.

Hickson, R.C., Foster, C., Pollock, M.L., Galassi, T.M., Rich, S. (1985). Reduced training intensities and loss of aerobic power, endurance and cardiac growth. *Journal of Applied Physiology: Respiratory, Environmental, and Exercise Physiology*, **58**, 492–499.

Kyle, C. (1987). Mechanics and aerodynamics of cycling. In E. Burke & M. Newsom (Eds.), *Medical and scientific aspects of cycling* (pp. 227–243), Champaign, IL: Human Kinetics.

Mitton, J.B., Carey, C., & Kocher, T.D. (in press). The relation of enzyme heterozygosity to standard and active oxygen consumption and body size of tiger salamanders, ambystoma tigrinum. *Physiological Zoology*.

Mitton, J.B., & Grant, M.C. (1984). Associations among protein heterozygosity, growth rate and developmental homeostasis. *Annual Reviews of Ecological Systems*, **15**, 479–499.

Pollock, M.L., Jackson, A.S., & Pate, R.R. (1980). Discriminant analysis of physiological differences between good and elite distance runners. *Research Quarterly for Exercise and Sport*, **51**, 521–532.

Sjodin, B., & Svedenhag, J. (1985). Applied physiology of marathon running. *Journal of Sports Medicine*, **2**, 83–99.

Van Handel, P.J. (1987). Periodization of training. *Bike Tech, 6*(1), 6–10.

Van Handel, P.J., Katz, A., Morrow, J.R., Troup, J.P., Daniels, J.T., & Bradley, P.W. (1988). Aerobic economy and competitive performance of US elite swimmers. In B. Ungerechts, K. Wilke, & K. Reischle (Eds.), *Swimming science V* (pp. 225–234). Champaign, IL: Human Kinetics.

Ergometric and Glycemic Comparisons of Glucose, Fructose, and Sweet Placebo Ingestion Before Exhaustive Exercise

Ed Price

Mike Menke

Phil Banda

Dan Holly

Steve Gall

Due to the recent commercial availability of pure crystalline fructose and the increased use of high-fructose corn sweeteners in the soft drink industry, there is a growing interest in the biochemistry of fructose metabolism. Athletes and diabetics have been encouraged to consume fructose as a sugar substitute before exercise to avoid the reactive hypoglycemia so common with the ingestion of glucose.

Koivisto, Karonen, and Nikkila (1981) compared glucose, fructose, and sweet placebo ingestion 30 min before exhaustive exercise (75% $\dot{V}O_2$max) and found that the rise in plasma glucose and plasma insulin was 3- and 2.5-fold greater after the ingestion of glucose as compared to the ingestion of fructose. In addition, the fall in plasma glucose was directly related to the preexercise levels of plasma glucose and insulin. Exercise time to exhaustion was not significantly different between the solutions, perhaps because of the relatively high intensity used.

Levine, Evans, Cadarette, Fisher, and Bullen (1983) compared glucose, fructose, and water ingestion 45 min before a 30-min treadmill run at 75% $\dot{V}O_2$max. As in the previous study by Koivisto et al. (1981), the increase in plasma glucose and plasma insulin was significantly greater following the ingestion of glucose solution as compared to the ingestion of fructose or water. The respiratory exchange ratio (RQ) during exercise was significantly higher following the ingestion of glucose as compared to fructose or water. This indicates that carbohydrates were oxidized at a greater rate during exercise following glucose ingestion, suggesting that fat was used less efficiently. As expected from the RQ data, muscle glycogen depletion was significantly greater following glucose ingestion, and although exercise was not continued to exhaustion, a faster rate of glycogen depletion would translate to reduced exercise performance.

Keller, Kirk, Schwarzkopf, and Robert (1984) compared exercise time to exhaustion on the cycle ergometer (85% $\dot{V}O_2$max) following glucose or water ingestion in highly trained college distance runners and found that exercise time to exhaustion was 25% longer with the placebo as compared to glucose. Fructose was not studied.

In another study by Koivisto, Harkonen, Karonen, and Groop (1985), comparisons were made between glucose, fructose, and placebo ingestion 45 min before 2 hr of exercise at 55% $\dot{V}O_2$max. The rise in plasma glucose and plasma insulin was 2.4- and 5.8-fold greater after glucose ingestion, as compared to fructose ingestion. Glycogen depletion rates were not significantly different between the groups; however, this could have been due to the low work loads used.

Costill, Katz, Fink, and Hargreaves (1985) compared the effects of pre-exercise fructose and glucose ingestion on the depletion of skeletal muscle glycogen. In agreement with the other studies, plasma glucose was significantly greater following the ingestion of glucose as compared to fructose; however, in contrast to the study by Levine, the RQ was not significantly different between the solutions. Skeletal muscle glycogen depletion was significantly greater following the glucose solution as compared to fructose or placebo. Decombaz, Sartori, Arnaud, and Thelin (1985) compared the effects of glucose and fructose intake before exercise on the oxidation of the substrate, the rate of glycogen depletion, and physical working capacity. Using radioisotopes of the sugars, they found both sugars were oxidized to the same degree. The RQ and blood lactate were higher at rest for fructose, but during exercise these differences disappeared. There was a tendency for greater glycogen depletion following glucose ingestion, but it was not statistically significant. There were no differences in physical working capacity.

In summary, there is general agreement in the literature that glucose ingestion before exercise increases the serum glucose and serum insulin to a greater degree than fructose ingestion. In addition, the fall in serum glucose during exercise is more pronounced following glucose ingestion. The RQ during exercise following glucose ingestion is generally higher, and the rate of muscle glycogen depletion is greater as compared to fructose ingestion. Total work capacity has not been consistently shown to be different between the sugars, perhaps due to the differences in exercise intensity used. However, the information does strongly suggest that glucose should be avoided the last hour before exercise based upon its glycemic effects alone.

Materials and Methods

Twenty-four male students between the ages of 20 and 45 volunteered for the study. The subjects had no history of glucose intolerance, diabetes, or liver disease. The study was conducted as part of the regular biochemistry laboratory taught at San Jose State University.

For at least 3 days prior to each test ride the subjects consumed a weight-maintaining diet consisting of at least 300 g of carbohydrate. This ensured adequate glycogen stores necessary for long-term exhaustive exercise. No exercise was allowed the day before, and no food 4 hr prior to each test ride. The test rides always were performed in the early afternoon to control for circadian rhythms and separated by 2 weeks to permit recovery and allow deconditioning to occur. Each subject served as his own control in a cross-over design.

Glucose, fructose, or sweet placebo solutions (250 ml) were ingested double-blind, 30 min prior to exhaustive exercise on the ergometer. Work loads were set at 60% of the subject's predetermined maximal oxygen consumption rate. This averaged 150 W. Pedal cadence was determined by what the subject felt was the most comfortable during previous tests on the ergometer to measure maximal oxygen consumption rate. Pedal cadence averaged 70 rpm.

Blood was drawn and assayed in a blind design for serum glucose spectrophotometrically (Sigma Blood glucose kit no. 115) three times: just prior to oral ingestion (T1), 30 min later just prior to exercise (T2), and at the end of exhaustive exercise (T3).

Exhaustion was defined as a combination of maximal heart and breathing rates in the subjects, inability to maintain pedal cadence, subjective feeling of the subject, and subjective analysis of the major investigator, who supervised every test ride providing encouragement and motivation to ensure that complete exhaustion had been reached in the subject.

Repeated measures analysis of variance were performed using the BMD2pv statistical package, and scatterplots, frequencies, and condescriptive and Pearson correlations were performed using the SPSS-X statistical package available for the IBM 3038.

A repeated measures analysis of covariance (ANCOVA) was performed. Because all subjects participated in all experimental conditions using SG at Time 1 as the covariate, and although it did partition a significant amount of subject variance in the analysis of variance, the covariate procedure did not alter the main effects or interaction obtained by the repeated measures analysis of variance without the covariate of SG at Time 1.

Results

Before the ingestion of the blind solutions, the blood glucose concentrations were statistically the same, an average of 97 mg/D1 with a standard deviation of 7 mg/D1.

The mean serum glucose concentrations for the placebo solution did not change in the 30 min after ingestion. At the end of exhaustive exercise it fell 20%, to an average of 76 mg/D1 with a standard deviation of 6 mg/D1.

The mean serum glucose concentrations for the fructose solution increased 14% in the 30 min after ingestion, to an average of 110 mg/D1 with a standard deviation of 6 mg/D1. At the end of exhaustive exercise it fell 20%, to an average of 89 mg/D1 with a standard deviation of 6 mg/D1.

The mean serum glucose concentrations for the glucose solution increased 71% in the 30 min after ingestion, to an average of 169 mg/D1 with a standard deviation of 11 mg/D1. At the end of exhaustive exercise it fell over 100%, to an average of 63 mg/D1 with a standard deviation of 4 mg/D1.

The fructose solution averaged the longest exercise time to exhaustion, a mean of 89 min with a standard deviation of 28 min. This is significant by repeated measures of ANOVA $(F = 6.32, df = 2.46, p < .004)$. The placebo solution averaged an intermediate time of 76 min with a standard deviation of 20 min. The glucose solution averaged the shortest time to exhaustion at 72 min, with a standard deviation of 18 min.

Conclusion

The data clearly indicate that glucose ingestion before exhaustive exercise is associated with large swings in the blood glucose levels. Thirty minutes after glucose ingestion, the SG levels approach hyperglycemic values, whereas at the end of exhaustive exercise the SG levels are near hypoglycemic. Fructose ingestion, on the other hand, causes a small but significant increase in the SG levels just prior to exercise and is not associated with hypoglycemia at the end of exhaustive exercise. In addition, fructose ingestion significantly increased, and glucose ingestion significantly decreased, endurance performance as measured by exercise time to exhaustion. The athlete should therefore avoid glucose containing solutions prior to exercise and consider the use of fructose solutions instead.

References

Costill, D.L., Katz, A., Fink, W.J., & Hargreaves, M. (1985). Effect of fructose ingestion on muscle glycogen usage during exercise. *Medicine and Science in Sports and Exercise, 17*(3), 360–363.

Decombaz, J., Sartori, D., Arnaud, J., & Thelin, L. (1985). Oxidation and metabolic effects of fructose or glucose ingested before exercise. *International Journal of Sports Medicine, 6*(5), 282–286.

Keller, K., & Schwarzkopf, R. (1984). Preexercise snacks may decrease exercise performance. *The Physician and Sportsmedicine, 12*(4), 89–93.

Koivisto, V.A., Karonen, S.L., & Nikkila, B.A. (1981). Carbohydrate ingestion before exercise: Comparison of glucose, fructose, and sweet placebo. *Journal of Applied Physiology, 51*(4), 783–787.

Koivisto, V.A., Harkonen, M., Karonen, S.L., & Groop, K.A. (1985). Glycogen depletion during prolonged exercise: Influence of glucose, fructose, or placebo. *Journal of Applied Physiology, 58*(3), 731–737.

Levine, L., Evans, W.J., Cadarette, B.S., Fisher, E.C., & Bullen, B.A. (1983). Fructose and glucose ingestion and muscle glycogen use during submaximal exercise. *Journal of Applied Physiology, 55*(6), 1767–1771.

Noninvasive Determination of the Anaerobic Threshold in Cyclists

Francesco Conconi

Chiara Borsetto

Ilario Casoni

Michele Ferrari

Anaerobic threshold (AT) is defined as the highest level of exertion or oxygen uptake ($\dot{V}O_2$) beyond which blood lactate concentration increases sharply, causing metabolic acidosis, with associated alterations in gas exchange (Caiozzo et al., 1982; Davis, Frank, Whipp, & Wasserman, 1979; Davis, Vodak, Wilmore, Vodak, & Kurtz, 1976; Davis et al., 1983; Wasserman & McIlroy, 1964; Wasserman, Whipp, Koyal, & Beaver, 1973; Wells, Balke, & Von Fossau, 1957).

Blood lactate measurements during muscular work have been utilized to identify AT as the level of effort at which lactate concentrations significantly exceed resting levels (Davis et al., 1976; Farrell, Wilmore, Coyle, Billings, & Costill, 1979; Wasserman & McIlroy, 1964; Wasserman et al., 1973; Yoshida, Nagata, Muro, Takeuchi, & Suda, 1981) or reach a given concentration (Kindermann, Simon, & Keul, 1979; La Fontaine, Londeree, & Spath, 1981; Londeree & Ames, 1975; Rusko, Rahkila, & Karvinen, 1983). AT can also be determined by measuring selected respiratory gas exchange variables (Davis et al., 1976, 1979; Wasserman & McIlroy, 1964; Wasserman et al., 1973).

Recently Conconi, Ferrari, Ziglio, Droghetti, and Codecà (1982) developed a noninvasive field test for the indirect evaluation of AT in runners, which relates running speed (RS) to heart rate (HR). The same authors adapted this field test to other sports, including cycling (Cellini et al., in press; Conconi, Ferrari, Ziglio, Droghetti, Borsetto, et al., 1982; Droghetti et al., 1985). AT, as determined by means of one of the several available methods, has been correlated with performance in aerobic running events (Conconi, Ferrari, Ziglio, Droghetti, & Codeca, 1982; Farrell et al., 1979; Kumagai et al., 1982; Sjodin & Jacobs, 1981; Tanaka, Matsumura, & Moritani, 1981; Thorland, Sady, & Refsell, 1980); in walking races (Conconi, Ferrari, Ziglio, Droghetti, Borsetto, et al., 1982; Hagberg & Coyle, 1983); and in swimming (Cellini et al., 1986), as well as with work time to exhaustion on the cycle ergometer (Jacobs, Sjodin, & Schele, 1983; Stegmann & Kindermann, 1982).

In the present study we have further developed the noninvasive field test and applied it to trained cyclists. In addition, we have evaluated the relationship between the test results and performance in several track and road events.

Methods

Subjects

This study involved 310 trained male cyclists whose ages ranged from 16 to 36. All were road or track racers who trained 300 to 600 km per week, and 32 raced professionally.

Cycling Speed, Heart Rate, and Identification of Deflection Speed

Conconi, Ferrari, Ziglio, Droghetti, and Codecà (1982) found that the relationship between running speed (RS) and heart rate (HR) is linear up to a velocity at which a deflection occurs. The deflection coincides with AT, identified as the level of effort beyond which lactate concentration increases sharply. The same relationship between work intensity and heart rate has been found in cycling (Conconi, Ferrari, Ziglio, Droghetti, Borsetto, et al., 1982; Droghetti et al., 1985) and has been used to determine AT in the present study.

The relationship between cycling speed (CS) and HR was determined while the cyclists progressively increased their CS. The test was usually performed on a 335-m velodrome. The cyclists rode their own bicycles in the racing position and selected their own test gears. After warming up for 15 to 30 min, the cyclists rode 15 to 20 laps without interruption. They began at 28 to 30 km • h^{-1}, and increased their CS slightly after each lap (average increase 1.0 km • h^{-1}), reaching their submaximal velocity in the final lap. The CS of the last lap ranged from 42 to 54 km • h^{-1}, depending on the subject's athletic level. HR was measured at the end of each lap by means of an ECG or a heart rate monitor (Sport Tester TM PE 3000, Polar Electro, Kempele, Finland). Because the frictional air resistance increases relative to the square of the velocity (Di Prampero, 1986), the power output of the cyclist increases proportionally to the velocity raised to the third power; this was taken into account in plotting the data. As in running, a deflection speed (CS$_d$) was identified from the graph of CS versus HR.

The CS-HR relationship was also determined in 57 cyclists as they ascended a 10% constant grade. An ascent of 1.8 km was divided into 12 sections of 150 m each. The cyclists began at a slow pace (approximately 12 km • h^{-1}), increased their CS slightly after every 150 m, and reached their submaximal velocity (22 to 27 km • h^{-1}) in the 12th section. At the velocities reached during the ascending test the air resistance is negligible; therefore, the power output of the cyclist increases proportionally to the velocity. This was also considered in plotting the data. As in the velo-drome test, a CS_d was identified from the graph of ascending CS versus HR.

Speed of Deflection and Blood Lactate Concentrations

CS_d was determined for 8 cyclists. Each cyclist was then asked to reach gradually and maintain, for 2,000 m, each of six speeds—three below and three above CS_d—in increasing order. Blood samples were collected at rest and 5 min after the conclusion of each segment. The cyclist rested for 20 min between segments. Blood lactate was measured twice for each sample with the Roche Model 640 Lactate Analyzer.

Speed of Deflection and Average Cycling Speed in Competition

The correlation between CS_d and average CS was analyzed in the following events (performed within a week after CS_d determination): 1-km individual time trial (flying start) for 82 cyclists, 1 of whom was tested 19 times over a 16-month period; 4-km pursuit for 44 cyclists; 16-km time trial for 1 cyclist who was tested 17 times over a 16-month period; and a 1-hr individual time trial for 6 cyclists. The correlation between ascending CS_d (10% constant grade) and average ascending speed was also studied in two time trials: 2 km (10% constant grade) for 57 cyclists and 10 km (6% average grade) for 18 cyclists. Correlations were evaluated by linear regression analysis.

Results

Cycling Speed and Heart Rate

Figure 1 shows a typical relationship between CS and HR: The two variables are linearly related up to 43.1 km $\cdot$ h^{-1}, whereas at higher speeds there is a definite decrease in slope and the linearity of the CS-HR relationship is lost. The speed at which the linearity is lost is the speed of deflection (CS_d). The HR corresponding to this value is designated HR_d. CS_d was identified for all 310 cyclists.

When the field test was repeated by the same subject within a few days and under similar experimental conditions (clothing, air temperature and humidity, absence of wind), nearly identical data were obtained.

Figure 2 shows the relationship between CS and HR as determined for a cyclist ascending a 10% constant grade. A linear relationship exists between CS and HR, and a deflection occurs at submaximal velocities. Ascending CS_d was identified for all 57 cyclists.

Speed of Deflection and Lactate Concentration

Figure 3 shows the CS-HR relationship and the blood lactate concentrations for one cyclist at six speeds, three below and three above CS_d. The

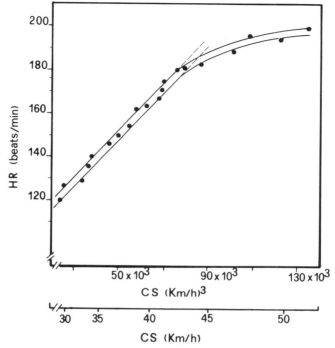

Figure 1   Relationship between CS³ and HR for an amateur cyclist. An abscissa with the actual velocities is also provided for clarity.

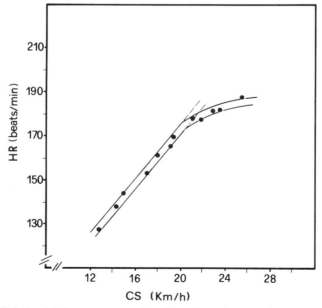

Figure 2   Relationship between ascending CS and HR for a professional cyclist.

lactate concentrations increase sharply at velocities above CS_d. The intersection of the lines (LI) connecting the lactate concentrations below and above CS_d coincides with CS_d. Figure 4 shows the correlation $(r = .99)$ between LI and CS_d for 8 cyclists.

Speed of Deflection and Performance in Cycling Events

The correlation between CS_d and average speed in competition, previously established for several running, walking, and swimming aerobic events, has been evaluated in cycling.

Figure 5 illustrates the correlation between CS_d and average speed in a 1-km individual time trial (flying start) for 82 cyclists. The correlation coefficient is .84. For one novice cyclist, the same relationship was determined 19 times over a 16-month period of continuous training; the correlation coefficient is .96 (see Figure 6).

The correlation between CS_d and average CS in a 4-km pursuit for 44 cyclists appears in Figure 7; the correlation coefficient is .90.

Figure 8 shows the correlation between CS_d and average CS in a 16-km time trial for 1 novice (same subject as Figure 6) who was tested 17 times over a 16-month period of continuous training; the correlation coefficient is .97.

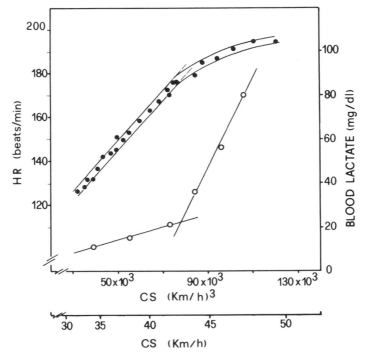

Figure 3 CS^3-HR relationship and blood lactate concentrations at six speeds for an amateur cyclist. An abscissa with the actual velocities is also provided for clarity.

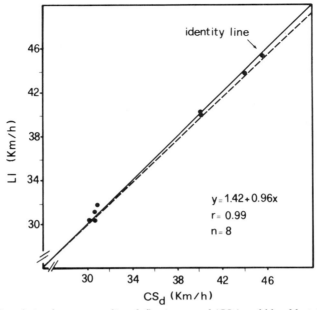

Figure 4   Correlation between cycling deflection speed (CS_d) and blood lactate line intersections (LI) for 8 cyclists.

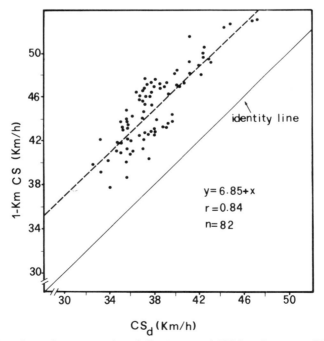

Figure 5   Correlation between cycling deflection speed (CS_d) and average CS in a 1-km individual time trial (flying start) for 82 cyclists.

Figure 9 depicts the correlation between CS_d and average CS in a 1-hr individual time trial for 6 cyclists; the correlation coefficient is .99. Finally, the correlation between ascending CS_d and average ascending speed was measured in time trials of 2 km for 57 cyclists and 10 km for 18 cyclists and found to be .85 and .91, respectively (see Figures 10 and 11).

Discussion and Conclusions

The field test relating speed and heart rate, developed in running, has been adapted to cycling as well as to walking, canoeing, rowing, skating, cross-country skiing, and swimming. For all cyclists tested, a linear relationship occurred between CS and HR, with a definite decrease in slope at high work intensities.

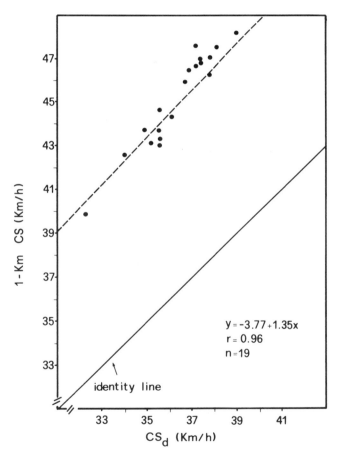

Figure 6 Correlation between cycling deflection speed (CS_d) and average CS in a 1-km individual time trial (flying start) for 1 novice. This cyclist was tested 19 times over a 16-month period of continuous training.

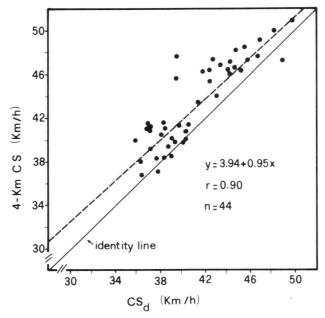

Figure 7   Correlation between cycling deflection speed (CS_d) and average CS in a 4-km pursuit for 44 cyclists.

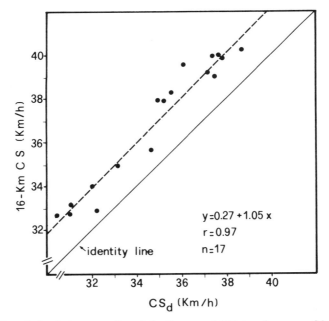

Figure 8   Correlation between cycling deflection speed (CS_d) and average CS in a 16-km time trial for 1 novice. This cyclist was tested 17 times over a 16-month period of continuous training.

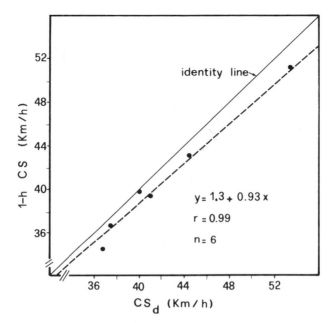

Figure 9 Correlation between cycling deflection speed (CS_d) and average CS in a 1-hr individual time trial for 6 cyclists.

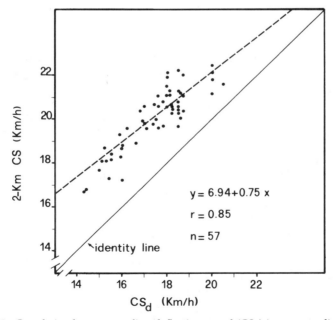

Figure 10 Correlation between cycling deflection speed (CS_d) in an ascending test (10% constant grade) and average CS in a 2-km ascending time trial (10% constant grade) for 57 cyclists.

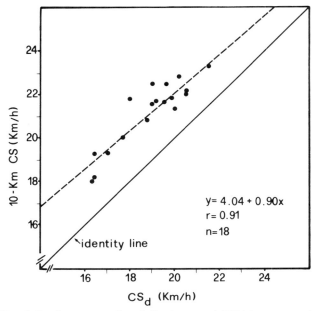

Figure 11   Correlation between cycling deflection speed (CS_d) in an ascending test (10% constant grade) and average CS in a 10-km ascending time trial (6% average grade) for 18 cyclists.

As in other sports, the speed at which the linearity of the CS-HR relationship is lost, called CS_d, coincides with the onset of blood lactate accumulation and therefore with the so-called anaerobic threshold. Similarly, CS_d is closely correlated with average speed in aerobic events. The longer (and therefore the more aerobic) the event lasts, the higher the correlation coefficient (range of .84 for the 1-km to .99 for the 1-hr individual time trial).

The CS_d determination can be used to establish the training intensities (or heart rates) above which the anaerobic mechanisms of ATP production are utilized in individual cyclists.

Other applications of the test to cycling include equipment optimization (aerodynamics, gearing, etc.) and evaluation of the effects of such factors as air temperature and humidity and barometric pressure (especially at altitude).

The test presented in this paper has been reproduced on a bicycle windload trainer by Argentieri, Ennis, and Piper, 1988. We have also performed the test on both a windload trainer and traditional cycle ergometers; in the latter case, the incremental test was performed starting with a 50-W load that increased by 50 W each minute.

Acknowledgments

We acknowledge the technical and financial support of the Italian Cycling Federation (FCI) and of the Scuola dello Sport of the Italian Olympic Committee (CONI), and also the assistance of Patricia Ennis in editing the manuscript.

References

Argentieri, M.P., Ennis, P.S., & Piper, L. (1988). Deflection velocities in heart rate and end-tidal oxygen graphs during incremental exercise on a windload trainer. In E.R. Burke & M.M. Newsom (Eds.), *Medical and scientific aspects of cycling* (pp. 97–103). Champaign, IL: Human Kinetics.

Caiozzo, V.J., Davis, J.A., Ellis, J.F., Azus, J.L., Vandagriff, R., Prietto, C.A., & McMaster, W.C. (1982). A comparison of gas exchange indices used to detect the anaerobic threshold. *Journal of Applied Physiology, 53,* 1184–1189.

Cellini, M., Vitiello, P., Nagliati, A., Ziglio, P.G., Martinelli, S., Ballarin, E., & Conconi, F. (1986). Noninvasive determination of the anaerobic threshold in swimming. *International Journal of Sports Medicine, 7,* 347–351.

Conconi, F., Ferrari, M., Ziglio, P.G., Droghetti, P., & Codecà, L. (1982). Determination of the anaerobic threshold by a noninvasive field test in runners. *Journal of Applied Physiology, 52,* 869–873.

Conconi, F., Ferrari, M., Ziglio, P.G., Droghetti, P., Borsetto, C., Casoni, I., Cellini, M., & Paolini, A.R. (1982). Determination of the anaerobic threshold by a noninvasive field test in running and other sport activities (abstract). *International Journal of Sports Medicine* (Suppl.), 15.

Davis, J.A., Vodak, P., Wilmore, J.H., Vodak, J., & Kurtz, P. (1976). Anaerobic threshold and maximal aerobic power for three modes of exercise. *Journal of Applied Physiology, 41,* 544–550.

Davis, J.A., Frank, M.H., Whipp, B.J., & Wasserman, K. (1979). Anaerobic threshold alterations caused by endurance training in middle-aged men. *Journal of Applied Physiology, 46,* 1039–1046.

Davis, J.A., Caiozzo, V.J., Lamarra, N., Ellis, J.F., Vandagriff, R., Prietto, C.A., & McMaster, W.C. (1983). Does the gas exchange anaerobic threshold occur at a fixed blood lactate concentration of 2 or 4 mM? *International Journal of Sports Medicine, 4,* 89–93.

Di Prampero, P.E. (1986). Energy cost of human locomotion on land and in water. *International Journal of Sports Medicine, 7,* 55–72.

Droghetti, P., Borsetto, C., Casoni, I., Cellini, M., Ferrari, M., Paolini, A.R., Ziglio, P.G., & Conconi, F. (1985). Noninvasive determination of the anaerobic threshold in canoeing, cross-country skiing, cycling, roller, and ice-skating, rowing and walking. *European Journal of Applied Physiology, 53*, 299–303.

Farrell, P.A., Wilmore, J.H., Coyle, E.F., Billings, J.E., & Costill, D.L. (1979). Plasma lactate accumulation and distance running performance. *Medicine and Science in Sports and Exercise, 11*, 338–344.

Hagberg, J.M., & Coyle, E.F. (1983). Physiological determinants of endurance performance as studied in competitive racewalkers. *Medicine and Science in Sports and Exercise, 15*, 287–289.

Jacobs, I., Sjodin, B., & Schele, R. (1983). A single blood lactate determination as an indicator of cycle ergometer endurance capacity. *European Journal of Applied Physiology, 50*, 355–364.

Kindermann, W., Simon, G., & Keul, J. (1979). The significance of the aerobic-anaerobic transition for the determination of work load intensities during endurance training. *European Journal of Applied Physiology, 42*, 25–34.

Kumagai, S., Tanaka, K., Matsuura, Y., Matsuzaka, A., Hirakoba, K., & Asano, K. (1982). Relationship of the anaerobic threshold with the 5, 10 km and 10 mile races. *European Journal of Applied Physiology, 49*, 13–23.

La Fontaine, T.P., Londeree, B.R., & Spath, W.K. (1981). The maximal steady state versus selected running events. *Medicine and Science in Sports and Exercise, 13*, 190–192.

Londeree, B.R., & Ames, S.A. (1975). Maximal steady state versus state of conditioning. *European Journal of Applied Physiology, 34*, 269–278.

Rusko, H., Rahkila, P., & Karvinen, E. (1983). Anaerobic threshold skeletal muscle enzymes and fiber composition in young female cross-country skiers. *Acta Physiologica Scandinavica, 108*, 263–268.

Sjodin, B., & Jacobs, I. (1981). Onset of blood lactate accumulation and marathon running performance. *International Journal of Sports Medicine, 2*, 23–26.

Stegmann, H., & Kindermann, W. (1982). Comparison of prolonged exercise tests at the individual anaerobic threshold and the fixed anaerobic threshold of 4 mmol • l⁻¹. *International Journal of Sports Medicine, 3*, 105–110.

Tanaka, K., Matsuura, Y., & Moritani, T. (1981). A correlational analysis of maximal oxygen uptake and anaerobic threshold as compared with middle and long distance performance. *Journal Physiological Fitness Japan, 30*, 94–102.

Thorland, W., Sady, S., & Refsell, M. (1980). Anaerobic threshold and maximal oxygen consumption rates as predictors of cross-country running performance. *Medicine and Science in Sports and Exercise, 12*, 87.

Wasserman, K., & McIlroy, M.B. (1964). Detecting the threshold of anaerobic metabolism. *American Journal of Cardiology, 14*, 844–852.

Wasserman, K., Whipp, B.J., Koyal, S.N., & Beaver, W.L. (1973). Anaerobic threshold and respiratory gas exchange during exercise. *Journal of Applied Physiology, 35*, 236–243.

Wells, F.J., Balke, B., & Von Fossau, D.D. (1957). Lactic acid accumulation during work: A suggested standardization of work classification. *Journal of Applied Physiology, 10*, 51–55.

Yoshida, T., Nagata, A., Muro, M., Takeuchi, N., & Suda, Y. (1981). The validity of anaerobic threshold determination by a Douglas bag method compared with arterial blood lactate concentration. *European Journal of Applied Physiology, 46*, 423–430.

Prediction of Oxygen Consumption From Heart Rate During Cycling

Philip S. Clifford

J. Richard Coast

David P. Swain

Martin C. Milliken

Paul R. Stricker

James Stray-Gundersen

Knowledge of the oxygen cost of cycling during various racing events is potentially valuable information in designing training programs for competitive cyclists. Oxygen consumption ($\dot{V}O_2$) values during racing events are not presently available, undoubtedly because it has not been logistically feasible to make such measurements under racing conditions due to the equipment required and the nature of the sport. However, it has long been known that heart rate (HR) is a linear function of $\dot{V}O_2$. We hypothesized that this relationship might be used to allow prediction of $\dot{V}O_2$ from HR measurements that could be accomplished under racing conditions with minimal interference. Thus, the purpose of this investigation was to compare measurements of HR and $\dot{V}O_2$ made during an incremental ergometer test in the laboratory with like measurements made while cycling outdoors on a level road. We reasoned that if the HR/$\dot{V}O_2$ relationship on the ergometer was identical to that on a moving bicycle, then one could record HR during cycling on the road and predict O_2 consumption from the HR/$\dot{V}O_2$ relationship determined in the laboratory.

Methods

The subjects for this study were 10 experienced male cyclists recruited from local touring and racing clubs. Selected anthropometric and physiological characteristics of the subjects are listed in Table 1.

Two studies were performed on each subject: one outdoors on the subject's own bicycle on a level road and the other in the laboratory on a calibrated cycle ergometer (Monark). The studies were performed on different days, with some subjects tested in the laboratory first and others tested first on the road.

Road Tests

For the road tests, the subjects rode beside a parallel moving vehicle with the front of the bicycle slightly ahead of the vehicle to avoid the effects of wind turbulence created by it. A mouthpiece and lightweight breathing valve (Hans Rudolph #2000) connected by plastic tubing to a modified Douglas bag in the accompanying vehicle permitted the collection of expired air. Gas samples were later analyzed with a Perkin-Elmer mass spectrometer (MGA 1100A) and a Tissot spirometer (120 L). Heart rate was measured with a lightweight, battery-powered telemetry system (Quantum XL Fitness Monitor). Measurements were taken with the subjects cycling at 16.1, 24.2, and 32.2 kph (10, 15, and 20 mph) over a course 1,100 m long. Computerized bicycle speedometers were used by the subjects to control their speed over the length of the course, and this was verified by timing them over a 300-m section. Gear ratios were chosen to enable the subjects to pedal at approximately 60 rpm at the lowest speed and at 75 to 80 rpm at the two highest speeds. These pedal rates have been shown to be optimal at these moderate power outputs (Coast & Welch, 1985). Prior to each set of runs, 4 to 5 min of warm-up at the test speed were used to ensure relatively steady-state conditions. Four runs were made at each speed, two in each direction, to compensate for the slight elevation change (0.9 m) and the presence of light winds. Wind speed was measured with an anemometer (Dwyer Instruments), and runs were not included if the wind speed exceeded 8 kph (5 mph).

Ergometer Tests

The cycle ergometer in the laboratory was modified with pedals, handlebars, and seat from a racing cycle, adjusted to approximate the dimensions of each subject's bicycle. Oxygen uptake was measured on-line using O_2 and CO_2 analyzers (Ametek S-3AI and CD-3A), which sampled from an

Table 1 Subject Characteristics

Trait	Measure
Age (years)	30.8 ± 2.5
Height (cm)	179.4 ± 4.0
Weight (kg)	71.9 ± 4.3
Fat (%)	10.9 ± 1.3
$\dot{V}O_2$max ($ml \cdot kg^{-1} \cdot min^{-1}$)	59.9 ± 2.2

expiratory mixing chamber, and a dry gas meter (Rayfield Equipment) connected to the inspiratory port of a Hans Rudolph breathing valve (#2000). This system was interfaced with an Apple computer that calculated and printed values at 30-s intervals. Both analyzers used in these tests and the mass spectrometer used in the road tests were calibrated with Scholander-analyzed gases. In addition, the dry gas meter employed for the ergometer tests in the laboratory was calibrated against the Tissot spirometer utilized for the road tests.

As in the road tests, HR was measured via telemetry. The protocol for the ergometer tests was designed to allow measurement of HR and $\dot{V}O_2$ at several different steady state levels. The initial work load was 75 W (450 kpm), and work load was increased by 75 W at 3-min intervals until volitional fatigue. If $\dot{V}O_2$ had not reached a plateau within 3 min, the work load duration was increased by 1 min. Both $\dot{V}O_2$ and HR were averaged over the last minute of each work load.

Statistics

The regression of HR on $\dot{V}O_2$ was calculated for each individual subject for the road tests and for the ergometer tests. No resting data were included in the analysis. A paired t test was then performed on the slopes and intercepts of the regression lines to determine if significant differences existed between the two conditions.

Results

Data from an individual subject are shown in Figure 1. Simultaneous measurements of HR and $\dot{V}O_2$ from the road tests are depicted by the

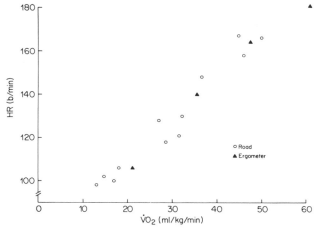

Figure 1   Heart rate (HR) plotted as a function of oxygen consumption ($\dot{V}O_2$) for an individual subject.

open circles with measurements from the ergometer tests represented as closed triangles. For each subject there were 10 to 12 values for the road tests and 4 to 5 values for the ergometer tests.

Figure 2 contains the data for all subjects studied. The regression lines pictured were obtained by determining the regression for each individual subject, then calculating the mean for all the slope and intercept values. The regression equation for the road tests (solid line) was

$$HR = 2.09 \ \dot{V}O_2 + 67.88$$

and that for the ergometer tests (dashed lines) was

$$HR = 2.00 \ \dot{V}O_2 + 70.86$$

with HR given in beats/min and $\dot{V}O_2$ in $ml \cdot kg^{-1} \cdot min^{-1}$. R values for these regression equations were .99 for the ergometer tests and .96 for the road. There were no significant differences between the slopes of the lines or between their intercepts, as assessed by paired t tests $(p > .05)$.

Discussion

Our measurements of O_2 consumption on the road were similar to values reported previously by Brooke and Davies (1973) and Pugh (1974). In addition, the $\dot{V}O_2$ values (expressed in L/min) for the ergometer tests were on the order of those expected for the work loads employed (Åstrand & Rodahl, 1977).

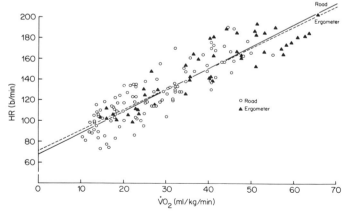

Figure 2 Heart rate (HR) versus oxygen consumption ($\dot{V}O_2$) for all 10 subjects. The solid line is the regression line for the road tests, and the dashed line is the regression line for the ergometer tests.

The linear relationship between HR and $\dot{V}O_2$ is readily discernible from the data points shown in Figure 1 from a single subject. This relationship has been described previously, at least as early as 1922 when it was demonstrated by Douglas and Haldane. Dill (1942) reported a close, linear relationship between HR and $\dot{V}O_2$ but also showed that this relationship was altered by environmental temperature. The road and ergometer tests comprising this report were performed at similar ambient temperatures. From the data of Dill, it would appear that similar temperatures are requisite to allow accurate prediction of $\dot{V}O_2$ from HR.

Advances in electronics, particularly in miniaturization, have expanded the possibilities in many areas of scientific endeavor. Indeed, the piece of equipment that made the present study feasible was the existence of the lightweight, battery-powered telemetry unit employed for measurement of HR. This telemetry device should also be particularly applicable for monitoring work levels during training sessions.

The empirical equations that describe the linear relationship between HR and $\dot{V}O_2$ were derived for this particular group of cyclists and are not necessarily generalizable to a different population. In order to predict O_2 consumption from HR, the HR/$\dot{V}O_2$ relationship must be determined in the laboratory for each individual cyclist. We would caution that there may be some variability in predicting values for a given individual, but the above results suggest that group values should be predicted accurately.

Conclusion

The key finding of this study is that the slopes and intercepts of the regression of HR on $\dot{V}O_2$ for the road tests were not significantly different from the corresponding parameters for the ergometer tests. We conclude from this that there is no significant difference between the relationship of HR and $\dot{V}O_2$ on a moving bicycle on the road compared with that on an ergometer in the laboratory. Therefore, determination of the HR/$\dot{V}O_2$ relationship for each subject on an ergometer in the laboratory should allow accurate prediction of O_2 consumption from HR measured by telemetry during cycling on the road.

Acknowledgments

The authors would like to express their sincere appreciation to the subjects who participated in this study and to Robert Vaughan who assisted in data collection. We also thank Ms. M. Mick for preparing the manuscript and Dr. Jere Mitchell for his support of the study.

References

Åstrand, P.O., & Rodahl, K. (1977). *Textbook of work physiology.* New York: McGraw-Hill.

Brooke, J.D., & Davies, G.J. (1973). Comment on "Estimation of energy expenditure of sporting cyclists." *Ergonomics,* **16**, 237–238.

Coast, J.R., & Welch, H.G. (1985). Linear increase in optimal pedal rate with increases power output in cycle ergometry. *European Journal of Applied Physiology,* **53**, 339–342.

Dill, D.B. (1942). Effects of physical strain and high altitudes on the heart and circulation. *American Heart Journal,* **23**, 441–454.

Douglas, C.G., & Haldane, J.S. (1922). The regulation of the general circulation rate in man. *Journal of Physiology* (London), **56**, 69–100.

Pugh, L.G.C.E. (1974). The relation of oxygen intake and speed in competition cycling and comparative observations on the bicycle ergometer. *Journal of Physiology* (London), **241**, 795–808.

PART II

Research: Techniques and Results

Deflection Velocities in Heart Rate and End-Tidal Oxygen Graphs During Incremental Exercise on a Windload Trainer

M.P. Argentieri

P. Ennis

L. Piper

The speed at which a deflection occurs (deflection velocity, or V_d) in heart rate (HR) graphs during incremental exercise has been used to predict running performance (Conconi, Ferrari, Ziglio, Droghetti, & Codecà, 1982). Similarly, deflection velocities have been used to predict the endurance performance of walkers, cross-country skiers, and cyclists (Droghetti et al., 1985).

Endurance performance is usually assessed through measurements of blood lactate and/or ventilation parameters during incremental exercise testing (Ward, Davis, & Whipp, 1982). At low power loads, changes in lactate and ventilation parameters match the increases in effort in a linear fashion. At high power loads, oxygen delivery can no longer meet the metabolic demand, and anaerobic work increases. As a result, lactate levels and ventilation parameters quickly change, causing simultaneous deflections in their respective graphs (Wasserman, 1978).

At power levels above this deflection, metabolic acidosis occurs, and performance is limited. Thus, the power level at which deflections occur defines the limit of endurance performance. Conconi et al. (1982) and Droghetti et al. (1985) have found an excellent correlation between deflections in lactate and HR graphs and have considered this deflection point to be the anaerobic threshold.

A good correlation usually exists between deflections in lactate and ventilation parameters. However, errors in these measurements can result in a poor correlation between them and thus an inaccurate assessment of endurance performance. Statistical errors in sampling and analytical technique can affect lactate measurements (Ward et al., 1982). The use of inaccurate flow and volume transducers can cause measurement errors in volume-dependent ventilation parameters (Gardner, Hankinson, & West, 1980). Further errors have been introduced by difficulties in the subjective interpretation of a deflection point (Yeh, Gardner, Adams, Yanowitz, & Crapo, 1983).

In contrast to the above methods, end-tidal oxygen (ETO_2) and end-tidal carbon dioxide ($ETCO_2$) can be precisely and easily measured on a breath-to-breath basis using a fast-response mass spectrometer. Deflections in ETO_2 and $ETCO_2$ graphs have been found to correlate well with deflections in lactate levels and other ventilation parameters (Wasserman, Whipp, Koyal, & Beaver, 1973). These correlations, and the accuracy and ease with which ETO_2 and $ETCO_2$ measurements can be made, make them ideal parameters for assessing performance during incremental exercise testing.

During incremental exercise testing, oxygen uptake ($\dot{V}O_2$) increases linearly with increases in power. With a shift to anaerobic work, the rate of change of lactate, CO_2 production ($\dot{V}CO_2$), and total ventilation (VE) increases, causing deflections in VE/$\dot{V}O_2$ and ETO_2 graphs (see Figure 1). Due to a period of isocapnic buffering, VE/$\dot{V}CO_2$ and $ETCO_2$ temporarily remain constant. However, at higher power loads, VE further increases, causing deflections in VE/$\dot{V}CO_2$ and $ETCO_2$ graphs. The occurrence of the $ETCO_2$ deflection after the ETO_2 deflection indicates that the ETO_2 deflection was evoked by a large shift toward anaerobic

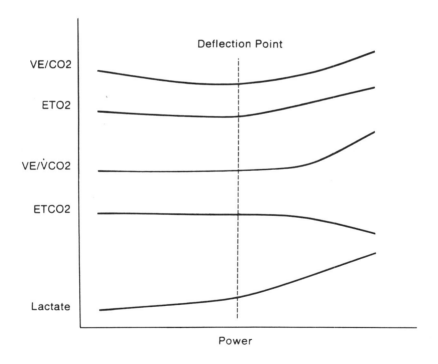

Figure 1   Deflections in lactate, ventilation parameters (VE/$\dot{V}O_2$; VE/$\dot{V}CO_2$, ETO_2, and $ETCO_2$ during incremental exercise where VE = total ventilation, $\dot{V}O_2$ = oxygen uptake, $\dot{V}CO_2$ = carbon dioxide production, ETO_2 = end-tidal oxygen, $ETCO_2$ = end-tidal carbon dioxide.

metabolism rather than by another stimulus, such as pain or anxiety (Wasserman et al., 1973).

Our group previously reported an incremental test for windload trainers that used deflections in HR graphs to determine V_d; 53 subjects were tested, and 87% yielded an HR deflection (Ennis, 1985). This test is easily performed using a heart rate monitor, bicycle computer, and windload trainer, with no influence on V_d from weather and track conditions. The primary purpose of this study was to compare the HR method to the more accepted ETO_2 method for determining V_d during incremental exercise on a windload trainer. We also compared target training HR ranges based on HR deflections to ranges computed from an age-based formula.

Methods

We tested 10 experienced cyclists who rode a minimum of 100 mi per week; their ages ranged from 26 to 51 years. All cyclists were tested with their own bicycles mounted on the same windload trainer. Heart rates were trended with an HR monitor/recorder. Velocity and time were measured with a bicycle computer. Inhaled and exhaled oxygen and carbon dioxide levels were measured with a Perkin-Elmer mass spectrometer and were continuously recorded. The mass spectrometer's sampling tube was connected to a face mask that had two large, unrestricted openings to prevent any increase in the work of breathing. All subjects confirmed that this apparatus did not inhibit their breathing. The windload trainer's rolling resistance was standardized by adjusting its tension on the rear wheel so that it took 4.0 s for it to coast to a stop from 15 mph (coast-down test).

The test began with a 20-min warm-up, during which the correct gearing was selected to prevent excessive cadences at higher velocities. Testing started at 10 mph, and no gear changes were allowed. Our test protocol consisted of holding a constant velocity for a 1-min interval, after which the velocity was increased by 1 mph for the next interval. This procedure was repeated until the designated velocity could no longer be maintained or the subject elected to end the test. Heart rate, ETO_2, and $ETCO_2$ levels were continuously recorded.

The relationship between velocity and power output for a cyclist riding a windload trainer is similar to that for riding on the road (Firth, 1981). Therefore, the power needed to drive a windload trainer is proportional to the velocity cubed. To obtain graphs of HR, ETO_2, and $ETCO_2$ versus relative power, we plotted the values recorded at the end of each interval against velocity cubed.

A numerical routine, programmed into a hand-held calculator, was used to identify V_d as indicated by deflections in HR and ETO_2 data. We then compared target training HR ranges based on HR deflections or HR_d (defined by .90 [HR_d] to HRd) to target HR ranges defined by the following age-based formula: .75(MPHR) to .85(MPHR), where maximal predicted HR (MPHR) equals 220 minus age in years (Hansen, Giese, & Corliss, 1980).

Results

Our numerical routine identified deflections in HR and ETO_2 graphs for all 10 subjects. Figure 2 shows a typical HR graph with V_d and its corresponding HR_d. Table 1 lists the deflection heart rates independently determined from deflections in HR and ETO_2 graphs. Deflections in the $ETCO_2$ graphs all occurred after ETO_2 deflections, indicating that a period of isocapnic buffering had occurred and that endurance performance would be limited at power levels above the ETO_2 deflection.

No statistically significant difference was found $(p < .01)$ between the HR and ETO_2 methods for determining V_d; the correlation coefficient for V_d was $r = .99$ with $y = 1.0x - .9$.

Figure 3 compares the target training HR ranges as defined by HR_d and the age-based formula. For all but 1 cyclist, the HR_d-based HRs were higher than the age-based HRs. For 4 cyclists, there was no overlap between the target HR ranges as defined by the two methods. A statistically significant difference was found $(p < .05)$ between the HR_d and .85(MPHR) heart rates and between the .90(HR_d) and .75(MPHR) heart rates. No statistically significant difference was found between .90(HR_d) and .85(MPHR).

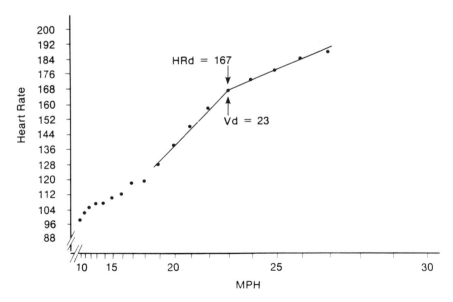

Figure 2 Typical heart rate (HR) graph from an incremental exercise test on a windload trainer with calculator-identified deflection velocity (V_d) and HR (HR_d). Velocity has been plotted on a velocity-cubed scale that is proportional to power.

Table 1   Comparison of Heart Rate and End-Tidal Oxygen Methods for Determining Deflection Velocities (V_d) in mph

Subject	Age	Heart rate method		End-tidal oxygen method
		HR_d	V_d	V_d
1	26	158	23	25
2	27	172	19	19
3	29	167	23	23
4	30	175	24	24
5	30	180	25	24
6	35	164	19	19
7	36	160	20	20
8	39	172	24	24
9	45	172	22	22
10	51	169	23	23

Note. HR_d is the heart rate at which a defection occurred in a HR graph.

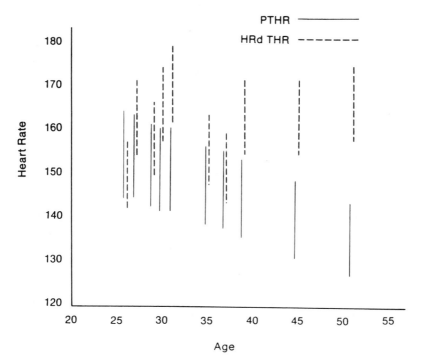

Figure 3   Comparison of target training HR ranges as defined by deflection heart rates (HR_d THR) and an age-based formula (PTHR).

Discussion

Our work demonstrates an excellent agreement between the HR and ETO_2 methods for determining V_d during incremental exercise testing on a windload trainer. Deflection velocity has been shown to be a good predictor of endurance performance (Conconi et al., 1982). Our results lend support to the concept of predicting a cyclist's endurance performance using a windload trainer, bicycle computer, heart rate monitor, and hand-held calculator. This test can be easily performed in a controlled manner without a laboratory or expensive equipment.

The power needed to drive a windload trainer is a function of its rolling resistance and its fan's aerodynamic drag. Because changes in either function can alter V_d, both must be controlled. The trainer's aerodynamic drag is a function of its fan's dimensions, drag coefficient (which remains constant), and velocity. Thus, for any given velocity, the aerodynamic drag will remain constant and should not influence V_d, provided that the same windload trainer is used.

Rolling resistance depends on the characteristics of the wheel and its pressure on the fan's roller. The time needed to coast to a stop is a function of the wheel's dimensions, mass distribution, and rolling resistance. We controlled the rolling resistance by using the same wheel and by performing a timed coast-down test.

With control over drag and rolling resistance, the work load of the windload trainer may be standardized. Thus any changes in V_d reflect changes in performance of the bicycle-cyclist combination. Use of a numerical routine further ensures that changes in V_d are not due to subjective interpretations. It must be remembered that, because it is derived from a relative power measurement, V_d is an indicator of relative and not absolute performance.

The formulas that are commonly used to prescribe optimal training HRs are usually based on a predicted maximal heart rate (MHR) computed from age. Londeree and Moeschberger (1984) found errors of $\pm$ 22 beats/min in age-predicted MRHs for 95% of the population. Maximal heart rate was also found to vary with the type of exercise and conditioning. Thus, age-based formulas are likely to yield incorrect training HRs. We found little agreement between HR_d-based and age-based HR training ranges.

Training at HRs close to one's endurance limit has been shown to result in optimal increases in endurance performance (Gibbons, Jessup, Wells, & Werthmann, 1983). Conconi (personal communication) found optimal increases in performance when the training HR range was between 0.9 (HR_d) and HR_d. These findings support the concept that by determining V_d and HR_d with a windload trainer, one can also identify an optimal HR training range.

References

Conconi, F., Ferrari, M., Ziglio, P.G., Droghetti, P., & Codecà, L. (1982). Determination of the anaerobic threshold by a noninvasive field test in runners. *Journal of Applied Physiology*, **52**, 869–873.

Droghetti, P., Borsetto, C., Casoni, I., Cellini, M., Ferrari, M., Paolini, A.R., Ziglio, P.G., & Conconi, F. (1985). Noninvasive determination of the anaerobic threshold in canoeing, cross-country skiing, cycling, roller and ice skating, rowing, and walking. *European Journal of Applied Physiology*, **54**, 299–303.

Ennis, P. (1985). Do-it-yourself test Conconi. *Velo-news: A Journal of Bicycle Racing*, **14**(10), 6–7.

Firth, M.S. (1981). A sport-specific training and testing device for racing cyclist. *Ergonomics*, **24**, 565–571.

Gardner, R.M., Hankinson, J.L., & West, B.J. (1980). Evaluating commercially available spirometers. *American Review of Respiratory Diseases*, **121**, 73–82.

Gibbons, E.S., Jessup, G.T., Wells, T.D., & Werthmann, D.A. (1983). Effects of various training intensity levels on anaerobic threshold capacity in females. *Journal of Sports Medicine*, **23**, 315–318.

Hanson, P.G., Giese, M.D., & Corliss, R.J. (1980). Clinical guidelines for exercise training. *Postgraduate Medicine*, **67**, 120–135.

Londeree, B.R., & Moeschberger, M.L. (1984). Influence of age and other factors on maximal heart rate. *Journal of Cardiac Rehabilitation*, **4**, 44–49.

Ward, S.A., Davis, J.A., & Whipp, B.J. (1982). The physiologic basis of exercise testing: Part 2. Design and interpretation. *Journal of Cardiovascular and Pulmonary Technology*, **9**(5), 21–24.

Wasserman, K. (1978). Breathing during exercise. *New England Journal of Medicine*, **298**, 780–785.

Wasserman, K., Whipp, B.J., Koyal, S.N., & Beaver, W.L. (1973). Anaerobic threshold and respiratory gas exchange during exercise. *Journal of Applied Physiology*, **35**, 236–243.

Yeh, M.P., Gardner, R.M., Adams, T.D., Yanowitz, F.G., & Crapo, R.O. (1983). "Anaerobic threshold": Problems of determination and validation. *Journal of Applied Physiology*, **55**, 1178–1186.

Metabolic Requirements of Riding Windload Simulators as Compared to Cycling on the Road

J. Richard Coast

David P. Swain

Martin C. Milliken

Philip S. Clifford

Paul R. Stricker

James Stray-Gundersen

Windload simulators have become increasingly popular as both casual exercise devices and as training tools for bicyclists in the off-season and during inclement weather. With this popularity, many styles and brands have become available to the public, all of which presumably attempt to approximate the resistance a rider experiences on the road. Little published research deals with the individual types of simulators or with simulators as a group, or with the degree to which the aerobic demands of riding these devices compare with outdoor cycling.

In addition, a problem incurred in testing cyclists in the laboratory is the use of an appropriate testing device. Cycle ergometers have been widely used and tests on them are standardized, but cyclists train on individualized equipment and bicycles are purchased to fit each athlete. The use of a windload simulator allows cyclists to use their own bicycles, rather than attempting to duplicate the fit of a bicycle on a standard exercise testing device. Thus, the windload simulator may prove to be a superior means of evaluating exercise physiological parameters in cyclists when compared with other methods currently in use.

With these ideas in mind, the primary purpose of this study was to determine how effectively several windload simulators duplicate the aerobic requirements of riding a bicycle of the road. Additionally, we tested two of the simulators to determine whether different degrees of rolling resistance affected the oxygen consumption at a given speed.

Methods

Subjects

Nine adult males participated in the tests, all experienced bicyclists recruited from local touring and racing clubs. Their physical characteristics are presented in Table 1. Informed written consent was obtained from each subject prior to commencement of testing.

Road Tests

Oxygen consumption was measured on the road at riding speeds of 16.1, 24.2, and 32.2 kph (10, 15, and 20 mph). Each subject rode his own bicycle while in a dropped position on the handlebars. Gear ratios were chosen such that pedaling rate was maintained between 60 and 75 rpm at each speed. These rates have been shown to be optimal at these moderate power outputs (Coast & Welch, 1985).

The subjects rode beside and slightly ahead (1 to 1.5 m) of an accompanying vehicle. They breathed through a mouthpiece and low resistance valve (Hans Rudolph #2000) connected by tubing to a Douglas bag in the vehicle. In order to prevent drag on the subject by the hose and mouthpiece, the hose was secured to a boom held by one of the experimenters. Expired air was collected for 45 to 60 s and analyzed with a Perkin-Elmer 1100A mass spectrometer (which had been calibrated with known gases) and a Tissot spirometer. Heart rate was monitored by telemetry.

At each speed, the subject warmed up for 4 to 5 min at the test speed and then immediately began the test. A test consisted of four runs over a straight flat road approximately 1,100 m in length. Two runs were made in each direction at each speed to account for the minor elevation change (0.9 m) and the presence of any light winds. Runs performed in winds of greater than 8 kph (5 mph) were not used. The subjects used cycle computer speedometers to gauge their speed, but they were also timed over a 300-m portion of the course as an independent check on the speed. Any run that varied by more than 0.8 kph (0.5 mph) from the chosen speed was discarded and the run repeated.

Table 1   Characteristics of the Subjects Used in the Study

Variable	Mean	Range
Age (years)	31.8	22–46
Height (cm)	180.7	161–198
Weight (kg)	73.4	53–89
$\dot{V}O_2max$ (L $\cdot$ min^{-1})	4.13	3.42–5.22
(ml $\cdot$ kg^{-1} $\cdot$ min^{-1})	58.3	49.3–65.4

Oxygen consumption and heart rate values were calculated for each run at each speed. The values used in the analysis were the means of those obtained for all four runs.

Windload Simulator Tests

Four simulators were used in the experiments. The simulators used were of different designs. Numbers 1 and 4 were designed such that the rear wheel of the bicycle rested upon the axle of the wind resistance turbines, the difference being the method of mounting the bicycle. Number 2 utilized a drum-and-belt system to drive a turbine mounted in front of the rider. This simulator was adjustable with respect to air resistance by opening or closing a cover over the turbine housing. For the test, only the highest and lowest resistances were used. Simulator Number 3 consisted of a pair of turbines mounted behind the saddle. The axle between the turbines rested on the top of the rear wheel.

The subjects used gears identical to those used in the road tests and monitored their speed with the cycle computers. In addition, cadence was counted to ensure that the proper speed was maintained. Heart rate was obtained using the same telemetric device as used on the road. Oxygen consumption was measured via an on-line open circuit system using Ametek O_2 (S-3AI) and CO_2 (CD-3A) analyzers, a Rayfield spirometer, and an Apple II computer. Checks had been performed previously in which the analyzers had been calibrated with the same gases used to calibrate the mass spectrometer, and the Rayfield and Tissot spirometers were calibrated against each other. These checks assured that identical $\dot{V}O_2$ and $\dot{V}CO_2$ values were obtained with the separate methods.

The windload simulators were assembled and the bicycles mounted according to the manufacturers' instructions. The riders performed all tests on each simulator in one session with 30-min intervals between each test. The order of the simulators was assigned randomly. Each test consisted of a 2-min rest period seated on the bicycle, following which the rider began pedaling. Each test speed lasted for 4 min, and the previous speed was used as a warm-up for the subsequent speed. Oxygen consumption was measured every 30 s and heart rate was monitored at each minute. The values for the 2nd to 4th min, when a steady state was achieved, were averaged and used for subsequent analysis.

Two of the simulators were studied repeatedly to assess test-to-test variability. We adjusted the windload simulators to provide different levels of pressure on the tires. These levels were made subjectively to produce levels of pressure that ranged from just touching the roller to very hard pressure, a wider range than would normally be used. At each adjustment, the subject pedaled at 32.2 kph for 4 min while the oxygen consumption was monitored by the on-line technique. Following each test, the subject was asked to pedal at 32.2 kph and stop pedaling. After stopping, the time required for the wheel to stop rotating (the roll-down time) was measured. This was repeated at least 3 times, and the average roll-down time used. The oxygen consumption at each setting was then graphed against the roll-down time for that setting.

Statistics

Data are reported as mean ± *SEM*. Two-way analysis of variance with repeated measures was used to assess any overall difference. Where an overall difference at a given speed was found, Newman-Keul's post hoc test was used to determine which of the simulators differed from values obtained on the road.

Results

During the road tests, the oxygen consumptions averaged 1.14 ± 0.04 (*M* ± *SEM*), 1.84 ± 0.06, and 2.82 ± 0.08 L • min⁻¹ at 16.1, 24.2, and 32.2 kph, respectively. Heart rates for the road tests were 100.2 ± 6.1, 119.4 ± 5.1, and 155.2 ± 6.3 bpm.

Oxygen consumption and heart rate values obtained from testing on the windload simulators are presented in Figures 1 and 2, respectively, and Table 2. Both increased with speed, as was expected. Surprising, though, was the range of values measured at each speed. At 16.1 kph, oxygen consumption varied from 0.8 to 1.2 L • min⁻¹ and heart rate from 91 to 107 bpm between the individual simulators. This difference was magnified at 32.2 kph, at which speed V̇O₂ ranged from 1.5 to 3.9 L • min⁻¹ and heart rate from 112 to 179 bpm.

As assessed by analysis of variance, the difference in V̇O₂ and heart rate was highly significant ($p < .001$) at each speed. When the average V̇O₂ values obtained using the individual windload simulators were compared to those on the road, two simulators (Numbers 1 and 4) were not different at any speed (Table 2). The rest were different at both 24.2 and 32.2 kph. None were different at 16.1 kph. The post hoc comparisons of heart rate revealed the same differences as did the V̇O₂ values (Table 2).

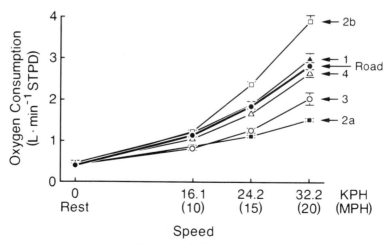

Figure 1 Oxygen consumption during road riding and riding on windload simulators. ● = road; ▲ = Number 1; ■ = Number 2a; □ = Number 2b; ○ = Number 3; and △ = Number 4.

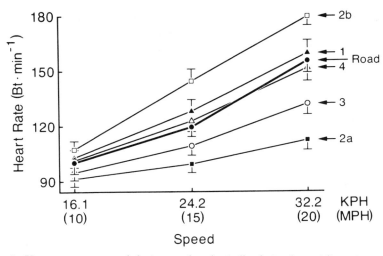

Figure 2 Heart rates measured during road and windload simulator riding. ● = road; ▲ = Number 1; ■ = Number 2a; □ = Number 2b; O = Number 3; and △ = Number 4.

Table 2 Oxygen Consumption and Heart Rate Values Measured on the Road and Using Windload Simulators

Test device	Speed (kph)		
	16.1	24.2	32.2
Oxygen consumption (L • min⁻¹)			
Road	1.14 ± .04	1.84 ± .06	2.82 ± .08
1	1.21 ± .05	1.88 ± .08	2.98 ± .14
2a	0.87 ± .03	1.12 ± .03**	1.52 ± .04**
2b	1.23 ± .04	2.37 ± .07**	3.89 ± .15**
3	0.82 ± .04	1.26 ± .06**	2.02 ± .15**
4	1.05 ± .05	1.66 ± .06	2.64 ± .09
Heart rate (beats • min⁻¹)			
Road	100 ± 6	119 ± 5	155 ± 6
1	103 ± 4	128 ± 6	159 ± 7
2a	91 ± 4	99 ± 5**	112 ± 5**
2b	107 ± 5	146 ± 6**	179 ± 5**
3	95 ± 4	109 ± 5*	132 ± 6**
4	101 ± 4	123 ± 6	151 ± 7

Note. All values are $M \pm SEM$, $n = 9$.
*$p < .05$. **$p < .01$; differences between road and individual simulators as assessed by Newman Keul's post hoc test.

The two simulators that most closely approximated the metabolic cost of road riding were tested at different levels of rolling resistance. The levels, although set subjectively, were characterized by the roll-down times from 20 mph. The simulators had widely divergent roll-down times. Those of Number 1 ranged from 4.4 to 9.8 s and of Number 4 from 1.7 to 3.4 s (Figure 3). The difference in roll-down time was probably due to the presence of a flywheel on Number 1. Both, though, yielded similar $\dot{V}O_2$ values (Number 1: 2.4 to 3.1 L • min^{-1}; Number 4: 2.4 to 3.3 L • min^{-1}). An important note is that both simulators yielded a large range of $\dot{V}O_2$ values at levels of resistance that might be used by a cyclist or investigator.

Discussion

The values we measured for oxygen consumption on the road (Figure 1) were in close agreement with those of Pugh (1974), who measured $\dot{V}O_2$ on racing cyclists. They were also similar to measurements made by Brooke and Davies (1973) for racing cyclists but slightly higher than estimates made by Whitt (1971). At the highest speed (32.2 kph) the cyclists were stressed, but well within their aerobic capacity, averaging 65% of $\dot{V}O_2$max.

All of the simulators yielded increased $\dot{V}O_2$ and heart rate values with increased speeds, as was expected, although the absolute values were widely divergent at the higher riding speeds (Figures 1 and 2). Simulators 1 and 4 produced similar $\dot{V}O_2$ and heart rate results to those of pedaling on the road, whereas Number 3 was consistently less than road cycling. One possible reason for the difference, because the size of the turbines was

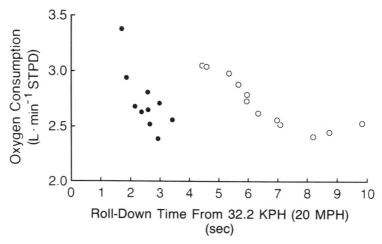

Figure 3   Oxygen consumption versus roll-down time from 32.2 kph for two windload simulators. O = Number 1 and ● = Number 4.

similar for these three simulators, may be that the bicycle wheel rested upon the turbine roller in Numbers 1 and 4, thus providing some rolling resistance as well as the air resistance of the turbines. On Simulator 3, however, the turbine roller rested lightly on top of the rear wheel of the bicycle, restricting the resistance to the windloading effect. This finding is in agreement with the work of Oude Vrielink, Vissers, and Binkhorst (1984) and Firth (1981). Oude Vrielink et al. (1984) tested a windload simulator of the same brand as Number 3 and found that when combined with riding on rollers (as it is often used and which provides rolling resistance), the simulator duplicated road values, but when used alone the simulator yielded values that were lower than those of riding on the road. Therefore, some rolling resistance in addition to the wind resistance provided by the turbines seems to be necessary to duplicate road riding with a windload simulator.

Simulator 2 was tested at two different settings, because it had a cover on the turbine that enabled the user to increase or reduce the amount of air moved by the fan and thus the air resistance. Only the fully closed (2a) and fully open (2b) settings were used, yielding the highest and lowest possible $\dot{V}O_2$ and heart rate values (Figures 1 and 2) for that apparatus. Neither setting duplicated values obtained on the road, but instead they were the highest and lowest values measured on any of the simulators at 24.2 and 32.2 kph. This indicates that although Simulator 2 did not duplicate road conditions in our test, an intermediate position of the turbine cover might do so. Further study would be needed to evaluate the optimum position.

The roll-down tests of Simulators 1 and 4 gave an indication of the variability inherent in these machines. This is an important concept, especially in quantitative exercise testing, that has not been mentioned previously by other investigators or in the lay press. Our settings were able to yield differences in oxygen consumption of almost 1 L • min^{-1} at 32.2 kph within the simulators. These settings, however, included extreme differences in the subjective pressure with which the tire rested on the turbine shaft. But even within normal ranges, differences in VO_2 of about 0.5 L • min^{-1} were noted. This is an area in which further investigation is merited, but in any event the bicycle should probably be installed on the simulator and adjusted so that similar roll-down times are achieved to minimize differences between subjects and between tests.

Conclusion

In this study, we measured oxygen consumption and heart rate during bicycling on the road and on four different windload simulating devices. We found wide differences in the oxygen cost of cycling between several of the simulators, with two of the simulators approximating the road closely. We also found that values obtained on a single simulator could be varied substantially by differences in the installation of the bicycle on the simulator. The results indicate that although any of the devices may be useful as a training device, care should be taken prior to assuming that a windload simulator duplicates the resistance seen in road riding.

Acknowledgments

The authors thank Robert Vaughan for his technical assistance and Christine Smith for manuscript preparation. We also thank the companies that furnished the machines tested: Jim Blackburn Designs, Eclipse Corp., Al Kreitler Custom Rollers, Inc., and Racer Mate, Inc.

References

Brooke, J.D., & Davies, G.J. (1973). Comment on "Estimation of energy expenditure of sporting cyclists." *Ergonomics, 16*, 237–238.

Coast, J.R., & Welch, H.G. (1985). Linear increase in optimal pedal rate with increased power output in cycle ergometry. *European Journal of Applied Physiology, 53*, 339–342.

Firth, M.S. (1981). A sport-specific training and testing device for racing cyclists. *Ergonomics, 24*, 565–571.

Oude Vrielink, H.H.E., Vissers, A.C.A., & Binkhorst, R.A. (1984). Oxygen consumption and speed of cycling using an air-resistance simulator on a hometrainer roller. *International Journal of Sports Medicine, 5*, 98–101.

Pugh, L.G.C.E. (1974). The relation of oxygen intake and speed in competition cycling and comparative observations on the bicycle ergometer, *Journal of Physiology* (London), *241*, 795–808.

Whitt, F.R. (1971). A note on the estimation of the energy expenditure sporting cyclists. *Ergonomics, 14*, 419–424.

The Use of Windload Simulators for $\dot{V}O_2$max Determination and Bicycling Research

John G. Seifert

Mark E. Langenfeld

While cycling, if riders cannot position themselves according to personal preferences, the amount of effective work output can be decreased (Firth, 1981). Experienced bicyclists involved with cycling research often express a dislike for a cycle ergometer due to its frame geometry in comparison to their own bicycle's frame. The windload simulator (WS) provides an alternative method to testing bicyclists on cycle ergometers. Windload simulator devices allow a bicycle to be mounted on a stand; thus, the cyclist does not have to change from the normal riding position or alignment as may be the case on an ergometer. On the WS, the bicycle's rear wheel is in contact with a freely rotating axle. Attached to each side of the axle are fans that impel air, creating resistance that is exponentially related to the wheel speed. The faster the rear wheel spins, the more air that is impelled into the fan, creating the corresponding resistance.

Previous investigators (Firth, 1981; Kyle, 1979; Pugh, 1974) have shown that rolling and wind resistance comprise virtually all of the total resistance while cycling (mechanical resistance is negligible). According to Firth (1981), the wind resistance created by the WS provides a similar work load condition to the resistance encountered at various speeds while cycling on the road.

In a comparative study between a WS and bicycle rollers, Burke, Langenfeld, and Kirkendall (1982) reported that only the WS stressed the cyclists enough to elicit a training effect. While riding on a WS, it is possible to vary the work load by gear selection to achieve the desired physiological effects.

The purpose of this study was to compare maximal oxygen uptake ($\dot{V}O_2$max) values attained on a friction-braked ergometer (FBE; Monark) to those values attained on a WS (TurboTrainer by Skid-Lid Corp.).

Methods

Seven experienced cyclists voluntarily consented to participate in the study (see Table 1). All trials were performed in a counterbalanced design in the Human Performance Laboratory at Miami University. Bicycles were

Table 1   Subject Characteristics and Results

Subject	Age	Weight (kg)	FBE ml/kg/min	l/min	WS ml/kg/min	l/min
A	26	75	54.4	4.1	53.6	4.0
B	31	73	56.8	4.2	56.3	4.1
C	25	80	51.8	4.2	53.6	4.3
D	28	79	56.5	4.5	56.7	4.4
E	24	70	59.1	4.2	58.2	4.2
F	21	78	57.6	4.5	60.0	4.7
G	21	84	59.3	5.0	57.0	4.8
Mean	25.1	77.1	56.5	4.4	56.5	4.4
± SD	3.6	4.2	2.7	0.3	2.3	0.3

Note. FBE = friction-braked ergometer; WS = windload simulator.

fitted with high gearing (121.5-in. gear; 53 T × 13 T gear combination) to ensure a high enough work load without requiring subjects to exceed their normal pedaling cadence. Pedaling cadence for WS and FBE was 90 (± 3) rpm throughout the duration of the tests.

A cycling computer (CC; Cateye Mate by Tsuyama Mfg. Co.) was attached to the bicycle to monitor speed. Calibration of the CC was made by rolling the bicycle, with the rider on the saddle, along a tape measure to obtain the loaded rear wheel circumference. This value was then entered into the CC. Upon initial contact with the rear tire, the axle of the WS was moved back into the tire 1 cm to ensure that no slippage between the tire and axle would occur. The FBE was fitted with toe clips on the pedals, drop handlebars, and racing saddle. Prior to the test, the FBE saddle height was adjusted to the subject's preference.

Expired air was sampled through a mixing chamber and analyzed by an Applied Electrochemistry S-3A oxygen analyzer and an Applied Electrochemistry CD-3A carbon dioxide analyzer. Gas volumes were measured with a Parkinson-Cowan CD-4 volume meter. The two analyzers and volume meter were interfaced with a Rockwell AIM-65 microcomputer using Rayfield REP-100 software for the determination of $\dot{V}O_2$max. Printouts from the computer were obtained for each 30-s segment throughout the duration of the test. The analyzers were calibrated during the warm-up phase of the test with a known gas concentration of 16.95% O_2 and 5.05% CO_2. Prior to the testing, $\dot{V}O_2$max was defined as the highest attained $\dot{V}O_2$ (ml/kg/min) value for any 30-s time segment.

A 10-min warm-up was performed on either the FBE (1.5 kp) or WS (68-in. gear) prior to the start of each test. The test on the FBE began at 2.0 kp and was continued by increasing the resistance in 0.5-kp increments every minute until $\dot{V}O_2$max was reached. After the warm-up on the WS, resistance was increased every minute by shifting through the five highest gears until the cyclist's $\dot{V}O_2$max was attained.

Results and Discussion

Table 1 contains the $\dot{V}O_2$max values attained on the FBE and WS. There were no significant differences in mean $\dot{V}O_2$max values between FBE and WS. For the FBE, the values were 56.5 ± 2.7 ml/kg/min and 4.4 ± 0.3 l/min. Values for the WS were 56.5 ± 2.3 ml/kg/min and 4.4 ± 0.3 l/min.

The results of this study indicate that experienced cyclists attained similar $\dot{V}O_2$max values on WS and FBE. Subjectively, however, subjects expressed a strong preference for riding their own bicycles on the WS, rather than riding the FBE, because of the preferred "feel" of their own bicycles. This concept of "feel" is related in part to the fit and flexing characteristics of their own bicycles. For studies involving experienced cyclists, the selection of a testing apparatus with a clearly higher subject acceptance and preference may be critical for allowing applied research that best simulates real riding conditions.

Burke et al. (1984) reported that by proper selection of gears while cycling on a WS, work loads can be varied throughout the range of physiological values needed to stress the cardiorespiratory system. Thus, by shifting to the appropriate gears, investigators can have cyclists ride at steady state or at various intensities to attain a desired effect.

Pugh (1974) notes that power development during road cycling increases as the square of the speed, not as the cube as would be expected. According to Pugh (1974), this is due to the variable contributions of the wind and rolling resistances, because both resistances are functions of body size. Thus, a curvilinear function of $\dot{V}O_2$ with speed (Pugh, 1974) and work load (Firth, 1981) will occur during steady-state cycling while on the road and on a WS. At speeds greater than 16 kmh, wind resistance becomes dominant in overall cycling resistance (Firth, 1981). Kyle (1979) reported that at speeds over 32 kmh, wind resistance comprises over 90% of total resistance on a bicycle. The curvilinear outputs that are needed to overcome the wind resistance at various speeds have been reported by previous investigators (Brooke & Davies, 1973; Pugh, 1974). These values are quite similar to those of Firth's (1981) WS calibration curve of power outputs and calculated road speeds.

In a study conducted by Seifert, Langenfeld, Rudge, and Bucher (1986), 14 subjects rode three 80-mi time trials on a WS in order to test the effects of carbohydrate feedings. The WS performed without incident through all of the trials, which lasted approximately 4 hr each. Prior to the study, subjects performed a $\dot{V}O_2$max test on a FBE. Subjects strongly preferred riding their own bicycles on the WS instead of riding the FBE and indicated that the WS made the trials feel much more like actual road riding.

Results from the present study, as well as those from other investigators, indicate that a WS is a useful device in the research setting and that further consideration should be given to a WS when research involves experienced cyclists.

Summary

The present study elicited the following conclusions:

- There was no significant difference in $\dot{V}O_2$max between the FBE and WS in absolute and relative values.
- WS are suitable for determining $\dot{V}O_2$max values of experienced cyclists.
- Large gearing (of at least 121.5 in.) must be used to ensure a high enough resistance without requiring the subjects to exceed their normal pedaling cadence.
- Subjects expressed a strong preference for riding their own bicycles mounted on a WS rather than riding the FBE during a $\dot{V}O_2$max test and an ultraendurance study.

References

Brooke, J.D., & Davies, G.J. (1973). Comment on "Estimation of the energy expenditure of sporting cyclists." *Ergonomics, 16*(2), 237–238.

Burke, E.R., Langenfeld, M.E., & Kirkendall, D. (1982). Physiological responses to submaximal bicycle exercise: Comparison of rollers and the Racer-mate Windload simulator. *Australian Journal of Sports Medicine and Exercise Sciences, 14*(3), 104–106.

Firth, M.S. (1981). A sport-specific training and testing device for racing cyclists. *Ergonomics, 24*(7), 565–571.

Kyle, C.R. (1979). Reduction of wind resistance and power output of racing cyclists and runners traveling in groups. *Ergonomics, 22*(4), 387–397.

Pugh, L.G.C.E. (1974). The relation of oxygen intake and speed in competition cycling and comparative observations on the bicycle ergometer. *Journal of Physiology, 241*, 795–808.

Seifert, J.G., Langenfeld, M.E., Rudge, S.J., & Bucher, R.J. (1986). Effects of glucose polymer ingestion on ultraendurance bicycling performance. *Medicine and Science in Sports and Exercise, 18*(2), S5.

Physiological Changes Riding a Bicycle Ergometer With and Without Toe Stirrups

Paul S. Visich

The bicycle ergometer is often used to evaluate physiological responses to exertion, because work load can be monitored and maintained easily. The bicycle ergometer has also been used as a training tool to improve cardiovascular fitness. In situations where obtaining constant training heart rate is important, such as in cardiac rehabilitation, the bicycle ergometer is a valuable device.

The bicycle ergometer is fairly inexpensive and portable as compared to a treadmill. Energy cost is proportional to work load and is constant, regardless of age, sex, extent of training, and body size (Åstrand & Rodahl, 1970; McArdle & Magel, 1970).

The bicycle ergometer has been widely used to evaluate an individual's physical condition and work capacity. Measuring the maximal amount of oxygen utilized ($\dot{V}O_2$max) or calories expended per unit of time when exercising is the most accepted method of determining physical condition. Karpovich and Sinning (1971) stated that $\dot{V}O_2$max is considered the best single physiological indicator of the capacity of man for sustained muscular work. However, $\dot{V}O_2$max is not the only indicator in performance of an aerobic event. The quality of skill performance is also an important criterion. Åstrand and Rodahl (1977) found that $\dot{V}O_2$ at submaximal levels were equivalent between Olympic cyclists and untrained subjects. The authors suggested that the lack of difference may be due simply to the uncomplicated movement of cycling. However, when an activity was unfamiliar and complicated, higher $\dot{V}O_2$ values were found at submaximal levels. This suggests less efficiency of performance.

Mechanical efficiency (ME) is a ratio of energy expenditure in performance of a task to the energy required to perform that task. The less the required energy, the higher the ME. Individuals skilled in the performance of a task have lower $\dot{V}O_2$ at a given work load than the unskilled. This suggests less energy utilization and thereby greater ME (Vokac & Rodahl, 1976).

In addition to skill performance, ME is affected by levels of training. The higher the training level, the more muscles have adapted to perform the required movement. Therefore, previously used extraneous musculature for performance of the task are no longer required. Less musculature used to perform a task requires less energy, thereby increasing ME.

Researchers have evaluated modifications in the bicycle ergometer in an attempt to find the most optimal cycling conditions to maximize ME. Nordeen-Snyder (1977) studied the effect of seat height on ME and found that an individual was most efficient when the seat height was 100% of trochanteric height, versus 95 and 105%. Faria, Dix, and Frazer (1978) compared cycling efficiency with racing handlebars in the up and down positions. They found a 7% increase in $\dot{V}O_2$max using handlebars in the down position. Pedaling frequency at 60 to 80 rpm was found to be the most efficient for average cyclists (Åstrand & Rodahl, 1970; Noble & Pandolf, 1973).

A popular device being used on bicycles are toe stirrups on the pedals. When the correct size is used, the ball of the foot is held over the center of the pedal. Stirrups enable the cyclists not only to push down on the crank to provide forward momentum but also to pull on the upswing side of the crank. This increases the total musculature involvement in the activity, which will produce a higher level of work. In addition, the stirrup offers positional support to the foot in the down phase of pedaling, directing all exerted forces in the proper direction, and maximizing efficiency of effort. Lavoie, Mahoney, and Marmelic (1978) studied the effects of using toe stirrups on $\dot{V}O_2$max. A significant increase in $\dot{V}O_2$max was found riding with stirrups. The authors suggested that a greater use of musculature on the upside of the pedal revolution caused a greater increase in $\dot{V}O_2$. However, they presented no data concerned with submaximal effort.

Wilde (1978) compared cycling with and without stirrups at maximal and submaximal levels. No significant differences were found in the $\dot{V}O_2$ at either level of exertion. This finding was unexpected. The author suggested that with the use of toe stirrups at submaximal or maximal levels there were additional muscles involved in an upward pulling motion on the pedal. This caused an increase in oxygen extraction by the larger active muscles. Therefore, $\dot{V}O_2$ values contrary to the finding of Wilde's study would be expected to be higher when using stirrups. The author suggested that the use of toe stirrups may have increased the ME of performance of the work load over that of not using stirrups. Therefore the higher $\dot{V}O_2$ expected with stirrups at the submaximal level due to larger musculature utilization may have been less due to higher ME. The subjects used in Wilde's study were not experienced in using toe stirrups; therefore their technique may not have been good enough to produce a $\dot{V}O_2$ difference.

No research concerning the physiological benefits of toe stirrup use has been found for experienced and nonexperienced cyclists at the submaximal level. It is speculated that experienced cyclists should obtain physiological benefits from toe stirrup use. Therefore, the purpose of this study was to investigate physiological response of trained and nontrained cyclists riding a bicycle ergometer with and without the use of toe stirrups.

Methods

Eighteen male subjects, between the age of 22 to 33 (mean = 25.72 years) were used in this study. Subjects were placed in two groups: cyclists, who rode more than 100 mi per week, and noncyclists, who rode less than 5 mi per week. Each subject read and signed an informed consent form.

Prior to testing, subjects reported to the laboratory for an orientation to the study. At this time, subjects became familiar with the bicycle ergometer. The correct technique for using toe stirrups was also shown to the noncyclists at this time. A modified Monark (model #688) bicycle ergometer was used. Rubber pedals were replaced with metal pedals, so that stirrups could be mounted on the pedals. Racing handlebars and a racing seat replaced the standard equipment for a more comfortable ride.

Seat height was adjusted to 100% of trochanteric height, and handlebar height was adjusted to equal the seat height. All subjects rode in the down bar position.

Each subject performed a battery of four tests, consisting of a maximal test with toe stirrups, maximal test without toe stirrups, submaximal test with toe stirrups, and a submaximal test without toe stirrups. The subjects were tested over a period of 8 weeks. In the first 4 weeks, the two maximal tests were administered, and during the last 4 weeks the two submaximal tests were randomly assigned. Subjects were asked to refrain from any physical activity 4 hr prior to testing.

Each subject completed two maximal discontinuous tests on the bicycle ergometer, with and without toe stirrups. Each test was performed at a pedaling rate of 80 rpm. Cadence was controlled by a metronome set at 80 beats per minute.

Each maximal exertion test consisted of 4-min work bouts, followed by 4-min rest periods. The first work load was set at 480 kpm/min, followed by an increase of 480 kpm/min each additional work phase. The subject continued until exhausted or until symptoms appeared that would cause termination of the test according to the American College of Sports Medicine guidelines. The subject was considered exhausted when he voluntarily stopped exercising, or when he could no longer continue the work load at the required cadence. Once the subject reached 70% of predicted maximal heart rate (HR), expired gas was collected each minute until exhaustion.

Each subject completed two randomly assigned submaximal tests with and without toe stirrups. The test was performed at 70% of maximal HR as obtained from the maximal exertion test.

The subjects sat on the bicycle for 10 min without pedaling, so that a resting oxygen uptake ($\dot{V}O_2$) could be determined. Gas samples were collected the last 3 min of the rest period. The subjects than cycled for 20 min at 70% of maximal HR. Work load was adjusted and recorded each minute to maintain 70% of maximal HR throughout the test. Gas samples were collected each minute for the 20 min of exercise. Following the 20-min work bout, the subjects sat in a chair, where recovery values were collected each minute for 20 min.

Measurement of $\dot{V}O_2$max was determined by the open circuit method (Mathews & Fox, 1976). The subjects wore a Welder's countered balance head support (model #2766), which supported a Rudolph (#2700) three-way breathing valve. One end of a 4-ft hose was connected to the valve, and the other end to a holder of five 120-L meteorological balloons. The balloons collected expired gas and were connected by rubber hoses, connected to low turbulence three-way Y valves (P-319).

Expired gas was analyzed for carbon dioxide (CO_2) and oxygen (O_2) concentration by the Beckman LB-2 and OM-11, respectively. Expired gas volumes were measured using a Pneumoscan S-301 spirometer. Oxygen consumption and $\dot{V}CO_2$ were calculated according to the formulas presented by Mathews and Fox (1976).

Submaximal $\dot{V}O_2$ collection technique was different from the $\dot{V}O_2$max method. Measurement of submaximal $\dot{V}O_2$ was collected each minute for a total of 40 min. Expired gas passed through a 6-ft hose into a 5-L mixing chamber and the other end into a Costill-Wilmore valve, from which air samples were collected each minute and analyzed through the OM-11 and LB-2. Gas volumes were measured using a Pneumoscan S-301 spirometer.

A Life Pack EKG recorder was used to record the electrocardiogram. Electrodes were attached to four limb leads and one chest lead. Lead V_5 was constantly monitored on the oscilloscope throughout the test.

Heart rate was recorded the last 15 s of each minute throughout the exercise and recovery period. Measurement of HR was calculated by the distance between 10 R-R intervals.

Blood pressure (BP) was measured primarily for safety purposes. Measured values were not recorded and therefore will not be included as results of this investigation. Blood pressure was determined by ausculatatory technique and was taken the last 30 s of each work phase for the maximal tests and every 5 min for the submaximal tests. The subjects were asked to release the grip while BPs were being measured. First and fifth sounds were recorded.

Mechanical efficiency (ME) was determined for submaximal tests with and without toe stirrups. Net efficiency was calculated according to Equation 1:

$$\text{Net} = \frac{\text{Work output in kilograms}}{\text{Total work input } - \text{ resting input in kilograms}} \tag{1}$$

The dependent variables that were examined in the statistical analysis were $\dot{V}O_2$, HR, physical work capacity (maximal and submaximal), ME, and body weight. A 2 × 2 factorial analysis of variance (ANOVA) with repeated measures on one factor was used to test for the effects due to variations in cycling experience, use of toe stirrups, and the interaction of these variables. An independent t test was used to determine if there was a significant difference in body weight between the two groups. The .05 level of significance was used to reject the null hypothesis.

Results

Mean $\dot{V}O_2$max values for the two experimental treatments are shown in Figure 1. Mean $\dot{V}O_2$ (L/min) values for the noncyclists with and without toe stirrups were 4.01 and 3.81 L/min respectively. Mean $\dot{V}O_2$max values for the cyclists were 4.31 L/min with and 4.32 L/min without toe stirrups. The F ratios were not significant for experimental conditions, groups, or interaction.

When $\dot{V}O_2$max values were expressed per unit of body weight, the $\dot{V}O_2$max mean values for the noncyclist group with and without toe stirrups were 48.90 and 46.82 ml/kg/min^{-1}, respectively. The mean $\dot{V}O_2$max values for the cyclist group were 59.97 with and 60.14 ml/kg/min^{-1} without toe stirrups (see Figure 2). The F ratios were significantly higher than the noncyclist group $(p < .05)$.

Mean submaximal $\dot{V}O_2$ (L/min) values in subjects riding at 70% maximal HR for the total exercise and recovery periods for the two experimental treatments are shown in Figure 3. The mean values for the noncyclist group were 68.81 with and 71.20 L/min without toe stirrups. F ratios were not significant for conditions, groups, or interaction.

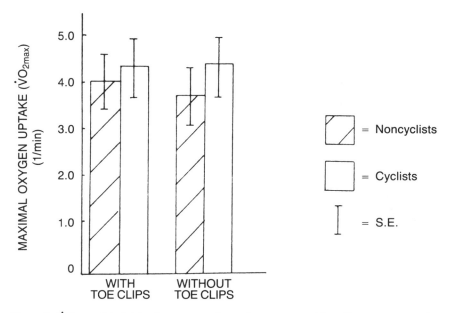

Figure 1 $\dot{V}O_2$max (1/min) for the two experimental treatments with cyclist versus noncyclist groups. No significant difference was found for conditions, groups, or interaction.

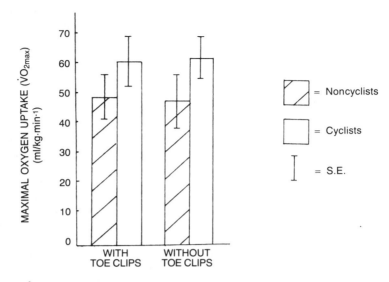

Figure 2 $\dot{V}O_2$max (ml/kg • min^{-1}) for the two experimental treatments with cyclist versus noncyclist groups $\dot{V}O_2$max (ml/kg • min) for the cyclist group was significantly higher. No significant difference was found for conditions or interaction.

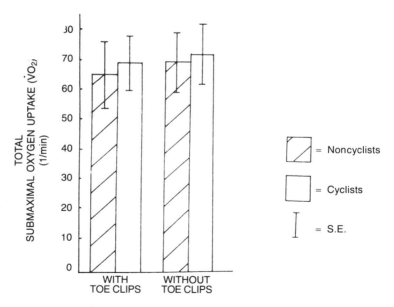

Figure 3 Submaximal $\dot{V}O_2$ (1/min) for the two experimental treatments with cyclist versus noncyclist groups. No significant difference was found for conditions, groups, or interaction.

Mean values for the noncyclist group during submaximal exercise with and without toe stirrups were 52.29 and 57.37 L/min, respectively. Mean values for the cyclist group during submaximal exercise were 58.79 with and 60.52 L/min without toe stirrups. Mean values for the noncyclist group during the recovery period with and without toe stirrups were 11.12 and 12.11 L/min, respectively. The mean values for the cyclist group during the recovery period were 10.02 with and 9.29 L/min without toe stirrups.

When submaximal $\dot{V}O_2$ values for the exercise period were expressed per unit of body weight, the mean values for the noncyclist group with and without toe stirrups were 31.88 and 33.48 ml/kg/min^{-1}, respectively. The mean submaximal values for the cyclist group were 39.86 with and 40.27 ml/kg/min^{-1} with toe stirrups (Figure 4). The F ratio for the groups was significant ($p < .05$), but no difference was found for conditions or interaction. Submaximal $\dot{V}O_2$ values for the cyclist group with and without toe stirrups were higher than the values found for the noncyclist group.

Mean maximal physical work capacity (PWC) values for the noncyclist group with and without toe stirrups were 1,813.33 and 1,813.33 kpm/min, respectively. The mean maximal PWC values for the cyclist group were not significant for conditions, groups, or interaction.

Total mean submaximal work performance for the 20-min exercise period for the noncyclist group with and without toe stirrups were 19,413.30 and 20,786.67 kpm/min, respectively. The mean submaximal work performance values for the cyclist group were 24,360.00 with and

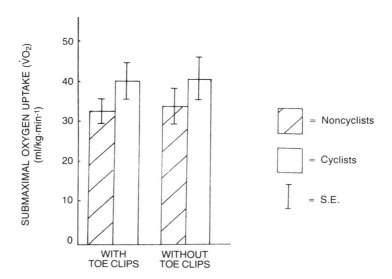

Figure 4   Submaximal ($\dot{V}O_2$max (ml/kg • min^{-1}) for the two experimental treatments with cyclist versus noncyclist groups. Submaximal $\dot{V}O_2$ (ml/kg • min^{-1}) for the cyclist group was significantly higher. No significant difference was found for conditions or interaction.

24,360.00 kpm/min without toe stirrups. F ratios were significant for groups ($p < .05$); however, no significant differences were found for conditions or interaction. Submaximal mean work performance values expressed in kilopond meters per minute for the cyclist group were significantly higher than for the noncyclist group.

Mean maximal HR values for the noncyclist group with and without toe stirrups were 188 and 189 bpm, respectively. The mean maximal HR values for the cyclist group were 193 with and 190 beats per minute without toe stirrups. F ratios were not significant for groups, conditions, and interaction.

Mean submaximal HR values for the noncyclist group with and without toe stirrups were 154 and 152 bpm, respectively. The mean submaximal

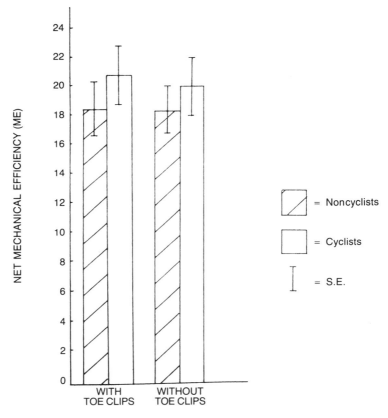

Figure 5   Net mechanical efficiency for the two experimental conditions, with cyclist versus noncyclist groups. Net ME for the cyclist group was significantly higher. No significant difference was found for conditions or interaction.

HR values for the cyclist group were 154 with and 153 bpm without toe stirrups. F ratios were not significant for conditions, groups, or interaction.

Mean net ME values for the two experimental treatments are shown in Figure 5. Mean ME values for the noncyclist group with and without toe stirrups were 18.21 and 18.04%, respectively. The mean ME values for the cyclist group were 20.73 with and 19.86% without toe stirrups. F ratios were shown to be significant for groups $(p < .05)$. However, no significant differences were found for conditions or interaction. Net ME for the cyclist group was significantly higher than for the noncyclist group.

Discussion and Conclusion

Results of this study reveal that there was no difference in $\dot{V}O_2$, HR, ME, and PWC for both the cyclists and noncyclist groups during the use and during the nonuse of toe stirrups. Because toe stirrups are standard equipment used by experienced cyclists, it was speculated that there would be an increase in physiological performance and a higher level of efficiency. This was not found to be true in this investigation. Manifested differences were between the population sample of cyclists who, by definition, rode at least 100 mi/week (this is assumed to provide a training effect) and noncyclists, who rode less than 5 mi/week. Maximum oxygen intake, when adjusted for body weight in ml/kg/min^{-1}, was significantly higher in the cyclist group than the noncyclist group but when expressed in liters per minute showed no difference between the two groups. This difference was due to a 11.3-kg lower mean body weight for the cyclist group. Body weight values between the two groups, however, were not found to be significantly different. This nonsignificant difference may be due to the small sample size. However, it is suggestive of a trend for trained cyclists to have and maintain a lower body weight than noncyclists. Whitt (1971) estimated that vigorous cycling would utilize 912 kcal/hr at an average speed of 22.26 mph. This would be approximately 4104.00 kcal for 1 week. Therefore, it would be expected that an individual who cycles at least 100 mi/week would exhibit a lower body weight than an individual who cycles less than 5 mi/week.

Submaximal physiological responses were recorded at 70% maximal exertion determined by HR. The findings, similar to those for maximal data, showed no significant difference in $\dot{V}O_2$, PWC, HR, and ME between the use and nonuse of toe stirrups. The only difference observed was again due to the population sample. Submaximal $\dot{V}O_2$, PWC, and ME were significantly higher in the cyclist group than in the noncyclist group. This is to be expected as the trained cyclists were able to perform more work at a given HR. The finding concerning ME suggests that the ratio of total work performed to energy provided was also higher in the cyclist group. This is apparently due to the benefit derived from training. A higher $\dot{V}O_2$max, cardiac output (Q_c), stroke volume (SV), and arteriovenous difference (a-$\bar{v}O_2$) that improve with regular training support this submaximal finding (Åstrand & Rodahl, 1977).

It would be expected that cyclists who ride at least 100 mi/week and use toe stirrups regularly would show a more enhanced physiological performance than noncyclists, due specifically to the utilization of toe stirrups. This is assumed to be true mainly due to the familiarity and skill in toe stirrup use that should be possessed by cyclists. However, the use of toe stirrups in the cyclist group appeared to be of no more benefit than to the noncyclist group. One reason for this lack of benefit could be that toe stirrups provide no benefit at the rate of 80 rpm. The major benefit of toe stirrups is believed to be due to the increase in muscle utilization on the upswing side of the pedal revolution. This provides force in both pulling and pushing directions to enhance pedaling, allowing for faster cadences at greater ratios or resistance. If the cadence is too fast or too slow, it is believed that the benefits of toe stirrups may be hindered. Lavoie et al. (1978) showed significantly higher $\dot{V}O_2$max values with toe stirrups at 60 rpm. Contrary to the findings of Lavoie et al., this study showed no benefit in the use of toe stirrups. This suggests that 80 rpm may have been too fast to enhance the pulling motion to produce differences in the use of toe stirrups on a bicycle ergometer.

In addition to toe stirrups, cyclists use cleated cycling shoes that secure the foot to the pedal so that it may not slide during the pulling phase of the pedal revolution. In this study, only toe stirrups were used. It is speculated that only half of the essential equipment to maximize cycling performance was used. Toe stirrups alone do not appear to provide benefit at a cadence of 80 rpm or above. However, it is assumed that coupled with cleated shoes, positive benefits are derived. This is apparent as experienced competitive cyclists who crank at rates from 90 to 120 rpm never use toe stirrups alone. This same reason may explain why no benefit was found due to the use of toe stirrups in the noncyclist group.

In summary, the findings of this study suggest that there is no benefit derived from the use of toe stirrups in either cyclists or noncyclists when riding at 80 rpm. It may be that toe stirrups provide little or no benefit unless coupled with cleated shoes. Differences that were observed in this investigation were due to the inherent physiological capabilities of the groups used.

References

Åstrand, P.O., & Rodahl, K. (1977). *Textbook of work physiology*. New York: McGraw-Hill.

Faria, I., Dix, C., & Frazer, C. (1978). Effect of body position during cycling on heart rate, pulmonary ventilation, oxygen uptake, and work output. *Journal of Sports Medicine*, **18**, 49–56.

Karpovich, P.V., & Sinning, W.E. (1971). *Physiology of muscular activity*. Philadelphia: W.B. Saunders.

Lavoie, N.F., Mahoney, M.D., & Marmelic, L.S. (1978). Maximal oxygen uptake on a bicycle ergometer without toe stirrups and with toe stirrups versus a treadmill. *Canadian Journal of Applied Sports Sciences*, **3**, 98–102.

Mathews, D.K., & Fox, E.L. (1974). *Physiological basis of physical education and athletics*. Philadelphia: W.B. Saunders.

McArdle, W.D., & Magel, J.R. (1970). Physical work capacity and maximum oxygen uptake in treadmill and bicycle exercise. *Medicine and Science in Sports, 5*, 132-136.

Noble, B.J., & Pandolf, K.B. (1973). The effect of pedalling speed and resistance changes on perceived exertion for equivalent power outputs on the bicycle ergometer. *Medicine and Science in Sports, 5*, 132-136.

Nordeem-Snyder, K.S. (1977). The effect of bicycle seat height variation upon oxygen consumption and lower limb kinematics. *Medicine and Science in Sports, 9*, 113-117.

Whitt, F.R. (1971). A note on the estimation of the energy expenditure of sporting cyclists. *Ergonomics, 14*, 419-427.

Wilde, S.W. (1978). *Cardiovascular and metabolic responses to toe clip use during bicycle ergometer work*. Unpublished master's thesis, Southern Illinois University, Carbondale.

Supercompensation in External Power of Well-Trained Cyclists

Leo P.V.M. Clijsen

Jaar van de Linden

Erwin Welbergen

Ruud W. de Boer

In training practice it is well known that heavy training will result in decreased performance. After a subsequent period of rest the performance will increase above the original level. This effect is called *supercompensation* (Figure 1).

Physiological research (Åstrand & Rodahl, 1977; Bowers, Branam, & Sparks, 1971; Costill, Sparks, Gregor, & Turner, 1971; Konopka, 1981) has shown the occurrence of supercompensation in the storage of glycogen. Three days after depletion of glycogen by means of a heavy-training stimulus, a 6% increase of the muscle glycogen stores was found. Supercompensation was also found for concentration of enzymes of the aerobic

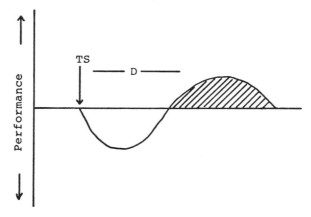

Figure 1 Heavy training (TS) will result in a decrease of performance. After a subsequent period of "rest" (D), performance will increase above the original level. The shaded area illustrates the supercompensation. From "Ausdauer und Ausdauertraining" by P. Konopka, 1981, *Deutsche Zeitschrift für Sportmedizin*, **4**. Reprinted by permission.

metabolic pathways (Schueler, 1981). This study also showed an increase in external power on a 2-hr bicycle ergometer test after 72 hr of rest following a training stimulus. This finding can be explained by the supercompensation in muscle glycogen stores. This effect could not be related to detraining because of the absence of a control group.

The purpose of this study was to answer the following questions:

• Does supercompensation occur in external power after a training stimulus?
• If so, how many days after the training stimulus?
• Is this supercompensation influenced by detraining?

Methods

Subjects

Twenty-five male subjects participated in this study. All of them were well-trained, national-level cyclists who trained at least 10 hr/week. Informed consent was obtained from all subjects. Table 1 shows some anthropometric data and mean maximal oxygen consumption.

Experimental Procedure

A preliminary test to familiarize the subjects with the experimental procedures and technical equipment was organized.

One day before the training stimulus (TS) the subjects came to the laboratory for a reference test (R). The training stimulus consisted of at least one competitive cycling event (at least 2.5 hr) during the 2 days following the reference test. In case a subject could not complete the cycling race, he performed a training of similar duration and intensity.

A test session (T) was held on 1 of the 5 days following the training stimulus. Normal training activities were allowed until the day of the test session. This period was characterized as the training period (Tr).

With an interruption of 1 week, the subject followed the same procedure. During this week, until the day of the next reference test, the subject

Table 1   Anthropometric Data and $\dot{V}O_2$max of the Subjects

	Height (m)	Body weight (kg)	Fat (%)	$\dot{V}O_2$max (ml/min/kg)
Mean	1.84	74.0	10.0	70.2
SD	0.06	6.1	2.3	4.4

Figure 2 The experimental procedure. TS = training stimulus, consisting of a competitive cycling event (at least 2.5 hr); R = reference test, on the day before TS; T = test session on 1 of the 5 days following TS; Tr = normal training activities during this period; D = minimal training activities during this period.

was asked not to perform training activities. This period was called the detraining period (D). The experimental procedure is shown in Figure 2.

Measurements

A modified electrically braked Mijnhardt bicycle ergometer with a parabolic function was used. The subjects were able to regulate external power by means of pedal frequency.

The following modifications were made:

A water cooling system to prevent the storage of heat was mounted, and a higher resistance setting was made possible. The bicycle ergometer was calibrated up to a level of 1,000 W and showed a maximal deviation of the linear relationship between pedal frequency and power output of only 2%.

Pedal frequency and power output were continuously registered. Heart rate was registered throughout the test with the use of a cardiotachometer. Oxygen consumption was measured with the conventional Douglas bag method. Temperature was kept constant at 18 to 20° C. For methodological reasons the population was divided into two groups. One group started with training (Tr), the other group with the detraining (D) conditions.

Bicycle Ergometer Tests

Every session consisted of two tests, separated from each other by at least 30 min.

30″ test. This was a modified Wingate test (Inbar, Dotan, & Bar-Or, 1976). A 10-min warm-up consisted of cycling at a cycling frequency of 90 rpm and a load of 150 W. Starting at Minutes 5, 7, and 9 the load was increased to 400 W for 30 s. Warming up was followed by a 2-min rest period, after which the subject was asked to perform maximally for 30 s. The subjects were encouraged verbally to do so. The resistance was individually adjusted to reach optimal power output with pedal frequencies between 90 to 120 rpm (Sargeant, Hoinville, & Young, 1981).

3' test. This test was based on the supramaximal test as proposed by Åstrand and Rodahl (1977). The warm-up consisted of 3 min of cycling at a work load of 100 W and another 3 min at 200 W. Pedal frequency was held at 90 rpm. After that the subject was asked to perform maximally for 3 min.

The resistance was individually adjusted to reach optimal power output with pedal frequencies between 90 and 120 rpm (Sargeant et al., 1981). During the last 2 min of this last period oxygen consumption was measured every 30 s, by means of the Douglas bag method.

The following parameters were derived:

30'' test: peak power	Pp30''
mean power	Pc30''
3' test: mean power	Pc3'
maximal aerobic power	$\dot{V}O_2max$

For each parameter the difference was calculated between reference test and test session, for training as well as detraining conditions. Differences between training and detraining conditions were also calculated and tested for significance ($p < .05$). Statistical analysis was performed by using the Student's t test.

Results and Discussion

Mean results for changes in external power are shown in Figures 3, 4, and 5 for Pp30'', Pc30'', and Pc3', respectively. External power appears to be the highest at the 2nd or 3rd day after training stimulus for all parameters. Standard deviation, however, was very large. The changes in Pp30'', Pc30'', and Pc3' were not different for training and detraining conditions. No difference was found in $\dot{V}O_2max$ between reference tests and test sessions, for both training and detraining conditions.

Two short-term tests, a 30'' modified Wingate test and a 3' supramaximal test, were used in this study to measure external power. It is likely that changes in anaerobic power can be detected by these tests. Hardly any changes in $\dot{V}O_2max$ occurred, and they were never significant. The differences found in external power must be explained, then, by changes in anaerobic power.

The supercompensation in external power on the 2nd and 3rd day is in agreement with the results found by Schueler (1981). Supercompensation appears at the 2nd or 3rd day after training stimulus. However, power output was much lower during his study (260 W). Moreover, our subjects had to perform during two short-term tests of 30 s and 3 min, respectively, whereas Schueler used a 2-hr test. In this study, because

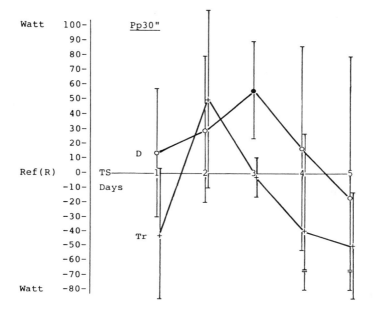

Figure 3   Difference in external power (W), between test session (T) and reference test (R) on each day (1 to 5) for training (Tr) and detraining (D) conditions, for Pp30''. Lines defined by "O" are for detraining (D) conditions ("●" = significant); lines defined by "+" are for training (Tr) conditions ("*" = significant).

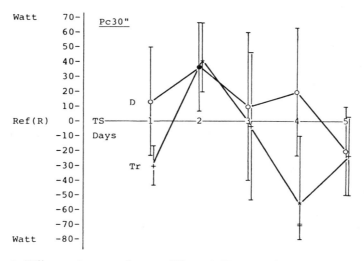

Figure 4   Difference in external power (W)—as in Figure 3—for Pc30''.

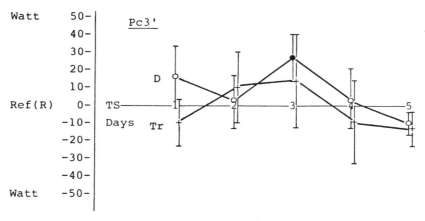

Figure 5 Difference in external power (W)—as in Figure 3—for Pc3'.

of the training stimulus the glycogen stores might have been depleted, but this could not have influenced the test results. Therefore, our findings cannot be explained by changes in aerobic power.

Conclusions

Supercompensation (4 to 7%) occurred in external power, 2 or 3 days after a heavy training stimulus. This supercompensation was not influenced by detraining. These results cannot be explained by changes in aerobic power.

References

Åstrand, P.O., & Rodahl, K. (1977). *Textbook of work physiology*. New York: McGraw-Hill.

Costill, D.L., Bowers, R., Branam, G., & Sparks, K. (1971). Muscle glycogen utilization during prolonged exercise on successive days. *Journal of Applied Physiology*, **31**(6), 834–838.

Costill, D.L., Sparks, K., Gregor, R., & Turner, C. (1971). Muscle glycogen utilization during exhaustive running. *Journal of Applied Physiology*, **31**(3), 353–356.

Inbar, O., Dotan, R., Bar-Or, O. (1976). Aerobic and anaerobic components of a 30-s supramaximal cycling test. *Medicine and Science in Sports*, (abstr.), **8**, 51.

Konopka, P. (1981). Ausdauer und Ausdauertraining. *Deutsche Zeitschrift für Sportmedizin* [Endurance and endurance training]. **4**, 104–109.

Sargeant, A.J., Hoinville, E., & Young, A. (1981). Maximum leg force and power output during short-term dynamic exercise. *Journal of Applied Physiology*, **51**(5), 1175–1182.

Schueler, K.P. (1981). Untersuchungen des Wiederherstellungsverlauf nach einer Langzeitdauerbelastung auf dem Fahrradergometer [Research on the recovery after an effort of long duration on the bicycle ergometer]. *Medizin und Sport*, **21**, 10–12.

$\dot{V}O_2$max of Competitive Cyclists Using a Conventional Cycle Ergometer Test Versus a Sport-Specific Bicycle Test

Norman F. LaVoie

Thomas H. Mercer

Michael A. Ciolfi

Specificity is a very important consideration when testing competitive athletes. A common method of testing many different athletes has been the use of a cycle ergometer pedaled at 60 rpm with the load being progressively increased until exhaustion. Such a test would seem to be very specific to cycling; however, in conversation with many competitive cyclists, most would agree that being tested on a cycle ergometer without toe stirrups, upright handlebars, sprung saddle, and pedaling at 60 rpm feels very uncomfortable and is not specific to the sport of cycling. Very often cyclists express a fear of being unable to maximize their physiological potential during conventional cycle ergometric assessment.

Various testing methods have been devised to test competitive cyclists in an attempt to obtain accurate physiological data. Hagberg (1979) had competitive cyclists riding their own racing bikes on a motor-driven treadmill and on the cycle ergometer. His results showed that both techniques done at 90 rpm produced no significant differences in maximum oxygen uptake ($\dot{V}O_2$max) measurements.

White, Quinn, and Darwalibi (1982) and Jurbala (1982) have developed similar systems of bicycle ergometry, both using a windload simulation device. White had his cyclists riding on rollers while a windload device was attached to the top of the rear wheel. The load was increased via the gear ratios on the bike. Jurbala's test is similar. He developed a field test to be used by coaches and trainers for a quick, inexpensive way of assessing the $\dot{V}O_2$max of cyclists. The test also requires the use of a wind load simulator (Racer-Mate or Racer-Mate II), a commonly used device by cyclists for indoor training. Jurbala's test was developed to predict $\dot{V}O_2$max from revolutions per minute and workload.

The purpose of this study was to investigate whether there were significant differences in $\dot{V}O_2$max and associated parameters during testing employing a conventional laboratory cycle ergometric (Monark) protocol (60 rpm) and also during a test employing more sport-specific apparatus (Vetta Trainer, subject's own bicycle) at a faster pedal cadence (90 rpm).

Methods

Five experienced male cyclists, all licensed with the Ontario Cycling Association and participating at the senior levels I, II, and III, volunteered to participate in the study. All subjects were informed of the exact details of the testing procedures and were told that they could withdraw from the experiment at any time.

Initially each subject completed a continuous incremental $\dot{V}O_2$max test on a Monark cycle ergometer equipped with toe stirrups and heel straps. Pedaling frequency was set at 60 rpm at an initial resistance of 150 W, and the resistance was increased 30 W every 2 min. A plateau in oxygen consumption between progressive loads indicated $\dot{V}O_2$max had been reached.

Each subject reported back to the laboratory 3 days after completing the conventional cycle ergometer test at or about the same time as the previous test. The subjects had been instructed to bring their own racing bicycle, cleats, and cycling shorts into the lab. Each bicycle was required to have a rear block having 18–13 teeth and a 53-tooth front chain ring. A Vetta trainer was provided by the laboratory for the second test. To standardize the setup of each subject's bicycle onto the Vetta trainer the following procedure was followed. The rear tire of each bicycle was inflated to 100 psi of pressure and then placed on the Vetta trainer with the tire sitting on the roller turbine with the forks in the front mounts and secured. The bottom bracket support foot was then set up. The foot was adjusted until it was touching the bottom bracket and was then securely fastened.

The test protocol using the Vetta trainer was the same as Jurbala's protocol (1982). Each subject pedaled at 90 rpm in the large chain ring and the large rear cog (53 × 17). The subject remained in the first gear for 4 min after which he was instructed to gear up one ratio while maintaining 90 rpm. Each successive gear was used for a 2.5-min period. At the end of this period in top gear (53-13), the pedaling frequency was increased to 100 rpm and the subject continued to exhaustion, which was defined as the point where the rider could no longer maintain a pedaling frequency of 70 rpm.

Oxygen consumption ($\dot{V}O_2$), ventilation, ($\dot{V}_E$), respiratory exchange ratio (RER), carbon dioxide output ($\dot{V}O_2$), and heart rate (HR) were measured during the conventional cycle ergometer test and the sport-specific test. Collection and analysis of metabolic data was done using a previously calibrated Beckman MMC Horizon II system. Previously a test-retest reliability coefficient of .988 had been established for the user of the metabolic cart. Heart rate responses were recorded electrocardiographically and then integrated by digital analog for presentation.

Means and standard deviations were computed for $\dot{V}O_2$, $\dot{V}_E$, RER, and HR. A Students' t test for related samples was utilized to examine differences between the variables.

Results

Anthropometric data ($M \pm SD$) for the 5 subjects who participated in the study are presented in Table 1. Tables 2 and 3 give the maximum physiological values attained during both the conventional cycle ergometer test and the sport-specific bicycle test using the Vetta trainer. The statistical analysis did not reveal any significant differences between the physiological variables.

Table 1   Anthropometric Data

Subject	Age (years)	Weight (kg)	Height (cm)
S.T.	18	79.0	184
G.D.	24	77.5	183
E.Z.	25	83.0	193
G.M.	20	71.0	177
M.C.	23	71.0	173
M	22	76.3	182
SD	3.28	6.24	7.62

Table 2   Maximum Values for $\dot{V}O_2$, $\dot{V}_E$, RER, and HR During the Conventional Cycle Ergometer Test

Subject	$\dot{V}O_2$max (l/min)	(ml/kg/min)	$\dot{V}_E$ (l/min)	RER	HR (bpm)
G.D.	5.14	66.2	167.3	1.08	200
E.Z.	4.58	55.7	117.1	1.10	170
G.M.	4.44	62.4	126.2	1.14	196
M.C.	4.77	67.0	174.5	1.13	199
S.T.	4.99	62.2	146.3	1.13	190
M	4.79	62.7	146.28	1.12	191
SD	0.29	4.48	24.97	0.03	12.4

Table 3 Maximum Values for $\dot{V}O_2$, $\dot{V}_E$, RER, and HR During the Sport-Specific Bicycle Test

Subject	$\dot{V}O_2$max (l/min)	$\dot{V}O_2$max (ml/kg/min)	$\dot{V}_E$ (l/min)	RER	HR (bpm)
G.D.	5.19	66.3	166.9	1.09	191
E.Z.	4.87	59.2	137.0	1.09	188
G.M.	4.53	63.6	140.9	1.14	197
M.C.	4.88	68.6	192.2	1.15	195
S.T.	4.93	62.1	127.9	1.07	183
M	4.88	63.95	152.9	1.11	190
SD	0.24	3.62	26.3	0.04	5.59

Discussion

The mean $\dot{V}O_2$max values and the anthropometric characteristics for the subjects place them within the reported range for elite cyclists (Bonger, 1974; Hagberg, 1979; Vrijens, Pannier, & Bouckcret, 1982).

There were no significant differences in any of the physiological variables obtained when the subjects performed a test using a conventional cycle ergometer or a test using a sport-specific bicycle. This suggests that to obtain accurate metabolic information on competitive cyclists the cycle ergometer is as valid and accurate as the Vetta trainer. The cycle ergometer used in this study was equipped with toe stirrups and heel straps that securely held the subject's feet in place. The modifications to the pedals made it possible for the subject to push down as well as pull up on the pedals, duplicating the action of competitive cycling.

Subjectively, all subjects expressed a greater degree of comfort both physically and psychologically when being tested on their own bikes. This can undoubtedly be attributed to familiarity with the apparatus, cleats, saddle, handlebars, revolutions per minute, and gear shifts. However, this study has aptly demonstrated that once cyclists are habituated to the laboratory equipment, determination of their $\dot{V}O_2$max can be accurately and reliably determined using conventional cycle ergometry.

Summary

This study tested highly trained competitive cyclists on two different types of equipment. The results obtained indicated that there was no significant difference in $\dot{V}O_2$max of subjects when tested on the cycle ergometer and when tested using the Vetta trainer.

From these results it can be concluded that cyclists need not fear a lab situation on the cycle ergometer provided it is equipped with toe stirrups and heel straps. Athletes and coaches must realize that the laboratory is meant to be a supportive facility to training and performance.

Despite the findings of this study, cyclists will undoubtedly continue to fear tests on the cycle ergometer while pedaling at 60 rpm. To accommodate these athletes it is recommended that the following modifications be made to the conventional cycle ergometer. The cycle ergometer should be equipped with racing-type pedals and toe clips to allow the athlete to use his or her cycling cleats. The handlebars should be dropped handlebars similar to those found on racing bicycles with various stem extension lengths available to accommodate individual arm lengths. The saddle should be a racing saddle that can be adjusted both backward and forward according to individual preference. Lastly the revolutions per minute used should be 90 because this is one of the most preferred pedal revolutions used by competitive cyclists.

References

Hagberg, J.M. (1979). Physiological profiles and selected psychological characteristics of national class American cyclists. *Journal of Sports Medicine and Physical Fitness*, **19**, 341–346.

Jurbala, P. (1982). *Fitness testing for racing cyclists*. Unpublished test development protocol, Canadian Cycling Association, Vanier, Ontario.

Vrijens, J., Pannier, J.L., & Bouckcret, J. Physiological profile of competitive road cyclist. *Journal of Sports Medicine and Physical Fitness*, **2**(22), 207–216.

White, J.A., Quinn, G.A., & Darwalibi, M. (1982). Seasonal changes in cyclists' performance: Part I. The British Olympic road racing squad. *British Journal of Sports Medicine*, **16**(1), 4–12.

Physiological and Psychological Responses of Pursuit and Sprint Track Cyclists to a Period of Reduced Training

Frank S. Pyke

Neil P. Craig

Kevin I. Norton

In many sports coaches often reduce the training load of athletes during the last few days before important competitions. This procedure, generally referred to as *tapering*, is designed to improve performance by optimizing the physiological, biomechanical, and psychological responses of the individual. A wide range of tapering regimes exist, depending on the importance of the competition, the nature of the performance, and the characteristics of the individual athlete. However, very few scientific studies have been conducted that have either systematically measured the benefits of tapering or clarified the mechanisms associated with it.

One of these studies was conducted by Costill, King, Thomas, and Hargreaves (1985) on a group of collegiate swimmers. Power output, measured both on a biokinetic swim bench and in tethered swimming, significantly increased throughout a 14-day period of reduced training. Performance in swimming events ranging from 50 to 1,650 yd improved by an average of 3.1%. However, blood lactic acid, pH, and bicarbonate levels measured in response to a 200-m swim at 90% of maximal speed did not alter during this period. The investigators were unable to identify the precise mechanisms underlying these improvements in muscular power and swimming performance but suggested that the period of reduced training may have allowed for an increase in maximal tension development through changes in the contractile mechanisms and/or neural controls on muscle fiber recruitment.

It was decided to extend these investigations from swimming to the sport of cycling where tapering regimes are not as common. Despite achieving outstanding international results in recent years without extensive use of tapered training loads just prior to competition, the coach of the Australian team was prepared to study the responses of members of his national squad throughout taper periods lasting from 4 to 10 days.

The purpose of this study was to compare the physiological and psychological responses of a group of elite track sprint and pursuit cyclists during exposure to intense and tapered training loads.

Methods

Subjects

The six cyclists who participated in the study were male members of a national squad training at the Sports Institute in Adelaide, South Australia under the direction of the national coach. Five of the cyclists were pursuiters, 2 of whom had won gold medals in the 4,000-m team pursuit event at the 1984 Olympic Games. In the absence of 1 pursuiter, who was competing overseas, the others won the team pursuit title at the 1986 National Championships. Three members of the group won individual and team pursuit gold medals at the 1986 British Commonwealth Games. The sprinter is the current Australian senior sprint champion and 1986 Commonwealth Games gold medalist. Due to commitments with overseas competition Pursuiter 1 was only able to taper for 4 days. Pursuiter 2 was ill with a gastrointestinal virus for 2 days and was forced to extend the taper to 10 days. The other cyclists each underwent a 7-day taper period. All cyclists were fully acquainted with the laboratory testing procedures, having been regularly assessed on a wide range of physiological variables during their stay at the Institute. All were informed of the risks and stresses associated with the experiment and gave written consent to participate. The physical characteristics of the cyclists are given in Table 1.

Rationale for Test Selection

The rationale for selection of suitable physiological tests is based on the estimated energy requirements of different cycling events. Jurbala (1983)

Table 1 Physical Characteristics of Cyclists

Subject	Age (years)	Height (cm)	Mass (kg)
Pursuiter 1	19.6	184.0	75.0
2	19.6	181.7	78.1
3	22.9	181.8	78.4
4	27.6	178.7	81.8
5	22.8	172.0	66.3
Sprinter	19.4	177.0	76.9
M	22.0	179.2	76.1
SD	3.2	4.3	5.3

suggested that 4,000-m track pursuit events demand a 70% aerobic, 25% glycolytic, and 5% high energy phosphate energy contribution. On the other hand, the short sprint (approximately 200 m, lasting about 12 s) and the sustained sprint (1,000 m, lasting 65 to 70 s) place far greater emphasis on the breakdown of high energy phosphate compounds and glycolytic energy release. As shown in Table 2, the involvement of the glycolytic energy pathway, indicated from blood lactate data, is high in both match sprints and 1,000-m time trial events. Although blood lactate levels are also substantial in 4,000-m pursuit events, the duration of the event makes it possible for the major energy contribution to come from aerobic sources.

After considering these estimates of the contributions of energy sources, it was decided to measure the power output of the pursuiters during a simulated pursuit ride lasting 4 min, 45 s on a bicycle ergometer. During the ride the capability of the aerobic energy pathways was assessed from the maximal oxygen consumption ($\dot{V}O_2$max) and the capacity of the glycolytic energy pathways from peak blood lactate concentrations. In addition, the mechanical and cardiovascular efficiency of the pursuiters was determined during a 5-min submaximal ride at a power output of 350 W. Their peak explosive anaerobic power and the ability to sustain this power were measured during 10- and 30-s bicycle ergometer sprints. The strength and explosive power of the leg muscles in noncycling activities were assessed from isokinetic leg extension and flexion strength tests at different movement velocities and a vertical jump. The sprint cyclist was only involved in tests oriented toward explosive power. Hence, he completed the 10- and 30-s bicycle ergometer sprints and the isokinetic leg strength and vertical jump tests.

In view of the well-known effect of hard training on the psychological state of the individual and the likely consequences of this on performance, the researchers also decided to administer a mood state profile to each cyclist.

Table 2   Blood Lactate Levels (mmol · l⁻¹) of Cyclists Involved in Match Sprint, 1,000-m Time Trial, and 4,000-m Individual Pursuit Events

Source	Match sprint	1,000-m time trial	4,000-m individual pursuit
Burke, Fleck & Dickson (1981)	11.40–15.11	15.69–18.22	13.55–17.31
Craig (1985/1986)	14.50	15.23–19.11	11.60–14.90

Test Protocols

The following laboratory tests were conducted in the order shown on 2 consecutive days at the end of both a 2-week period of hard training and the period of tapering:

- Day 1—submaximal bicycle test and maximal simulated pursuit test, with a recovery period of 30 min between them; and
- Day 2—determination of physical characteristics, isokinetic leg strength, and vertical jump ability; and 10- and 30-s bicycle tests.

The 5 pursuit cyclists completed each of the above tests, whereas the sprinter only undertook those listed on the 2nd day. The cyclists arrived at the laboratory for each test session at the same time of the morning, following a standardized warm-up ride on their own bicycles. They were carefully instructed in terms of the timing of meals, fluid intake, and rest patterns that are most likely to be associated with a best performance. Their coach was present at all test sessions.

Physical characteristics.   Height was measured to the nearest 0.1 cm with a wall stadiometer. Body mass was measured in riding knicks to the nearest 25 g with Avery scales. Skinfold thickness was measured to the nearest 0.1 mm with Harpenden calipers at the following sites: triceps, biceps, subscapular, iliac crest, abdominal, juxtanipple, axillary, front thigh, and medial calf. All sites, with the exception of the juxtanipple and axillary, were located in accordance with the procedures outlined by Ross and Marfell-Jones (1982). The methods of Withers, Craig, Bourdon, and Norton (in press) and Behnke and Wilmore (1974) were used to locate the juxtanipple and axillary sites, respectively. Predicted body density was computed from the regression equation of Withers et al. Subsequent estimations of percentage body fat were calculated by employing the Siri equation (1961).

Bicycle ergometer tests.   A Repco air-braked bicycle ergometer, geared so that each revolution of the pedal crank produced 6.49 wheel revolutions, was used in the simulated pursuit and the 10- and 30-s tests. This gearing permitted optimum pedal rates to be achieved in these tests. A Sportronic Pacer 2000 was used to monitor pedal cadence during each of the tests. A Repco work monitor recorded work done (kJ) and peak power generated (W). A standard Monark mechanically braked ergometer was used for the submaximal test. Each ergometer was equipped with a racing saddle, dropped handlebars, and toe clips, and extreme care was taken to ensure that the cyclist's body was in the same position on each test occasion. All cyclists wore cleated cycling shoes.

Maximal simulated pursuit test.   The main criterion of performance for the pursuit cyclists was the total work output (kJ) achieved in a simulated, self-paced 4-min, 45-s ride on a Repco air-braked bicycle ergometer. During the test the cyclists breathed through a Hans Rudolph valve into a 2.5-L mixing box from which expired gas samples were drawn continuously through fast response oxygen (Applied Electrochemistry Model S-3A1) and carbon dioxide analyzers (Beckman LB2). Precision-analyzed gas mixtures were used to calibrate the analyzers before and after each test. Pulmonary ventilation was measured by a Morgan ventilometer connected to the inspiratory side of the respiratory valve and calibrated at pulsatile flow rates using a syringe of known volume. The ventilometer and gas analyzers were connected to an Apple IIe microcomputer via a three-channel analog-to-digital converter. Values for $\dot{V}_E$, $\dot{V}O_2$, $\dot{V}CO_2$, R, $\dot{V}_E/\dot{V}O_2$ and $\dot{V}E/\dot{V}CO_2$ were computed and displayed every 30 s. Maximal oxygen consumption was determined as the peak value reached during a 1-min period of the test. Measurements made using the computerized system were previously checked against those made with the Douglas bag method and found to be accurate.

Heart rate was determined from electrocardiograms recorded by means of a Nihon Kohden telemetry system during each minute of the test. Maximal heart rate was that attained during the last 10 s of the test.

A 25 μl sample of arterialized capillary blood was taken from a hyperaemic fingertip after 1, 3, 5, and 7 min of recovery for the determination of peak blood lactate concentration using the enzymatic method of analysis (Gutmann & Wahlefeld, 1974). The cyclists remained seated in a chair during the recovery period.

10-s bicycle test.   Both the work done and peak power generated during a 10-s sprint on the bicycle ergometer were recorded from a Repco work monitor. In the same manner as for the pursuit test, blood samples were drawn from a fingertip during the recovery period following the sprint for determination of peak lactate concentration.

30-s bicycle test.   Ten minutes after completing the 10-s bicycle test the cyclists engaged in a 30-s test in which they were encouraged to reach maximal power output early in the test and maintain it for the remaining time. The work done in each 5-s period was read from the work monitor. Total work done, peak power, and power loss (percentage loss from 0 to 5 or 5 to 10 s to 25- to 30-s periods) were computed. Peak blood lactate concentration was determined as in the other tests.

Submaximal bicycle test.   A 5-min submaximal test was performed on a mechanically braked Monark bicycle ergometer. A pedaling rate of 100 rpm performed against a resistance of 3.5 kiloponds was used to produce a power output of 350 W. The bicycle was calibrated before each test, and an electronic digital recorder enabled close monitoring of pedaling rate throughout the test. Oxygen uptake, heart rate, and blood lactate concentration were measured using the methods described previously.

Vertical jump.   The method described by Verducci (1980) was used to determine the maximal height jumped above standing height.

Isokinetic leg strength test.   A Cybex isokinetic dynamometer was used for measuring leg extension and leg flexion torques at speeds of 60, 180, and 300° • s⁻¹. In each test the cyclist was braced against the seat and backboard to prevent the recruitment of additional muscle groups when performing the movement. The values obtained on the strongest leg were given as the criterion score.

Mood state profile.   Before the first test in each sequence the cyclist was asked to fill out the mood state profile established by McNair, Lorr, and Droppleman (1971). The profile assessed the individual in six categories: tension, depression, anger, vigor, fatigue, and confusion.

Training Loads

During the 5 days of the pretaper period, the cyclists covered 430 km of road work, two 1-hr intensive interval sessions (15- and 20-s sprints every 60 and 80 s), and a 1-hr continuous session on a Repco air-braked bicycle ergometer; two weight training sessions; and an evening in racing competition. During an equivalent 5-day period of the taper, the road distance was reduced by approximately 20% to 340 km, and the intervalized bicycle ergometer training was deleted. The remainder of the program was similar to that followed in the pretaper period. The cyclists trained as a group and with the exception of Pursuiter 2, who was ill and in bed for 2 days during the taper period, each completed the same training.

Results and Discussion

Due to the small number of cyclists involved in the study, the absence of a control group, and the investigators being confined to obtaining only two sets of observations on each man, it was not considered appropriate to apply inferential statistics to the data. The results are therefore presented as a series of case reports.

Table 3   **Physical Chracteristics of Cyclists Measured Before and After a Period of Reduced Training**

Subject	Body mass (kg)		Sum of eight skinfolds (mm)		Percentage body fat[a]	
	Before	After	Before	After	Before	After
Pursuiter 1	75.00	75.00	41.4	41.0	5.23	5.23
2	78.05	76.30	41.2	39.5	5.54	5.50
3	78.40	78.50	56.9	55.4	6.94	7.31
4	81.75	81.90	64.1	61.1	7.58	7.36
5	66.30	66.00	38.9	39.4	5.35	5.60
Sprinter	76.85	76.05	55.4	53.8	6.89	6.78
M	76.06	75.63	49.7	48.4	6.26	6.30
SD	5.27	5.32	10.5	9.5	1.00	0.96

[a]Using equation of Withers et al. (1986).

Physical Characteristics

With the exception of Pursuiter 2, who lost 1.75 kg (some of which was fat-free mass), the cyclists maintained similar body mass and composition throughout the study (see Table 3).

Table 4 Physiological Responses of Cyclists to a 4-Min, 45-s Simulated Pursuit Ride on a Bicycle Ergometer Measured Before and After a Period of Reduced Training

Subject	Total work (kJ)		Average power (W)	
	Before	After	Before	After
Pursuiter 1	119.7	123.4	420.0	433.0
2	118.0	123.0	414.0	431.6
3	114.6	118.7	402.0	416.5
4	120.0	120.6	421.1	423.2
5	102.9	99.0	361.1	347.4
M	115.0	116.9	403.6	410.3
SD	7.1	10.2	25.0	35.8

	Maximal oxygen uptake			
	$(1 \cdot min^{-1}$ STPD)		$(ml \cdot kg^{-1} \cdot min^{-1}$ STPD)	
	Before	After	Before	After
Pursuiter 1	5.92	6.01	79.4	80.5
2	5.55	5.86	71.1	77.1
3	5.76	5.97	74.1	76.4
4	6.04	6.06	75.2	74.7
5	4.74	4.91	71.3	74.4
M	5.60	5.76	74.2	76.6
SD	0.52	0.48	3.4	2.5

	Maximal heart rate (bpm)		Blood lactate (mmol $\cdot l^{-1}$)	
	Before	After	Before	After
Pursuiter 1	184	192	14.22	15.23
2	194	202	17.03	16.84
3	186	193	16.72	17.75
4	179	185	14.49	12.61
5	188	204	20.66	20.49
M	186	195	16.62	16.58
SD	6	8	2.59	2.93

Maximal Simulated Pursuit Test

Three of the 5 pursuiters (1, 2, and 3) showed significant gains (3.1 to 4.2%) in power output during the simulated pursuit (Table 4). Pursuiter

Table 5   Physiological Responses of Cyclists to a 5-Min Ride (350 W) on a Bicycle Ergometer Measured Before and After a Period of Reduced Training

| Subject | Oxygen uptake | | | |
| | (L · min⁻¹ STPD) | | (% max) | |
	Before	After	Before	After
Pursuiter 1	4.76	4.99	80.4	83.0
2	4.95	4.81	89.2	82.1
3	4.87	5.00	84.5	83.8
4	4.71	4.86	78.0	80.2
5	4.60	4.83	97.0	98.4
M	4.78	4.90	85.8	85.5
SD	0.14	0.09	7.6	7.3

| | Heart rate | | | |
| | (bpm) | | (% max) | |
	Before	After	Before	After
Pursuiter 1	161	169	87.5	88.0
2	169	180	87.1	89.1
3	166	173	89.2	89.6
4	157	162	87.7	87.6
5	180	188	95.7	92.2
M	167	174	89.4	89.3
SD	9	10	3.6	1.8

| | Blood lactate | |
| | (mmol · L⁻¹) | |
	Before	After
Pursuiter 1	5.98	4.71
2	6.44	5.41
3	6.36	7.37
4	4.71	4.42
5	14.20	14.03
M	7.54	7.19
SD	3.79	3.99

4 did not alter his performance, and Pursuiter 5, who had difficulty in maintaining the same training load as the others, produced a lower power output (3.8%) during the period of reduced training.

These changes in power output were accompanied by changes in maximal oxygen uptake and blood lactate concentration measured during the same test (Table 4) and in oxygen uptake measured during the submaximal ride at 350 W (Table 5). For example, Pursuiter 2, who increased average power output in the pursuit test by 4.2%, also improved maximal oxygen uptake (5.6%) and used less oxygen in the submaximal ride. On the other hand, the decrease in power output of Pursuiter 5 appeared to be associated with an increase in the amount of oxygen used in the submaximal ride as his maximal oxygen uptake actually increased slightly.

The exceptionally high maximal oxygen uptake values attained by 4 of the pursuiters (5.86 to 6.06 l • min^{-1}) bear testimony to their success in national and international pursuit cycling events and are among the highest reported on track cyclists (Faria, 1984; Sjøgaard, Nielsen, Mikkelsen, Saltin, & Burke, 1985).

Submaximal Ride

The oxygen uptake measured during the submaximal ride at 350 W permitted estimations of mechanical efficiency. The cyclists averaged between 20.5 and 21.0% gross mechanical efficiency, which is within the range previously reported on track cyclists (Faria, Sjøgaard, & Bonde-Petersen, 1982). However, it should be pointed out that these values are overestimations of efficiency as no account has been made of the contribution of anaerobic energy sources. When working between 80 and 85% of maximal oxygen uptake, the cyclists developed blood lactate concentrations between 4.5 and 7.5 mmol • l^{-1}, indicating that they had surpassed the threshold for anaerobic metabolism and were utilizing the glycolytic energy pathways to a significant extent.

The heart rates measured both during the submaximal ride and maximal simulated pursuit test increased as a result of undergoing a reduced training load. The physiological mechanisms responsible for this response are not known, particularly in the 3 pursuiters, who profited most from the taper. However, in view of Coyle, Hemmert, and Coggan's (1986) findings that significant decreases in blood volume (associated with increases in exercise heart rate) occur during brief periods of detraining, further investigations of the haemodynamics of the circulation during tapering appear warranted.

10- and 30-s Bicycle Tests

Among the pursuiters the most significant improvements in the 10- and 30-s sprint tests were made by Cyclists 2 and 3, who underwent tapering periods of 10 and 7 days, respectively (see Tables 6 and 9). These improvements were matched only by the sprinter in the 10-s test. The 4-day taper of Pursuiter 1 did not enhance his performance in these tests, and, as

Table 6 Maximal Explosive Power and Capacity of Cyclists Measured in a 10-s Bicycle Ergometer Test Before and After a Period of Reduced Training

Subject	Total work (kJ)		Peak power (W)		Peak revolutions (rpm)	
	Before	After	Before	After	Before	After
Pursuiter 1	7.9	7.7	945	925	153	152
2	8.4	8.8	1,005	1,060	156	159
3	8.6	9.4	1,025	1,080	157	160
4	8.8	8.4	1,050	1,000	159	156
5	8.2	7.7	1,010	965	156	154
Sprinter	9.9	10.2	1,190	1,240	165	167
M	8.63	8.70	1,038	1,045	158	158
SD	0.70	0.98	82	112	4	5

	Blood lactate (mmol · L^{-1})	
	Before	After
Pursuiter 1	4.73	4.70
2	4.50	4.73
3	5.51	6.44
4	4.77	4.44
5	6.46	5.06
Sprinter	6.58	6.40
M	5.43	5.30
SD	0.91	0.89

in the other tests, Pursuiter 5 produced worse performances after the taper than before it.

The quantity of blood lactate accumulated in 10 s attests to the significant involvement of the glycolytic energy pathways in short, explosive cycling efforts. This is obviously even greater in the 30-s test. However, if the glycogen stores are depleted, as could occur during hard training on consecutive days, the full power of glycolysis cannot be sustained (Jacobs, 1981). The detrimental effects of such fuel shortage on the capability for generating muscular tension, particularly in the fast-twitch fibers, have been demonstrated by Jacobs, Kaiser, and Tesch (1982). This suggests that cyclists with a higher proportion of fast-twitch muscle fibers and/or those engaged in sprinting will be the most impaired by substantial depletion of muscle glycogen. The significant decrease in explosive power demonstrated by Pursuiter 5 may have resulted from such fuel depletion.

The smallest loss of power in the 30-s test was observed in Pursuiters 1 and 4, who also had the highest maximal oxygen uptake. This is expected in view of the likelihood of their having a muscle fiber composition favoring endurance activities, that is, having more slow-twitch fibers that are more resistant to fatigue (Thorstensson & Karlson, 1976). By contrast the sprinter and Pursuiter 5 lost considerably more power during the 30-s test, a characteristic that did not improve as a result of reducing the training load.

Vertical Jump and Isokinetic Leg Strength Tests

Changes in performance on the vertical jump (Table 7) and isokinetic leg strength tests (Table 8) did not mirror those measured on the bicycle ergometer. This adds weight to the case for assessing the capabilities of muscle groups when they are involved in similar movements to those used in training.

Mood State Profiles

The cyclists who profited most from the taper period also produced the most significant changes in the psychological variables assessed by the mood state profile (Table 10). Pursuiters 1, 2, and 3 demonstrated heightened vigor and lowered fatigue and depression at the end of the taper period. On the other hand, Pursuiter 4, as in the physiological tests, produced an almost identical profile on these variables throughout the pretaper and taper periods. The responses of the sprinter were also quite consistent. Pursuiter 5 claimed that he felt less vigorous and more fatigued and depressed throughout the taper, again mirroring his physiological responses to the cycling tests. The close correlation of the mood state profile scores with cycling performance makes the former a quick and effective tool for monitoring adjustments to training loads.

Table 7   The Vertical Jump (cm) of Cyclists Measured Before and After a Period of Reduced Training

Subject	Before	After
Pursuiter 1	44.0	45.5
2	51.0	50.5
3	43.0	44.0
4	51.5	47.5
5	50.0	51.5
Sprinter	65.5	61.5
M	50.8	50.1
SD	8.1	6.3

A summary analysis of each of the cyclists responses to the reduced training load is given as follows:

Pursuiter 1. This cyclist is a world-class pursuiter who tapered for 4 days and achieved a 3.1% increase in power output in a simulated pursuit. This was associated with some reduction in the blood lactate accumulated during a submaximal ride at about 80% of maximal oxygen uptake and an increase in maximal blood lactate. No changes were evident in any of the tests of maximal explosive cycling power. There was a significant positive shift in his mood state profile throughout the taper period toward reductions in tension, depression, and fatigue and an elevation in vigor.

Pursuiter 2. This cyclist, a member of the national team pursuit squad, tapered for 10 days, including a 2-day period during which he was ill and in bed. Power output in a simulated pursuit ride increased by 4.2%, associated with a 5.6% increase in maximal oxygen uptake and a marked

Table 8 Leg Extension and Leg Flexion Torque (NM) of Cyclists Measured at Three Different Velocities of Movement ($60°·s^{-1}$, $180°·s^{-1}$, $300°·s^{-1}$) Before and After a Period of Reduced Training

| Subject | Leg extension | | | | | |
| | $60°·s^{-1}$ | | $180°·s^{-1}$ | | $300°·s^{-1}$ | |
	Before	After	Before	After	Before	After
Pursuiter 1	122.2	108.9	69.1	67.7	44.5	43.8
2	109.6	108.9	67.7	74.4	50.5	50.5
3	106.9	104.9	72.4	67.7	44.5	46.5
4	110.9	95.6	69.7	62.4	47.2	39.8
5	99.0	89.0	61.1	61.1	42.5	39.9
Sprinter	106.3	102.3	68.4	69.1	49.8	50.5
M	109.2	101.6	68.1	67.1	46.5	45.2
SD	7.6	7.9	3.8	4.8	3.2	4.8

| | Leg flexion | | | | | |
| | $60°·s^{-1}$ | | $180°·s^{-1}$ | | $300°·s^{-1}$ | |
	Before	After	Before	After	Before	After
Pursuiter 1	67.7	61.1	43.2	43.8	32.5	30.6
2	69.1	57.1	45.2	45.2	32.5	33.2
3	65.1	55.7	46.5	42.5	34.5	30.6
4	77.0	65.1	55.1	45.2	38.5	33.2
5	67.7	63.8	51.1	46.5	39.2	34.5
Sprinter	71.7	62.4	49.2	49.2	34.5	33.2
M	69.7	60.9	48.4	45.4	35.3	32.6
SD	4.2	3.7	4.3	2.3	2.9	1.6

reduction (16.0%) in blood lactate accumulation during a submaximal ride at 350 W. Significant elevations in power output in the 10- and 30-s bicycle tests and reductions in power loss in the latter also occurred. Positive shifts in mood state variables such as depression, anger, fatigue, and vigor

Table 9 Sustained Explosive Power and Capacity of Cyclists Measured in a 30-s Bicycle Test Before and After a Period of Reduced Training

Subject	Total work (kJ)		Peak power (W)	
	Before	After	Before	After
Pursuiter 1	21.4	21.6	925	930
2	22.7	23.1	1,030	1,080
3	23.3	24.2	1,025	1,070
4	22.8	22.0	1,050	1,025
5	20.1	19.8	1,010	940
Sprinter	25.7	26.1	1,265	1,240
M	22.7	22.8	1,051	1,048
SD	1.9	2.2	114	114

	Power loss (%)	
	Before	After
Pursuiter 1	780–600 (23.0)	820–600 (26.8)
2	920–580 (37.0)	900–600 (33.3)
3	920–620 (32.7)	920–640 (30.4)
4	880–620 (29.5)	900–580 (35.5)
5	820–460 (44.0)	800–460 (42.5)
Sprinter	1,040–660 (36.5)	1,040–620 (40.3)
M	893–590 (33.8)	897–583 (34.8)
SD	91– 69 (7.2)	85– 64 (5.9)

	Blood lactate (mmol · L^{-1})	
	Before	After
Pursuiter 1	11.12	11.39
2	13.46	11.29
3	14.22	14.96
4	11.10	11.50
5	15.23	13.56
Sprinter	14.40	15.04
M	13.26	12.96
SD	1.75	1.79

accompanied these physiological changes. The adjustments of this cyclist to the period of reduced training were the most marked of those studied.

Pursuiter 3.   This cyclist is a member of the national team pursuit squad and followed a 7-day taper program. During this period he achieved a 3.6% increase in power output in the simulated pursuit. This was accompanied by a 3.6% increase in maximal oxygen uptake and a 6.2% increase in maximal blood lactate. Average power output measured in the 10- and 30-s bicycle tests increased by 9.3 and 3.9%, respectively, and power loss in the 30-s test was 2.3% less. Large decreases in mood state responses

Table 10   Profile of Mood States of Cyclists Measured Before and After a Period of Reduced Training

Subject	Tension		Depression		Anger	
	Before	After	Before	After	Before	After
Pursuiter 1	5	4	1	0	4	0
2	9	10	11	7	14	10
3	17	7	8	0	21	1
4	3	3	0	4	4	12
5	4	9	0	7	1	4
Sprinter	11	15	11	18	15	14
M	8.2	8.0	5.2	6.0	9.8	6.8
U.S. Road Cyclists (Hagberg et al., 1979)	8.6		4.6		4.9	
College norms (McNair et al., 1971)	13.5		14.0		9.5	

	Vigor		Fatigue		Confusion	
	Before	After	Before	After	Before	After
Pursuiter 1	13	22	11	0	5	2
2	9	15	15	12	9	8
3	14	16	16	1	14	6
4	14	6	6	1	6	
5	23	16	3	10	1	9
Sprinter	19	18	11	11	8	10
M	15.3	16.8	10.3	6.7	6.3	6.8
U.S. Road Cyclists (Hagberg et al., 1979)	18.9		10.6		6.8	
College norms (McNair et al., 1971)	15.5		10.5		11.0	

such as tension, depression, anger, fatigue, and confusion and some elevation in vigor also occurred during the taper period.

Pursuiter 4.   This man is a world-class pursuiter with a 9-year history of competitive cycling. During the 7-day period of reduced training, he demonstrated little change on the physiological variables measured. His scores on the mood state variables were generally lower than the other cyclists, but, other than for some elevation in anger and confusion, the profile was similar throughout the taper period. He seemed to cope more easily with the training load than other members of the squad, all of whom were less experienced cyclists. He may only experience the full benefit of a taper if it follows a substantially increased volume and intensity of training.

Pursuiter 5.   This relatively inexperienced cyclist had some difficulty in maintaining the training loads of other members of the squad. This is understandable in view of his smaller physique and lower absolute aerobic and anaerobic power. It is likely that the negative residual effects of hard training were still in evidence even after the 7-day taper period and resulted in poorer performance in all the cycling tests conducted. The inability to produce as much lactic acid in the sprints may either reflect depletion in muscle glycogen levels and/or depression in the activity of glycolytic enzymes. These physiological responses are matched by decreases in mood state energy levels (vigor) and increases in depression, confusion, and fatigue. It seems that the downturn in his physiological performances was closely associated with an increasingly negative outlook.

Sprinter.   This champion sprinter was able to produce a 3.1% increase in power during the 10-s bicycle test throughout the course of the taper. However, in the 30-s test of sustained explosive power, changes in power output and power loss were only minimal. Only marginal variations were observed in the mood state profiles obtained before and after the period of reduced training.

Conclusion

Within the limitations of the foregoing case reports of champion track cyclists studied throughout a 4 to 10-day period when the training load was reduced or tapered, the following conclusions appear warranted. Since the study involved only males, conclusions will relate only to them.

The response to tapering is variable and seems to depend on the individual capability for handling the training load. This may, in turn, be related to factors such as the training history of the cyclist, his physiological and psychological attributes, and the volume and intensity of the training program being followed both before and during the taper.

The adjustments to the tapered training program are more easily observed in tests that simulate cycling movements rather than those that encourage a less specific expression of power.

Mood state changes tend to mirror the physiological state changes of the individual and could be used as a sign of the cyclist's preparedness to perform.

It is recommended that in order to optimize the performance of pursuiters of this class, at least a 7 to 10-day taper period be provided just prior to major competition. Sprinters may need to be given extra time (10 to 14 days) to reap the benefits of reduced training loads. These periods may need to be flexible depending on the responses of the individual cyclist and the volume and intensity of the full and reduced training programs being followed. It is worth noting that in this case the outcome of the testing program convinced both the coach and the cyclists that there are measurable benefits to be gained from participation in a tapering regime. Subsequently they have engaged in the procedure during recent international competitions.

Acknowledgments

The authors wish to acknowledge the contribution of Mr. Graham Winter, psychologist at the South Australian Sports Institute, for his analysis of the mood profile tests.

References

Behnke, A.R., & Wilmore, J.H. (1974). *Evaluation and regulation of body build and composition*. Englewood Cliffs, NJ: Prentice-Hall.

Burke, E.R., Fleck, S., & Dickson, T. (1981). Post-competition blood lactate concentrations on competitive track cyclists. *British Journal of Sports Medicine*, **15**(4), 242–245.

Coyle, E.F., Hemmert, M.K., & Coggan, A.R. (1986). Effects of detraining on cardiovascular responses to exercise: Role of blood volume. *Journal of Applied Physiology*, **60**(1), 95–99.

Costill, D.L., King, D.S., Thomas, R., & Hargreaves, M. (1985). Effects of reduced training on muscular power in swimmers. *The Physician and Sportsmedicine*, **13**(2), 94–101.

Craig, N.P. (1985/1986). [Blood lactate levels for cyclists in three events]. Unpublished raw data.

Faria, I.E. (1984). Applied physiology of cycling. *Sports Medicine*, **1**, 187–204.

Faria, I., Sjøgaard, G., & Bonde-Petersen, F. (1982). Oxygen cost during different pedalling speeds for constant power output. *Journal of Sports Medicine and Physical Fitness*, **22**, 295–299.

Gutmann, I., & Wahlefeld, A.W. (1974). Lactate determination with lactate dehydrogenase and NAD. In H.V. Bergameyer (Ed.), *Methods of enzymatic analysis* (2nd ed., pp. 1464–1468). New York: Academic Press.

Hagberg, J.M., Mullin, J.P., Bahrke, M., & Limburg, J. (1979). Physiological profiles and selected psychological characteristics of national class American cyclists. *Journal of Sports Medicine and Physical Fitness*, **19**, 341–346.

Jacobs, I. (1981). Lactate concentrations after short, maximal exercise at various glycogen levels. *Acta Physiologica Scandinavica*, **3**, 465–469.

Jacobs, I., Kaiser, P., & Tesch, P. (1982). The effects of glycogen exhaustion on maximal short-term performance. In P.V. Komi (Ed.), *Exercise and sport biology*, (pp. 103–108). Champaign, IL: Human Kinetics.

Jurbala, P. (1983). *Training and nutrition for racing cyclists*. Ontario Cycling Association, Toronto, Canada.

McNair, D.M., Lorr, M., & Droppleman, L.F. (1971). *Profile of mood states manual*. San Diego: Educational and Industrial Testing Service.

Ross, W.D., & Marfell-Jones, M.J. (1982). Kinanthropometry. In J.D. MacDougall, H.A. Wenger, & H.J. Green (Eds.), *Physiological testing of the elite athlete* (pp. 75–115). Ottawa, Canada: Canadian Association of Sport Sciences.

Siri, W.E. (1961). Body composition from fluid spaces: Analysis of methods. In J. Brozek, & A. Henschel (Eds.), *Techniques for measuring body composition* (pp. 223–244). Washington, DC: National Academy of Sciences, National Research Council.

Sjøgaard, G., Nielsen, B., Mikkelsen, F., Saltin, B., & Burke, E.R. (1985). *Physiology in bicycling*. New York: Mouvement Publications.

Thorstensson, A., & Karlson, J. (1976). Fatiguability and fiber composition of human skeletal muscle. *Acta Physiologica Scandinavica*, **98**, 318–322.

Verducci, F.M. (1980). *Measurement concepts in physical education*. London: C.V. Mosby.

Withers, R.T., Craig, N.P., Bourdon, P.C., & Norton, K.I. (1987). Relative body fat and anthropometric prediction of body density of male athletes. *European Journal of Applied Physiology*, **56**, 191–200.

Aerobic Capacity and Muscle Characteristics of Junior Road Cyclists

Jan Melichna

Nicolas Terrados

Eva Jansson

Zdeněk Bartůněk

Presently, insufficient data are available in respect to the relationship between successful physical performance and the properties of skeletal muscles in elite competitive road cyclists (Burke, Cerny, Costill, & Fink, 1977; Sjøgaard, 1984). Intensive training leads to adaptation responses of the organism that depend upon both the type of training and on the site of adaptation, that is, system, organ, cellular, and/or molecular level. The purpose of this study is to elucidate the relationships among different levels of adaptation and to identify which may represent the limiting factors of physical performance.

Methods

Characteristics of Subjects

Eight male road cyclists (elite junior group) with a mean age of 19.6 ± 1.2 years, body mass of 71.2 ± 2.2 kg, and height 1.79 ± 0.03 m were examined. The tests were performed at the end of the training period designed to prepare them for competition.

Exercise Test

Maximum values of oxygen consumption per kilogram of body mass per minute ($\dot{V}O_2$max, ml $\cdot$ kg^{-1} $\cdot$ min^{-1}), heart rate, work capacity, and blood lactate concentration were elicited by bicycle ergometry, using an incremental test described previously (Terrados, Mizuno, & Andersen, 1985). This test consisted of 6 min of warming up with a work load of 180 W followed by increments of 50 W until exhaustion. The $\dot{V}O_2$max was measured by means of the Beckman Metabolic Measurements Cart. Blood samples were taken from an antecubital vein immediately upon termination of maximal exercise, and serum lactate concentration was established by a fluorometric technique.

Tissue Samples

Needle biopsies were obtained from vastus lateralis muscle at rest according to Bergström (1962). The muscle sample was frozen in isopentane precooled with liquid nitrogen and used for histochemical analysis. Serial cross sections (10 μm thick) were cut at $-20°C$ and stained for myofibrillar ATPase activity with preincubation in varied pH to distinguish different types of muscle fibers as follows: Type I, Type II A and Type II B (Brooke & Kaiser, 1970). For calculation of the number of muscle capillaries these cross sections were stained for amylase-PAS reaction according to the method of Andersen (1975).

The second muscle sample was immediately frozen in liquid nitrogen, and the activities of enzymes were measured by fluorometric techniques (Kirk & Lowry, 1978; Shepherd & Garland, 1969), freeze-drying and homogenization in a 0.1 M phosphate buffer (pH 7.7). The following enzymes were assessed: phosphofructokinase (PFK), lactate dehydrogenase (LD), citrate synthase (CS), and 3-hydroxyacyl-CoA dehydrogenase (HAD).

Results

Results concerning work capacity, $\dot{V}O_2$max, and maximum blood lactate concentration are summarized in Table 1. The percentage distribution of

Table 1 Results of the Incremental Maximal Exercise Test

Subject	$\dot{V}O_2$max (ml $\cdot$ kg^{-1} $\cdot$ min^{-1})	HRmax (beats $\cdot$ min^{-1})	Work capacity (kJ)	LAmax (mmol $\cdot$ l^{-1})
1	73.33	197	217.2	10.38
2	60.06	180	164.4	10.08
3	64.97	186	141.6	7.87
4	69.81	176	157.8	10.30
5	76.54	205	189.9	11.00
6	73.97	198	184.2	9.62
7	71.37	182	171.1	6.65
8	71.84	175	119.4	10.44
Means	70.24	187	168.2	9.54
SEM	2.01	4	11.4	0.57

Note. $\dot{V}O_2$ = oxygen consumption; HR = heart rate; LA = blood lactate concentration.

muscle fiber types in vastus lateralis is given in Table 2. A predominance of slow oxidative muscle fibers may be observed in contrast to the small percentage of fast glycolytic fibers. Data regarding density of capillaries in muscle are presented in Table 3. Table 4 shows muscle enzyme activities. The ratios of PFK/CS and LD/CS are 0.66 and 17.2, respectively. Table 5 illustrates a significant positive correlation between percentage of Type I muscle fibers and $\dot{V}O_2$max, ml $\cdot$ kg^{-1} $\cdot$ min^{-1}, and between Type I muscle fibers and the activity of CS. A negative correlation exists between both

Table 2   Muscle Fiber Type Distribution in M. Vastus Lateralis

Subject	Muscle fiber type (%)		
	I	II A	II B
1	70.4	16.1	13.5
2	49.7	46.3	5.0
3	50.2	35.3	5.5
4	74.0	22.1	3.9
5	76.5	12.5	9.0
6	59.6	37.3	3.1
7	73.3	26.7	0.0
8	60.4	24.5	15.1
Means	65.6	27.5	6.9
SEM	3.7	4.2	2.0

Note.   Type I = slow oxidative fiber; Type II A = fast oxidative-glycolytic fiber; Type II B = fast glycolytic fiber.

Table 3   Capillary Density in Muscle

Subject	Muscle capillaries	
	per fiber	per area (mm^2)
1	3.01	470
2	3.75	461
3	3.80	370
4	2.15	340
5	3.24	400
6	3.87	493
7	3.69	405
8	3.75	457
Means	3.41	424
SEM	0.22	20

percentage of Type II A fibers and $\dot{V}O_2max$, ml • kg^{-1} • min^{-1} and between Type II A fibers and activity of CS. Moreover, a significant negative relationship exists between LD activity and HAD activity, and between percentage of Type I muscle fibers and percentage of Type II A fibers.

Table 4   Enzyme Activities in M. Vastus Lateralis

Subject	PFK	LD	CS	HAD
		(ukat • g^{-1} dry weight of muscle)		
1	1.02	21.3	1.65	0.62
2	0.98	26.0	1.30	0.62
3	1.17	36.0	1.30	0.47
4	0.87	23.4	1.62	0.63
5	0.90	25.5	1.60	0.58
6	0.85	23.6	1.08	0.50
7	0.85	25.0	1.55	0.62
8	1.05	18.8	1.50	0.77
Means	0.96	24.9	1.45	0.60
SEM	0.04	1.8	0.07	0.03

Note. PFK = phosphofructokinase; LD = lactate dehydrogenase; CS = citrate synthase; HAD = hydroacyl-CoA dehydrogenase.

Table 5   Correlation Coefficients

Selected parameters	LAmax	Work capacity	I fibers (%)	II A fibers (%)	II B fibers (%)	PFK	LD	CS	HAD
$\dot{V}O_2max$/kg	.24	.41	.73	−.77	.27	−.43	−.48	−.35	.01
LAmax		.18	.04	−.28	.63	−.05	−.51	.19	.34
Work capacity			.41	−.15	−.03	−.40	−.16	.18	−.32
I fibers (%)				−.90	0	−.45	−.20	.75	.08
II/A fibers (%)					−.34	.24	.32	−.77	−.32
II/B fibers (%)						.51	−.44	.38	.63
PFK							.45	−.08	−.04
LD								−.35	−.77
CS									.54

Note. For abbreviations see Tables 1, 2, and 3; $p = .05$ for $r = .71$.

Discussion

Elite road cyclists have exhibited the highest values of $\dot{V}O_2$max per kilogram of body mass observed in well-trained endurance athletes (Åstrand & Rodahl, 1977). In the present study the competitive road cyclists were members of the Swedish junior national team. They trained regularly and participated in races of various distances. Our mean value of maximal aerobic power is somewhat lower (70.24 ml • kg^{-1} • min^{-1}) than that recorded for other elite road cyclists (Burke et al., 1977; Sjøgaard, 1984) for example, for the champion bicycle racer Merckx (Veicsteinas, Samaja, Gussoni, & Cerretalli, 1984). However, our values of maximal oxygen uptake were determined during the preparatory period and elicited via a different exercise test.

Peak blood lactate concentration, which was measured at the end of maximal incremental exercise, was lower than that described by Sjogaard (1984) in elite road cyclists. It may be suggested that the anaerobic capacity in this group of cyclists is limited and similar to that observed in non-well-trained cyclists or that such a condition is typical of junior as opposed to senior cyclists.

With regard to fiber composition, number of muscle capillaries, and the activity of enzymes of muscle metabolism, previous studies of well-trained male endurance athletes have revealed a high percentage of slow muscle fibers, a relatively large number of muscle capillaries, and a high activity of oxidative enzymes (Burke et al., 1977; Sjøgaard, 1984). In line with this, our elite junior road cyclists were a homogeneous group with similar properties to those mentioned. Contrary to this observation, a higher percentage of fast glycolytic muscle fibers and a greater activity of enzymes regulating the anaerobic pathway have been reported in sprint cyclists (Macková et al., 1986).

A close relationship between $\dot{V}O_2$max, ml • kg^{-1} • min^{-1}, and the percentage of slow muscle fibers, capillary density, and/or the activity of oxidative enzymes has also been reported by other authors in endurance athletes and road cyclists (Ingjer, 1978; Macková, et al., 1983; Rusko, Rahkila, & Karvinen, 1980; Sjøgaard, 1984). The present study, however, supported only some of these relationships (i.e., the significant positive relationship between the number of Type I fibers and the CS activity, the $\dot{V}O_2$max, ml • kg^{-1} • min^{-1}, and the percentage of Type I fibers and the negative relationships between number of Type II A fibers and the $\dot{V}O_2$max, ml • kg^{-1} • min^{-1}, and the percentage of Type I fibers and CS activity. The other analyzed correlations were not statistically significant. From these results it is suggested that an endurance type of training program may increase the activity of key enzymes involved in oxidative metabolic pathways of skeletal muscles (Holloszy, 1975). However, some of the correlations are difficult to interpret, such as the inverse relationship between the LD and HAD activity. Some of these differences may be due to difference among studies in type of aerobic power tests or other procedural variations.

It may be concluded that elite junior road cyclists such as those examined in the present investigation exhibit adaptation of the cardiorespiratory system ($\dot{V}O_2$max, ml $\cdot$ kg^{-1} $\cdot$ min^{-1}) as well as adaptation at a muscular level, particularly as regards CS activity.

Acknowledgments

This study was approved by the ethical committee of Karolinska Hospital. The authors are grateful to Prof. C.W. Zauner, Miami Beach, Florida, for his editorial help.

References

Andersen, P. (1975). Capillary density in skeletal muscle of man. *Acta Physiologica Scandinavica*, **95**, 203–205.

Åstrand, P.O., & Rodahl, K. (1977). *Textbook of work physiology*. New York: McGraw-Hill.

Bergström, J. (1962). Muscle electrolytes in man. *Journal of Clinical Laboratory Investigation*, **14** (Suppl.), 68.

Brooke, H.M., & Kaiser, K.K. (1970). Muscle fiber types: How many and what kind? *Archives of Neurology*, **23**, 369–379.

Burke, E.R., Cerny, F., Costill, D., & Fink, F. (1977). Characteristics of skeletal muscle in competitive cyclists. *Medicine and Science in Sports*, **9**, 109–112.

Holloszy, J.O. (1975). Adaptation of skeletal muscle to endurance exercise. *Medicine and Science in Sports*, **7**, 155–164.

Ingjer, F. (1978). Maximal aerobic power related to the capillary supply of the quadriceps femoris muscle in man. *Acta Physiologica Scandinavica*, **184**, 238–240.

Kirk, K., & Lowry, O. (1978). Enzyme patterns in single human muscle fibers. *Journal of Biology and Chemistry*, **253**, 8269–8277.

Macková, E.V., Melichna, J., Šprynarova, S., Bass, A., Teisinger, J., Vondra, K., Bojenovský, I., & Jehlíková, A. (1983). Muscle enzyme activities and fibre composition (M. vastus lateralis) and efficiency of the cardiorespiratory system in cross-country skiers. *Physiology Bohemoslovaca*, **32**, 272–288.

Macková, E., Melichna, J., Havlíčková, L., Placheta, Z., Blahová, D., & Semiginovský, B. (1986). Skeletal muscle characteristics of sprint cyclists and non-athletes. *International Journal of Sports Medicine*, **7**, 295–297.

Rusko, H., Rahkila, P., & Karvinen, E. (1980). Anaerobic threshold, skeletal muscle enzymes and fiber composition in young female cross-country skiers. *Acta Physiologica Scandinavica*, **108**, 263–268.

Shepherd, D., & Garland, P. (1969). Citrate synthase from rat liver. In J.M. Lowenstein (Ed.), *Methods of enzymology* (Vol. 13, pp. 11–16). New York: Academic Press.

Sjøgaard, G. (1984). Muscle morphology and metabolic potential in elite road cyclists during a season. *International Journal of Sports Medicine, 5,* 250–254.

Terrados, N., Mizuno, M., & Andersen, H. (1985). Reduction in maximal oxygen uptake at low altitudes; roles of training status and lung function. *Clinical Physiology, 5* (Suppl. 3), 75–77.

Veicsteinas, A., Samaja, M., Gussoni, M., & Cerretelli, P. (1984). Blood O_2 affinity and maximal O_2 consumption in elite bicycle racers. *Journal of Physiology: Respiratory, Environmental, and Exercise Physiology, 57,* 52–58.

A Physiological Profile of the 1984 and 1986 Race-Across-America Winner

Randolph G. Ice

Phillip L. Millman

Diane C. Ice

John C. Camp

The Race Across AMerica (RAAM) is a nonstop competitive bicycle race that has been in existence since 1982. Except for 1982, it has started in Huntington Beach, California and finished in Atlantic City, New Jersey, with cyclists riding against the clock as well as other competitors for 8 to 12 days. Different routes from the West to East Coast have been used each year, and the length of the race has varied from 2,986 to 3,170 mi. Although relatively new, RAAM has gained widespread publicity and exposure in the United States through ABC television coverage on ''Wide World of Sports.''

Because of its nonstop nature, cyclists who train for and compete in the RAAM are, by the nature of the time required to finish the race, endurance athletes in the truest sense. Each athlete and his or her support crew determines riding pace, food and fluid intake, rest and sleep periods, and race tactics. Usually, two to three vehicles including a following vehicle (usually a small car or van) and a motorhome with 8 to 10 crew members are needed to keep the RAAM racer on the correct course throughout the race and tend to the needs of the competitor 24 hr a day. The term *ultramarathon cyclist* has become synonymous with the challenging nature of the RAAM.

From 1982 to 1986, only 3 male cyclists won the race. The finish times and race pace, as expected, have improved considerably. The male winners and their times are shown in Table 1. The purpose of this paper is to present a physiologic profile of a successful ultramarathon bicyclist and the 1984 and 1986 RAAM winner, Pete Penseyres.

Background Information

At the time of this study, the subject was a 43-year-old nuclear engineer at Southern California Edison's San Onofre Nuclear Generating Plant. He began his competitive cycling career at the age of 31, beginning with

Table 1 RAAM Male Winners, Distances, and Times for 1982 to 1986

Year	Male winner	Distance (mi)	Winning time	Overall race pace (mph)
1982	Lon Haldeman	2,986	9 days, 20 hr, 2 min	12.6
1983	Lon Haldeman	3,170	10 days, 16 hr, 29 min	12.4
1984	Pete Penseyres	3,048	9 days, 13 hr, 13 min	13.3
1985	Jonathan Boyer	3,120	9 days, 2 hr, 6 min	14.3
1986	Pete Penseyres	3,107	8 days, 9 hr, 47 min	15.4

USCF Category IV road races and progressing to longer road races such as the Spenco 500, where he won his age category in 1984. Prior to his cycling activities, he was active in motor cycling, dune buggy and drag racing, backpacking, and long-distance running. He ran a 2:47 marathon at the Mission Bay Marathon in San Diego when he was 35 years old.

Pete began commuting by bike to work in 1978, and in 1979, he trained for and set a tandem cross-country record of 10 days, 21 hr with Rob Templin, Brooks McKinney, and Bruce Hall. In 1982, after ABC's coverage of the Race Across America, Pete began training for the 1983 John Marino Open, an 800-mi qualifying race. He placed second and entered the 1983 RAAM. Despite severe dehydration the first day, Pete came from second-to-last place to finish second overall in 10 days, 22 hr, 2 min, a 12.1-mph average race pace.

With this in mind, Pete continued to train for the 1984 RAAM, cycling over 27,000 mi. Employing the same come-from-behind strategy during the race, he eclipsed the transcontinental record by 7 hr in the process of winning the race. Having accomplished his goal of winning the RAAM, he decided to "retire" from ultramarathon racing and assist his brother in training, qualifying, and competing in the 1985 RAAM.

In 1985, professional cyclist Jonathan Boyer entered and won the RAAM, setting a new transcontinental record of 9 days, 2 hr, 6 min. His disparaging remarks regarding the ability of ultramarathon cyclists in general provided fresh incentive for Pete to begin training for the 1986 RAAM and an expected head-to-head competition with Jonathan Boyer. Although Boyer elected not to race and withdrew 2 months before the 1986 RAAM, Pete subsequently went on to utilize new aerodynamic changes, a liquid diet, and additional sleep deprivation to establish a new record of 8 days, 9 hr, 47 min in winning the 1986 RAAM.

Prior to the 1984 RAAM, and before and after the 1986 RAAM, Pete underwent a series of physiologic tests to aid in training and race strategy. Testing was performed at the Human Performance Center in Whittier, California, except for body composition testing at the end of the 1986 RAAM, which was done in Atlantic City, New Jersey.

Results

The results of Pete's tests, including bicycle ergometer testing, body composition, blood chemistry, and pulmonary function, are summarized in Tables 2, 3, 4, and 5.

Discussion

Between the 1984 and 1986 RAAM, the subject attempted to improve his performance in four areas: (a) aerodynamics, (b) training, (c) nutrition, and (d) sleep deprivation/time on bike.

Table 2   Bicycle Ergometer Test

Variable	August 1984	April 1986
Max. workload (W)	425	402.5
Time (min)	23.0	22.2
$\dot{V}O_2$max (ml/min/kg)	79.6	—
Max HR (bpm)	200	185
Resting HR (bpm)	47	48
Max Minute Ventilation (L/m)	172.3	190
Body weight (kg)	62.6	63.5
Power/weight ratio (W/kg)	6.79	6.34

Table 3   Body Composition

Variable	Pre-1984 RAAM[a]	Pre-1986 RAAM[b]	Post-1986 RAAM[b]
Body weight (kg)	61.0	63.5	62.5
Body fat (%)	7.0	8.3	6.9
Lean body mass (kg)	56.73	58.2	58.2
Lean body mass (%)	—	75.3	81.1
Resistance (Ω)	—	479	439
Total body water (L)	—	43.2	47.2

[a]Densitometry method (August 17, 1984). [b]Bioimpedence technique (July 5, 1986 and July 14, 1986).

Aerodynamics

From an aerodynamic standpoint, skintight bodysuits were employed, and a special arm-trough platform creating a more forward flexed body position was mounted on custom-made Raleigh bicycles. The bike frames

Table 4 Blood Chemistry and Blood Count (Pre-RAAM)

Parameter	August 1984	June 1986
BUN (mg/dl)	25	26
Creatinine (mg/dl)	1.0	1.1
BUN/creatinine ratio	25	23.6
SGOT (U/L)	37	46
SGPT (U/L)	29	32
LDH (U/L)	227	235
Bilirubin (mg/dl)	0.8	0.6
Alkaline phosphatose (U/L)	40	48
Ca+ (mg/dl)	9.7	9.5
Phosphorus (mg/dl)	3.5	3.2
Na+ (meq/L)	139	140
Potassium (meq/L)	4.6	6.2
Chloride (meq/L)	101	105
Uric Acid (mg/dl)	4.6	5.8
Glucose (mg/dl)	99	85
Cholesterol (mg/dl)	142	180
HDL-Cholesterol (mg/dl)	58	78
Chol/HDL ratio	2.4	2.2
Triglycerides	36	57
Hemoglobin (g/dl)	14.2	14.8
Hemotocrit (%)	42.2	43.5

Note. BUN = blood urea nitrogren; SGOT = serum glutamic-oxaloacetic transaminase; SGPT = serum glutamic-pyruvic transaminase; LDH = lactate dehydrogenase; HDL = high-density lipoprotein; U/L = Microliters/Liter; meq/L = millequivalent/Liter.

Table 5 Pulmonary Function

Variable	August 1984	April 1986
Vital capacity (L)	4.38 (88% of predicted)	4.99 (100% of predicted)
Forced expiratory volume, second (L)	3.76 (100% of predicted)	3.38 (90% of predicted)

were made of aluminum, carbon fiber, and kevlar in layers at shallow angles to absorb road shock. The front wheel was radially spoked with 16, 18, or 24 bladed spokes, and for 400 of the first 1,000 mi of the 1986 RAAM, a rear disc wheel was used until it suffered mechanical failure. A bladed spoked rear wheel was employed from then on.

Training

Training consisted of riding 30 mi to and from work on Mondays, Wednesdays, and Fridays. On Tuesdays and Thursdays, additional speed work and interval training totaling 100 mi each day was added. In May and June, 380 to 440 mi overnight rides requiring 20 to 28 hr on Friday night and Saturday were done over a variety of terrains and weather conditions. Sunday was a recuperation day with no cycling done. Weekly mileage was 660 to 720 mi before the 1986 RAAM, approximately 100 mi/week less than before the 1984 race.

Nutritional Changes

Nutritional changes made in 1986 were considerably altered compared to the 1984 RAAM. In 1984, the subject ate mostly all solid food consisting of lasagne, baked potatoes with butter and cheese, grilled cheese sandwiches, french toast, cherries, ice cream and shakes, and so forth. He found it difficult to eat solid food as well as sufficient quantities due to the hot weather.

In 1986, a special liquid diet product ("UltraEnergy"$_{TM}$) was created by Chemique Pharmaceutical Services in Whittier, California. The product was in powder form and mixed with water to make 395 calories per 500-ml water bottle. By composition, it was 83% carbohydrates, 13.2% proteins, and 3.2% fat with 150 to 300% the RDA of all vitamins and minerals. The subject's crew kept track of all fluid, food, and UltraEnergy consumed throughout the race. Table 6 summarizes daily calorie consumption and the sources of these calories, as well as the percentage from the liquid diet. For the entire race, approximately 66,663 food calories were consumed (average calories = 7,965/day) with 79.7% (53,128 calories) coming from the liquid UltraEnergy product. Including 2 lb of fat stores utilized, total RAAM energy requirements are estimated to be 73,663. Subjectively, the subject reported a more stable blood sugar level without highs and lows experienced in 1984.

Sleep Deprivation

As shown in Table 7, sleep time was reduced by 3.5 hr to 11.5 hr in 1986 compared to 1984. This would have added 8 to 9 mi/day to the increased daily average. Likewise, an average of 40 min more per day was spent on the bike, accounting for approximately another 11 mi/day. Table

8 breaks down total off-bike time into the various reasons for stopping and time off bike for each category. Total time off the bike was 16.25 hr in 8.41 days (1.93 hr/day), or 8% of the total race time. Table 9 summarizes the day-by-day times, mileages, speed, and sleep time throughout the 1986 RAAM. Total time on the bike accounted for 92% of the time of the race.

Summary

The data presented indicates a highly motivated, world-class athlete, who through a scientific approach toward race strategy, aerodynamics,

Table 6 Food Summary 1986 RAAM

Food	Day								
	1	2	3	4	5	6	7	8	9
UltraEnergy liquid	17	18	14	11	14	16	16.5	21	7
395 cal/bottle	6,715	7,110	5,530	4,345	5,530	6,320	6,518	8,295	2,765
Baked potato w/cheese & butter	2	1	2	1	1	0	0	0	0
300 cal	600	300	600	300	300	—	—	—	—
Chicken soup w/crackers	0	0	2	2	1	2	2	1	0
350 cal/c	—	—	700	700	350	700	700	350	1
Lasagna	0	0.5	0	0	0	1	1	0	0
700 cal/c	—	350	—	—	—	700	700	—	—
Poached eggs (3)/toast (2 slices)	0	1	2	1	1	0	0	0	0
620 cal	—	620	1,240	620	620	—	—	—	—
Cherries	0	0	4	0	0	1	0	2	0
150 cal/c	—	—	600	—	—	150	—	300	—
Grilled cheese sandwich	0	0	1	1.5	0	0	0	1	0
350 cal	—	—	350	525	—	—	—	350	—
Fruit juice	0	0	0	0	1	0	0	0	0
150 cal/bottle	—	—	—	—	150	—	—	—	—
Diet Slice	0	0	0	5	2	1	2	2	2
40 cal/bottle	—	—	—	200	80	40	80	80	80
Date shake	0.25	0	0	0	0	0	0	0	0
400 cal/c	100	—	—	—	—	—	—	—	—
Total calories/day	7,415	8,380	9,020	6,690	7,030	7,910	7,998	9,375	2,845
% liquid	90.5	84.8	61.3	64.9	78.6	79.8	81.4	88.5	97.2

Total calories/1986 RAAM 66,663 (7,965 average)
Liquid calories 53,128 (6,347 average)
% liquid total = 79.7%

nutrition, training, and sleep deprivation was able to improve his race performance markedly between 1984 and 1986. Six months prior to the 1986 RAAM, Pete expressed the feeling that if he could add 1 mph average onto his overall 1984 race pace, he could win RAAM. His actual improvement was 2.1 mph faster as he improved his average daily mileage from 319.0 in 1984 to 369.5 in 1986. With perhaps 20 mi/day of this improvement due to less sleep and more time on the bike, the remainder is attributable to improved nutrition, training, and aerodynamic/bicycle changes. The ability to do prolonged submaximal work with minimal body fat loss suggests that the primarily liquid diet contributed significantly to optimal metabolic function and energy production. Total caloric expenditure in the 1986 RAAM was less than anticipated, averaging 7,037 cal/day.

Table 7   Sleep Deprivation and Time on Bike

Variable	1984	1986
Sleep time (total hr)	15.0	11.5
Time on bike (hr/day)	21.5	22.1
Average mi/day	319.0	369.5

Table 8   Off-Bike Time

Reason	Number of stops	Total time	Average time/day
Sleep breaks	7	13 hr, 20 min[a]	1 hr, 35 min[a]
Shower/rest	2	55 min, 30 s	6 min, 36 s
Bathroom	10	43 min, 52 s	5 min, 13 s
Clothing changes	6	13 min	1 min, 33 s
Bike changes	10	13 min, 20 s	1 min, 35 s
Bike trouble	12	15 min, 48 s	1 min, 53 s

[a]1.5 hr total "quality" sleep; remainder is clean up, clothing changes, getting down, and getting up.

Table 9 1986 RAAM Performance Summary

Day	Time off/day (hr)	Time on/day (hr)	Cumulative time on	Average speeds/mileage (miles/hour)						Average cumulative daily mileage	Actual sleep (hr)
				Day mileage	Cumulative mileage	Day on bike	Day total	Cumulative on bike	Cumulative total		
1	0:03:05	23:56:55 (23.94)	23.94	448.7	448.7	18.7	18.7	18.7	18.7	448.7	0
2	2:37:20	21:22:40 (21.37)	45.32	370.8	819.5	17.3	15.4	18.1	17.1	409.8	2:00
3	2:11:58	21:48:02 (21.80)	67.12	390.3	1,209.8	17.9	16.3	18.0	16.8	403.3	1:40
4	2:02:20	21:57:40 (21.96)	89.08	362.7	1,572.5	16.5	15.1	17.7	16.4	393.1	1:30
5	2:11:47	21:48:13 (21.80)	110.88	358	1,930.5	16.4	14.9	17.4	16.1	386.1	1:30
6	2:09:45	21:50:15 (21.83)	132.72	349.8	2,280.3	16.0	14.6	17.2	15.8	380.0	1:20
7	2:07:35	21:52:25 (21.87)	154.59	344.7	2,625.0	15.8	14.4	17.0	15.6	375.0	1:30
8	2:32:50	21:27:10 (21.45)	176.05	328.9	2,953.9	15.3	13.7	16.8	15.4	369.2	2:00
9	0:17:20	9:29:40 (9.49)	185.54[a]	153.1	3,107.0	16.1	15.6	16.75	15.4	369.5	
Total	16:14:00 (16.23 hr; 8% of total race time)										11.5

[a]Total cumulative time on calculated out to be 92% of total race time (total hours = 201.78).

The Effects of Long-Distance Bicycling on Heart Disease Patients

Randolph G. Ice

Diane C. Ice

John C. Camp

Adherence to exercise conditioning and risk factor reduction measures in cardiac rehabilitation programs is a well-documented problem. Failure to demonstrate improved survival or lower reinfarction rates in randomized exercise studies in part relates to compliance problems. In 1974, in the midst of a randomized exercise/risk reduction angiographic study in men less than age 50, the SCOR Cardiac Cyclists Club was formed at Rancho Los Amigos Hospital in Downey, California. From its inception, the goal was to improve compliance and to reduce the dropout rate by providing an outdoor, sociable exercise done on nonprogram days off the medical complex grounds.

Despite the premature ending of the government grant, the club has grown in size and scope as fitness levels, equipment knowledge, and goals of the cardiac patients in the club have changed. This retrospective, clinical study reports on the medical outcomes and risks of outdoor bicycling in a group of 68 self-referred heart disease patients who undertook bicycling as an adjunct to standard cardiac rehabilitation procedures.

Methods

Between October 1974 and September 1985, 68 patients (67 men, 1 woman) with various cardiovascular diagnoses voluntarily began a bicycling exercise program on Saturdays with the SCOR Cardiac Cyclists Club. The majority of these patients became involved after seeing or talking to other club members during either Phase II or Phase III cardiac rehabilitation programs between 1974 and 1985 at Rancho Los Amigos Hospital, Ross Loos Medical Center, Presbyterian Intercommunity Hospital, or the Human Performance Center in Whittier. A minority came to the club through word-of-mouth or press exposure in Southern California. Another 25 patients started with the club but dropped out within a month and are not included in this study.

The average length of participation in the club is 4.4 years, with a range of 2 months to 11 years. At entry 73% were employed, 15% retired, 6%

disabled, and 6% were working and subsequently retired. The average age of this group was 56.6 years.

Most patients began riding multigeared bicycles while enrolled in Phase II/III programs. They were encouraged to begin in our weekly Saturday riding sessions when they were able to ride 15 mi without excessive fatigue. For the purpose of this study, a definition of long-distance bicycling (LDB) was determined to be bicycle rides of 10 mi/ride, at least once/week. Weekly Saturday morning rides began in November 1974 with initial distances of 10 to 15 mi per session. Distance, not speed, was always emphasized. Distances ridden had increased to 25 to 50 mi by early 1976. In late 1976, 5 patients completed their first 100-mi "century" bike ride from Santa Barbara to Los Angeles. As a group, all 68 patients have averaged 60 mi/week with a range of 10 to 800 mi/week.

From direct observation, home training logs, and patient self-reports club members ride at peak heart rates of 120 to 135 bpm (range 90 to 170) an average of 3 to 4 times/week.

Average Saturday rides now are either 15 to 25 (short) or 35 to 50 (long) mi with 12 to 15 members riding each Saturday. As a group, 948,000 mi requiring 90,000 hr of bicycling have been accumulated.

Currently, 40 of 68 (59%) have rode a century in 1 day, the cycling equivalent of a marathon. A smaller number have completed double or triple centuries with the furthest distance being 380 mi in 32 hr in a 56-year-old post-Coronary Artery Bypass Graft (CABG) patient. In 1982, 14 patients rode a nonstop bicycle relay ride from Los Angeles to New York City in 12 days, 1 hr, and 50 min.

At entry into the club, the following cardiovascular diagnoses were observed. (No patient was denied access to participating in the club due to the severity of underlying Coronary Artery Disease (CAD) or left ventricular dysfunction.)

- CABG surgery—32 (47%)
- Myocardial infarction—one: 22 (32%); two: 2 (3%); three: 1 (1.5%)
- Angina pectoris—6 (9%)
- Atrial arrythmias—2 (3%)
- History of CHF—1 (1.5%)
- Heart transplant—1 (1.5%)

Among the 52 patients who had previously undergone coronary angiography, three-vessel CAD was present in 33 (64%), two-vessel CAD in 6 (12%), and single-vessel CAD in 13 (25%).

Ventricular function as defined by resting ejection fraction (EF) on ventriculography or echocardiography, or assumed to be greater than 50% if a normal ECG was present, revealed the following:

Good (EF > 50%)—51 patients (80%)
Fair (EF > 30 but < 50%)—7 (11%)
Poor (EF < 29%)—6 (9%)

Currently, of 62 survivors, 35 are active in the club while 27 have dropped out due to a variety of reasons including moving out of the area, increased vocational demands, retirement, progression of CAD, lack of interest, change in motivation (several became runners), and personality conflicts with other club members. The dropout rate among this self-selected group was 8% a year.

Results

During LDB, two episodes of cardiac arrest occurred (one fatal, one non-fatal) for an incidence rate of 1/45,000 patient-hours of exercise. One myocardial infarction occurred during a Saturday ride in a 57-year-old post-CABG patient for an incidence rate of 1/90,000 patient-hours of LDB. Two episodes of congestive heart failure occurred in 2 patients with EF < 35%. One was treated with diuretics, the other with rest, and both returned to bicycling without further episodes.

Orthopedically, LDB represents a different risk from traditional cardiac rehabilitation programs. No overuse syndromes were observed in any patient between 1974 to 1985. Traumatic injuries were observed 1/11,250 patient-hours of bicycling. Seven fractures resulted from falls off the bike, and 1 patient sustained a mild concussion when he ran into the back of a parked car while pedaling at a 17-mph pace, shattering the rear windshield. A hardshell helmet prevented certain brain damage, and the patient was discharged from an overnight hospital stay without complications.

Independent of LDB, primary fatal cardiac arrests were observed in 3 patients, each of whom had reduced ejection fractions of 20, 25, and 31%. Each was 19, 2, and 18 years post-myocardial infarction at the time of their deaths, respectively. Three other patients developed bladder, jaw, and lung cancer and died from advanced carcinoma (4.2%).

Among 62 survivors, 19 nonfatal cardiac events occurred during the 4.4-year follow-up:

Cardiac Arrest	Myocardial Infarction
3 (4.9%)	5 (4 pts) (8%)
New Onset Angina Pectoris	CABG Surgery
2 (3.2%)	6 (9.8%)
Second CABG Surgery	Pacemaker
1 (1.6%)	2 (3.2%)

Of 6 patients with exertional angina pectoris at the time of starting LDB, 4 (6.6%) became asymptomatic 1 to 5 years later requiring no antianginal drugs.

Table 1 lists the mortality and morbidity rates for 68 subjects. Based on natural history studies published in the last 5 years for patients who have equivalent medically or surgically treated CAD with good, fair, or

Table 1   Surgically (*n* = 36) Versus Medically (*n* = 32) Treated Patients

	Medical	Surgical
Mortality		
Cardiovascular	2	1
Cancer	1	2
Morbidity		
Primary cardiac arrest	1	2
Myocardial infarction	1	3
New onset angina pectoris	1	1
CABG surgery	6	—
Repeat CABG surgery	—	1
Pacemaker	2	0
Total (excluding cancer deaths)	13 (19%)	9 (13.2%)

poor left ventricular function, it was assumed that a 3%/year and 4%/year mortality and morbidity rate, respectively, would be observed among the 64 known CAD patients. The observed death rate was 1.1%/year, 35% of predicted. Repeat myocardial infarction rate was 1.7%/year, or 44% of predicted.

Conclusion

The cardiovascular risk of long-distance bicycling in a group of heart disease patients is comparable with published risks for supervised and unsupervised exercise programs in known CAD patients. Sudden death not associated with LDB was observed more frequently in patients with reduced ejection fractions (EF < 31%), confirming other reports that ventricular function is a major predictor of subsequent mortality.

The natural history of CAD may be beneficially altered by long-distance bicycling when done in conjunction with standard risk factor reduction measures.

PART III

Injuries and Psychology

Cycling Injuries in Triathloning

M.A. Boitano

Triathloning has become an increasingly popular sport, especially in the United States military, as it combines the "big three" endurance events: swimming, running, and cycling (usually in that order).

Triathlons vary in the length of the swimming, cycling and running events. The classic Ironman variety combines a 4-k swim, a 186.6-k bike ride, and a 43.6-k run.

Cycling and swimming are excellent aerobic sports and much less demanding physically on the body than is running. Also, cycling and swimming injuries are reported to be much less common than the over-use injuries of long-distance running. Most triathlon injuries have been noted to occur in the running phase, either during training or competition (Micheli, 1985). The majority of injuries reported from cycling are abrasions, followed by fractures (Bohlmann, 1981).

The purpose of this study was to document the injury pattern in three short-course triathlons held at Torii Station, Military Base, Okinawa, Japan over a 2-year period.

Materials and Methods

From January 1984 through December 1985, three short-course triathlons were held at Torii Station, Military Base, Okinawa, Japan. These comprised a 2-k swim, a 50-k bike ride, and a 25-k run (with the option of pairing up into teams for the events (see Figure 1).

Materials for the study were collected at the events. The injured participants were evaluated at a trackside ambulance. Fractures were documented by radiographs at the U.S. Naval Hospital.

Results

Injuries occurred in two of the three triathlon events, with all but one occurring during the bike race.

Eight participants sustained 11 injuries. During the cycling phase, 6 participants sustained abrasions, and 1 sustained a fracture. Peroneal tendinitis occurred in 1 participant at the conclusion of the running event (see Table 1).

Figure 1   Torii Station Triathlon course.

Table 1   Injuries in Triathloning

Injury	Number of participants
Abrasions	6[a]
Fracture	1[a]
Tendinitis	1[b]

[a]During the cycling phase. [b]During the running phase.

There were 9 abrasions in 6 participants (2 participants sustained more than one abrasion). Seven of the nine abrasions were on the left (see Table 2).

Three of the participants sustained injuries at the same location on the track during the most recent (October 1985) event, as they fell from their bikes at a sharp unmarked turn, preceded by a water station. Injuries included abrasions in three, and a corner avulsion fracture of the little finger proximal phalanx, all occurring on the left side (see Figure 2).

Table 2 Abrasions in Cycling Phase of Triathloning

Body area	Number	Left	Right
Knee	2	1	1
Thigh	4	3	1
Elbow	1	1	0
Upper arm/forearm	1	1	0
Flank	1	1	0

Note. Two participants sustained more than one abrasion.

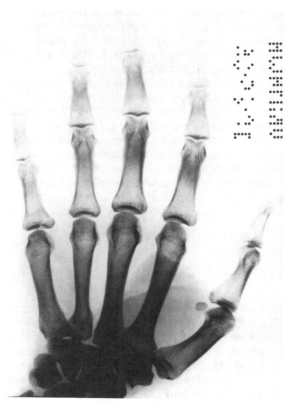

Figure 2 AP radiograph of the left hand showing corner avulsion fracture of the radial aspect of the little finger proximal phalanx.

During the most recent triathlon, 82 of 103 entrants (79.6%) completed the event. Japanese nationals, U.S. military, and their dependents competed. Future triathlons at Torii Station will conform to the standards of the short-course triathlons—1.5-k swim, 40-k bike ride, and 10-k run—all performed by one individual.

Discussion

A review of the literature showed no documented studies on the incidence and injury pattern in triathloning. It has been noted that in contrast to the overuse injuries of long-distance running, injuries associated with cycling and swimming are much less common. A recent comment concerning an injury survey of 7,150 New England triathloners noted that most triathlon injuries occur in the running phase, either during training or competition, with the swimming and bike phases having a protective effect (Micheli, 1985). In contrast, this study shows the majority of injuries to occur in the cycling phase. Abrasions are the most common injuries seen in competitive cycling, followed in frequency by fractures, with most of the injuries occurring to the left side of the cyclist. The abrasions in this study were of a minor nature without imbedded pavement particles, with the majority being on the left side.

A corner avulsion fracture of the little finger proximal phalanx occurred as a result of a fall from a bike, also on the left side of the cyclist (Table 2). This is an uncommon injury. As noted by Lee (1963), the majority unite in the original displaced position (see Figure 3).

The importance of preventive measures, including the mechanical condition of the bike, wearing appropriate clothing and a helmet, and knowing how to fall properly have been stressed (Bohlmann, 1981). Also of importance is the pavement and water spillage onto the racing surface, as three of the cycling injuries occurred at a sharp, unmarked left-handed corner preceded by a water station.

Summary

The injuries sustained during three short-course triathlons at Torii Station, Military Base, Okinawa, Japan during a 2-year period were reviewed. The majority of injuries occurred in the cycling rather than the running phase of the triathlon, with the most common injury being minor superficial abrasions to the left side of the cyclist. An uncommon injury, a corner avulsion fracture of the proximal phalanx, occurred secondary to a fall from a bike. Course layout and placement of water stations are important in injury prevention.

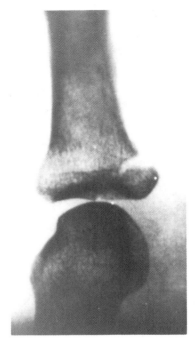

Figure 3 Oblique radiograph of the proximal phalanx showing fracture in displaced position 6 weeks after injury.

References

Bohlmann, J.T. (1981). Injuries in competitive cycling. *The Physician and Sportsmedicine,* **9**, 117–124.

Lee, M.L.H. (1963). Intra-articular and peri-articular fractures of the phalanges. *Journal of Bone and Joint Surgery,* **45B**, 103–109.

Micheli, L.J. (1985). Commentary. *Sports Medicine Digest,* **7**, 3.

Acute Mountain Sickness in Competitive Cyclists

Jon G. McLennan

James C. McLennan

John A. Ungersma

With the recent success of the U.S. Olympic team, cycling has seen a resurgence of interest. In 1985, over 78 million Americans rode a bicycle, half of which were females and greater than 40% were 16 years of age or older (Caille, 1986; Dillion, 1986). Eleven million adults were serious cyclists, riding at least once per week (Dillion, 1986). The United States Cycling Federation (USCF) reported over 19,000 amateur licensed racers in 1985, and the trend is likely to continue (Endicott, 1985; George, 1986).

The consensus of opinion is that injuries in competitive cycling are few and can rarely be avoided (Bohlman, 1981; Kruse & McBeath, 1980; Mayer, 1985a, 1985b). French insurance statistics report a 3.2% incidence of accidents in cycling (Goetchebuer, 1985), whereas Bohlmann (1981) has reported a 2% incidence in competitive cycling, which included criteriums, track, and road events.

In the West, there has been an increasing number of races at altitudes over 1,500 m, attracting many participants from sea level. Acute mountain sickness (AMS) is known to occur in this setting, impairing judgment and motor coordination (Hackett, 1979; McLennan & Ungersma, 1983). As a possible cause of accidents at altitude, AMS can be prevented by appropriate acclimatization and hydration.

Materials and Methods

The incidence of acute mountain sickness was evaluated in 1,502 Category I to IV cyclists in USCF-santioned races above 1,500 m, in an attempt to determine the incidence of acute mountain sickness and its possible effects on accidents. For controls, a similar group in numbers and experience was evaluated at races occurring at or near sea level.

All participants completed a postrace questionnaire, interview, and physical examination when indicated. The clinical criteria of Hackett (1980) was used to categorize the patients with acute mountain sickness.

Mild acute mountain sickness was defined as occurring at an altitude greater than 1,500 m in unacclimatized cyclists. Symptoms were mild headache, insomnia, anorexia, dyspnea, irritability, decreased visual acuity, and periodic breathing at night. Clinical signs were that of an increased respiratory and heart rate.

Moderate acute mountain sickness usually occurred within 1 to 3 days. Symptoms were similar; however, headaches were noted to be more severe. Lassitude, mild ataxia, nausea, vomiting, and shortness of breath at rest were more prominent. Clinical signs included those seen in mild acute mountain sickness with a decreased urinary outflow.

Hypothermia was defined as a core temperature of less than 35°C utilizing a core thermometer. Ward's (1975) clinical criteria and classification were utilized.

In addition, the type of injury sustained, helmet usage, type of pedal, race event, and rider category were considered. Also, the presence, response, and qualification of medical personnel were strictly scrutinized.

Results

Forty-five accidents (3%) occurred from falls secondary to flats, collision, or for unexplained reasons. When the event in which the accident was considered, 28 injuries (62%) occurred in criteriums, whereas 17 injuries (38%) occurred during road races. It was noted that 78% of the injuries involved Category III and IV riders (see Table 1).

There were 12 fractures (0.8%), 32 abrasions (2.1%), 2 head injuries (0.1%), 10 lacerations (0.7%), and 6 ligamentus injuries (0.4%). Two thirds of all injuries involved racers participating in criteriums (see Table 2). The

Table 1 Accident by Event and Category

Category	Road (n = 17)	Criterium (n = 28)
I	1	3
II	2	4
III	6	9
IV	8	12

Table 2 Type of Injury and Event

Event	Fracture	Abrasion	Head	Laceration	Ligamentus
Road	5	10	0	3	2
Criterium	7	22	2	7	4

most common fracture appearing in this series was that of the clavicle, (5) whereas ligamentus injuries primarily involved the anterior talofibular ligament of the ankle. By anatomic site, fractures occurred twice in both the wrist and ankle and one time each in the leg, hip, and humerus.

Three hundred seventy-five (25%) cyclists had documented evidence of acute mountain sickness. Of these individuals 324 (21.6%) had signs and symptoms of mild acute mountain sickness. The remaining 51 (3.4%) riders developed moderate acute mountain sickness.

Interestingly, 75 individuals (5%) incidentally had symptoms of exposure. However, only 11 individuals consented to core temperature readings and could be classified as having hypothermia. In contrast, the sea level control group demonstrated a 6% incidence (90 cyclists) of symptoms that could be loosely misinterpreted as acute mountain sickness.

Twenty accidents were directly associated with acute mountain sickness. Fourteen of these individuals were diagnosed as having the mild variety, and the remaining were moderate.

Only 330 riders (22%) were found to use ANSI- or SNELL-approved helmets, 96% of which were used by less experienced racers (Categories III and IV). Fortunately, the two head injuries that occurred were concussions with minor lacerations, though both riders withdrew from participation. Both riders wore hairnet "helmets."

At only 4 of the 10 races evaluated did the race sponsor provide even loosely adequate medical coverage. This consisted of paramedical health professionals with ambulance support.

Discussion

Most cycling accidents cannot be directly prevented. However, acute mountain sickness affects judgment and muscular coordination in a mountain setting and is a prime cause of accidents. This disease is prevented by acclimatization and appropriate hydration. Hypothermia is known to be more common in the mountains than previously thought and one of its key features is that of poor judgment. Therefore, it is not presumptive to anticipate that acute mountain sickness and hypothermia can increase the number of injuries in cycling events at altitudes greater than 1,500 m.

It was not surprising, then, that 375 individuals (25%) in the present study had signs of acute mountain sickness. However, the majority of these patients suffered only from the mild form. Correcting for the chance occurrence of similar symptoms arising from other causes, the incidence of acute mountain sickness should be diminished by 6% (from the control group).

Bohlman (1981) reported previously in a study on injuries to competitive cyclists that one could anticipate approximately a 2% accident rate, most occurring during criteriums. In the present study there were 45 accidents (3%) of which two thirds occurred in criteriums. Of those, 20 were directly related to acute mountain sickness. The occurrence of hypothermia, which is preventable with appropriate clothing and calorie intake, also may be expected to add to the overall incidence of accidents. Further investigation and better documentation of hypothermia will be necessary in the future if accidents are to be further lessened.

Those individuals who are susceptible to or have previously had a documented case of acute mountain sickness will require slightly longer acclimatization at altitude. Acetazolamide has been effectively used to prevent AMS in climbers; however, because this drug is a diuretic, potentially disastrous effects may result and it should be used with caution.

Our study supports the precept that most accidents (62%) occur during criteriums and in Category III and IV riders. In addition, abrasions were common and clavicles were the most frequently fractured bone.

Recent USCF legislation requiring the use of approved protective helmets in all category-licensed riders certainly should significantly decrease the incidence of head injuries.

The reliance on paramedical health professionals at one USCF-sanctioned race in our series, we believe, was below the standard acceptable practices of medicine in the community. As the USCF has required the use of helmets, we hope that in the future sponsors of USCF-sanctioned events are required to provide physician coverage.

The introduction of the look release pedal system last year is promising and should diminish the severity of injury. Unfortunately, we did have the opportunity to observe the release system in action on several occasions during race situations. It was noted that riders using this system released from their bike prior to impact—the bike going one way and the rider the other. This appeared to be beneficial as neither rider nor bike was severely damaged, and other riders in the pack were able to avoid a collision, in contrast to the usual situation.

Conclusion

As in all competitive sports, cycling has its own inherent risks, many of which are unavoidable. However, as interest surges many more races may be expected to occur at altitudes over 1,500 m. Therefore, the effects of acute mountain sickness and hypothermia must be dealt with if the incidence of accidents are to be diminished. This may be very important in the near future as the liability crisis worsens. Therefore, we recommend that all cyclists participating in races at high altitudes should be made aware of the potential effects of acute mountain sickness and hypothermia, as well as the guidelines for prevention. Susceptible individuals may require prolonged acclimatization. In addition, look release bindings should be considered, and all USCF-sanctioned races should have a qualified physician in attendance.

References

Bohlmann, J.T. (1981). Injuries in competitive cyclists. *The Physician and Sportsmedicine, 9*(5), 117–124.

Dillion, C. (1986). Cyclopedia. *Outside,* **11**(3), 51.

Caille, J. (1986). Cycling a favorite. *Winning Club News,* No. 6, p. 3.

Endicott, P. (1985). *Cycling USA,* **6**(2), 3.

George, B. (1986). Velo-news (newspaper). **15**(6), p. 3.

Goetchebuer, G. (1985). Cycling risks. *Winning,* **23**(6), 68–71.

Hackett, P. (1980). *Mountain sickness: Prevention, recognition and treatment.* New York: American Alpine Club.

Kruse, D.L., & McBeath, A.A. (1980). Bicycle accidents and injuries. *American Journal of Sports Medicine,* **8**(5), 342–344.

McLennan, J.G., & Ungersma, J.A. (1983). Mountaineering accidents in the Sierra Nevada. *American Journal of Sports Medicine,* **11**(3), 160–163.

Mayer, P.J. (1985a). Helping your patients avoid bicycling injuries. Part I. *Journal of Musculoskeletal Medicine,* **2**(5), 31–40.

Mayer, P.J. (1985b). Helping your patients avoid bicycling injuries. Part III. *Journal of Musculoskeletal Medicine,* **2**(6), 31–38.

Ward, M. (1976). *Mountain medicine.* London: Crosby, Lockwood, Staples.

Sport Psychology and Its Relationship to Cycling

Andrew A. Jacobs

Over the past decade, a tremendous amount of interest has developed in a new field of study, sport psychology. Since the early 1970s an emphasis in numerous sports has been to investigate what makes athletes tick, not only physically but also mentally. In the past, it was thought that when the body worked, the mind would follow. In reality, however, it's the other way around. For example, whenever the pain from that last sprint becomes so intense that the body screams to stop, it's always the mind that pushes the body ahead to the finish line. As both amateur and professional athletics have become more competitive, athletes and coaches have begun studying more of the factors that affect performance. The bottom line is that when you have two athletes who are of equal physical ability and are using the same equipment, quite often the factor determining who wins the race will be who has the stronger mind.

Sport psychology is concerned with the identification, assessment, and management of the psychological factors that directly impact an athlete's performance. This relates to athletic performance in two ways: training and competition. Issues specifically relating to training involve such areas as commitment, attitude, communication skills, and goal setting. These issues must be realistically attacked before the athlete can begin to work on the areas that directly impact competition, which include motivation, concentration/attention span, confidence, and stress management

In 1982, the U.S. Cycling Federation began its sport psychology program. Since that time a sport psychologist has been available at numerous training camps and competitions to work with riders on psychological skill training. Over 250 cyclists, many of them national team members, have worked with the sport psychologist during winter training camps and throughout the season to world championship competition. The psychologist has dealt with the athletes on a variety of issues, from counseling for personal problems to teaching specific focusing techniques that can be beneficial during a race.

Keys to Developing a Psychological Base

The first step in designing a psychological skills program must occur with the cyclist's personal training program. Just as a cyclist must build a mileage base before attacking speed work, he or she must first lay down a psychological base to ensure not only short-term results but long-term success. Once this program has been designed and structured, the manner in which the athlete advances in training will be set. Through discussions with athletes, I have identified three basic keys that act as the foundation for a mental game plan: commitment, attitude, and communication.

Commitment

Commitment is the willingness to strive for and obtain specific goals. The degree to which an athlete is willing to sacrifice certain aspects of a personal life for athletic training is often an indication of how committed that athlete will be toward success. The desire to reach a goal is often directly reflected by how dedicated one is at working for that goal. Consequently, the degree of commitment is determined by the level of the goal the athlete is attempting to reach.

For example, if the goal is simply to compete at the novice level, the commitment may be limited to training 3 to 4 times a week in order to build mileage each week until the body is ready to handle the physical stress of a race. In contrast, if the goal is to compete at a national level, the athlete will need to design a sophisticated training program that allows him or her to work not only on building mileage but also on developing the ability to climb and to sprint. As a result, the higher the goal, the more time and demands will be required to reach that goal.

Attitude

Emotions, feelings, thoughts, and actions all reflect an individual's attitude toward performance. A cyclist's everyday performance, both on and off the bike, is affected by the interactions with coaches, teammates, and support personnel. Almost all athletes strive to maintain a positive image and outlook on their daily performance; however, negative thinking, lack of confidence, and burnout are among the usual factors that make it impossible for one to be totally positive all of the time. It is very easy to suggest to a rider that he or she should be more positive, but it is more important to teach the athlete to develop a realistic attitude. When a problem develops that negatively influences an individual's attitude, the key to becoming positive again is to be realistic in attempting to identify the source of the problem.

For example, a sprinter with whom I have worked found it very difficult to maintain a positive perspective during competition because of internal and external sources of stress placed upon him to win. As a result, during competition he usually found himself tightening up and making very simple tactical mistakes. To help this athlete, we worked on identifying and learning to handle the pressure that affected his performance. Eventually, this athlete learned how to block out his negative thoughts so that he could think more clearly and thus make correct tactical decisions.

Communication

The third major key to success is open and honest communication. One of the major problems I have encountered with many cyclists (as well as other athletes) is that they are not honest and open with themselves in terms of their goals. Often they will attempt to achieve goals that are unrealistic. As a result, they may be consistently depressed or unsatisfied because they never reach those goals.

Communication problems can occur between athletes and coaches, most commonly in terms of training philosophies and team unity, especially when a team must work for the leader in a road race or when a group comes together to compete in team pursuit or team time-trial. The key to working on this area is to identify how committed the athlete is to working for the team's goals. Often an athlete will say that he/she wants to work for the team, but internally, he knows he really wants the gold medal all to himself. This kind of attitude can result in a variety of problems that have a detrimental effect on individual athletic performance and on the team's performance overall.

When the athlete is reluctant to discuss such issues with coaches or teammates, personal problems can arise (e.g., marital or family difficulties), which in turn affect performance on the bike. Often, the stress caused can lead to drug and/or alcohol abuse, a problem of growing dimensions in sports.

The solution to this problem? It basically comes down to the fact that the cyclist must learn how to communicate with coaches and teammates, either verbally or nonverbally. But more importantly, they need to be honest and open with themselves. When the person can deal directly with a problem, a lot of the negative stress, fear, anxiety, and lack of confidence that developed from the communication blockage can be eliminated. This almost always results in an improved performance, both from an individual and team standpoint.

Attention Span and Concentration

Over the past 5 years, an increasing number of research studies have been done regarding the role of attention span in performance. Many investigations have concluded that attention is an important factor affecting both arousal and concentration levels in an athlete's performance. Studies in this area have shown that there are two major attentional dimensions and an attentional control factor that have a significant effect on performance (Nideffer, 1976).

First, athletes need to be able to control the *width* of their attentional focus. Width deals with the amount and diversity of information being processed. In a situation requiring an athlete to attend to several different cues in order to perform effectively, the demand would be for a broad focus of attention. In contrast, a situation that demands intense, sustained concentration on one thing requires a narrow focus of attention.

Second, it is important to think of attention in terms of *direction* of focus. This characteristic involves an athlete's ability to have either an internal or external focus of attention. Making use of past race experience, anticipating the time for a break or sprint, and being sensitive to one's own body are examples of an internal attentional focus. On the other hand, reacting quickly and effectively to another rider's break and becoming aware of what opponents are doing in a race are examples of an external focus of attention.

Third, cyclists need the *ability to shift* their attentional focus as the race situation changes. This involves changing from a broad to a narrow focus and/or from an external to an internal focus, all in response to changing attentional demands in the competitive situation. Figure 1 demonstrates these attentional abilities. As a result, when the two attentional dimensions are put together, four separate attentional combinations necessary for competition will occur: (a) broad external, (b) broad internal, (c) narrow external, and (d) narrow internal.

A broad external focus is the ability to integrate many external stimuli effectively at one time. This is important in a criterium or points race where the rider needs to be aware of what is happening around him or her in the race, including the location of other riders and the condition of the course or track.

A broad internal focus is the ability to integrate ideas and information from several different areas. This is the type of attentional ability necessary when planning race strategy, as it involves decision making and analytical planning. Cyclists who compete in match sprints must be effective in this area as they need to plan what kind of race they will have to ride against different opponents.

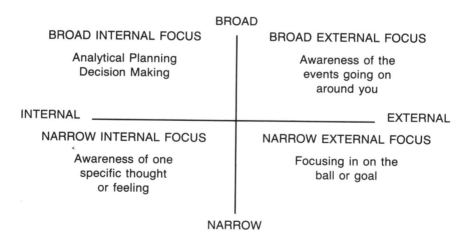

Figure 1 Graph of attentional abilities. *Note.* From *The Inner Athlete: Mind Plus Muscle for Winning* (p. 49) by R.M. Nideffer, 1976, New York: Crowell. Reprinted by permission.

A narrow focus of attention involves concentrating on one thing either externally (e.g., on another rider) or internally (e.g., on one specific thought or idea). Psychological research has determined that the most successful athletes are those who can narrow their attention under pressure. For example, in individual pursuit the cyclist will need to be able to concentrate on pushing him- or herself harder and harder throughout the race, focusing in on a goal (internally on a specific time or externally on catching his opponent).

In order to be successful, cyclists need to be aware of these different attentional abilities and should be able to shift from one focus to another.

During a recent training camp, a group of cyclists (44 males, 14 females) were tested with the Test of Attentional and Interpersonal Style (TAIS). The results of the testing, based on the averages of their results on attentional abilities, indicated that the cyclists tested consider themselves to be effective at all four attentional skills and are strongest at having the ability to narrow their focus of attention when necessary.

In 1984, 10 of the 11 track cyclists selected for the U.S. team were given the TAIS after the team had been chosen. The results of the testing are summarized next and have been analyzed into six factor scores compared to the standard norm group.

Factor 1, Intellectual Criticalness, measures an individual's ability to assume a leadership role in intellectual discussions, as well as the need to be critical, challenging, and confrontive to others. The team score of 55 indicates that the riders scored in the average range on this factor. This score demonstrates that the team would probably be fairly comfortable discussing the technical aspects of cycling and that they would likely be able to hold their own in discussions or classroom situations.

Factor 2, Overloaded-Impulsive, evaluates the tendency to become confused by having too many thoughts or too many events going on at one time. This confusion often contributes to a tendency to behave impulsively, to make decisions without adequate thought, and to act out in antisocial or unconventional ways. The score of 32.5 shows that the team scored in the low range, indicating that this should not be a problem for these athletes.

Factor 3, Extroverted, assesses an athlete's need to enjoy others, to express positive feelings, and to feel good about both him- or herself and others. The team score of 50 indicates that these athletes enjoy spending time with others just as much as having time to themselves.

Factor 4, Performance Anxiety, is associated with anxiety in high-pressure performance situations that can interfere with the ability to concentrate effectively. The team score of 60 falls in the average range and demonstrates that the team is quite capable of concentrating effectively in most athletic situations.

Factor 5, Physical Control and Competitiveness, relates to the athlete's need and desire to win and to be on top in athletic situations; this factor is often associated with self-confidence. The team score of 82.5 was the highest score and falls in the top 15% of all athletes. This indicates that the team members are extremely competitive and must feel in control of sport situations. It also demonstrates that they have the killer instinct required to make it to the top in athletic competition. It is important to emphasize that athletes who score high on this scale may find that the need to be in control and to win can become so important that it can result in frustration if goals are not achieved. Athletes with similar scores often may find themselves overtraining if they are not in charge and satisfied.

Factor 6, Attentional Effectiveness, measures an athlete's ability to analyze people and situations effectively. The team score of 77.5 indicates that the team is effective at the different attentional demands and was strongest at the narrow attentional ability.

Arousal, Stress, and Performance

In the past, it was typically believed that improvements in athletic performance resulted from increased levels of arousal. Coaches sometimes prepared athletes for competition by giving very emotional, arousing pep talks in an attempt to psyche up the athletes. Although such speeches may be the proper incentive for some competitors, they in fact have the opposite effect on many others.

Recent research on arousal and performance has shown that as arousal increases, an athlete's performance improves up to a certain level. This level is known as the optimum level of performance. However, when arousal increases past this optimum level, the quality of the athlete's performance decreases. This theory is known as the Inverted U Principle (see Figure 2).

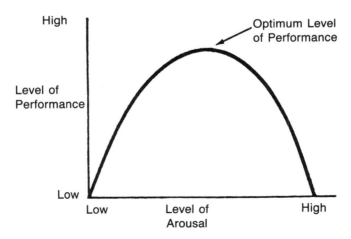

Figure 2   The inverted-U principle.

Conclusions drawn from the Inverted U indicate that some athletes will not be adequately aroused, whereas others may become too aroused or psyched before competition, either of which can have a detrimental effect on performance. As a result, it is important for each individual athlete to identify what he or she needs to do to reach his or her own optimum level of performance. If a rider is on the left side of the curve (not adequately aroused), he may need to use appropriate motivations to prepare himself for competition. For example, if competing against a group of riders whom he or she regularly beats, the athlete may need to focus on another goal such as a desired specific finishing time. This is where realistic goal setting is important.

On the other hand, those athletes who fall on the right-hand side of the curve, past optimum level, will need to apply appropriate relaxation techniques to calm themselves down. Cyclists typically find themselves on this side of the curve as a result of the wide variety of situations they are exposed to that can cause an abnormally high amount of stress. It is important to emphasize that a cyclist needs a certain amount of stress to get through any competition, whether it is a road race or a kilo. However, too much stress can have a detrimental effect on performance. For every cyclist, certain situations, called *situational stressors* and that may cause problems, can occur. Some examples of situational stressors are:

- performing in front of family or friends,
- racing against a rider of superior ability,
- competing in a qualifying or championship race,
- making a break in a road race,
- riding the last lap of a track event, and
- being the focus of a coach's or teammate's anger or criticism.

There are many different types of situational stressors that can occur, and their effect changes from one individual cyclist to another. The effect on one individual rider can also vary from race to race.

A wide variety of physical and mental changes will typically occur in response to situational stressors. Physical changes are generally associated with the "fight or flight" response and include increases in heart rate, blood pressure, respiration rate, skin conductance, and most importantly, muscle tension. In other words, while waiting for the start of a big race, the athlete may have sweaty palms, a dry mouth, a feeling of butterflies in the stomach, and may exhibit tension by squeezing the handlebars more tightly than usual.

Mental and emotional changes can also occur as a result of situational stressors. For example, an increased narrowing of attention often occurs, which can result in a reduced ability to analyze information both internally and externally. This is typically accompanied by an overall feeling of being rushed, confused, and overloaded. Additionally, the rider may lose the ability to shift attentional focus, resulting in an internal preoccupation with the physical changes that are occurring and causing the cyclist to begin to think negatively and worry about the decrease in performance.

Eventually, the physical and mental changes that occur can trigger a variety of performance problems. Muscle tension may cause motor coordination and timing to become impaired, resulting in uncoordinated or jerky movements. Increased perspiration may cause a rider's hands to slip off the handlebars. The lack of concentration accompanied by excessive muscle tension can increase the chances for injury. The mental changes that occur can result in a difficulty in decision making, causing some riders to react in an impulsive fashion (such as making a break too early in a race), while causing others to freeze and fail to respond at all (e.g., always hanging back in the pack because of negative thoughts or second guessing).

Situational stressors thus cause various physical and mental changes that can harmfully affect a rider's performance. For example, consider a cyclist who is competing in his or her first international competition. Here the pressures of competing against world-class cyclists from many countries for the first time may cause the rider to doubt his or her ability. When such an athlete finds him- or herself paired against the defending world champion, he or she may become so preoccupied with the competitor that the prerace instructions and plans are forgotten. As a result, when waiting for the gun to start the race, the athlete may notice tension in the neck and shoulders, shallow breathing, and/or difficulty in swallowing due to a very dry mouth. The athlete may as a result begin to wonder what he or she is doing competing against a world champion, and so much anxiety can result that the rider can become extremely distracted by internal negative thoughts and, as a result, fail to respond when the gun goes off.

Treatment Suggestions and Applications

The first step in learning how to approach competition is development of a mental game plan. Earlier it was mentioned that when two cyclists of equal physical ability compete, the cyclist with the stronger mental attitude will most likely come out ahead, because mental outlook has a tremendous impact on the ride.

One of the most important areas that should be investigated further is mental preparation before competition. Sport psychologists have applied several psychological techniques designed to assist athletes with their performance. These treatment modalities can be classified into the areas of relaxation/hypnosis and visualization exercises. The purpose of these techniques is to help the athlete calm down prior to competition and develop superior methods of concentration.

Relaxation/hypnosis exercises are used extensively in athletics and exist in many forms. The masters of the martial arts, for example, are experts at concentration because of their superior ability to relax and concentrate on the task at hand. Hypnosis, meditation, yoga, and biofeedback have all been used successfully worldwide in assisting athletes at further developing mental toughness.

One exercise that has been used successfully with several American cyclists involves four parts. This exercise should be done before competition, either the night before and/or before the race. The first part focuses on physical relaxation and requires the rider to lie down in a quiet, comfortable setting where he or she won't be disturbed for approximately 20 min. It is important to make sure that the arms and legs are not crossed and that no uncomfortable or restrictive clothing is being worn. The athlete should begin by concentrating on taking long, deep breaths and should continue this breathing pattern throughout the exercise. Next, the rider should begin to tighten and loosen sets of muscles from the head to the feet, one set at a time, including the forehead, teeth and jaws, neck and shoulders, biceps, triceps, forearms, wrists and hands, abdomen, thighs, calves, and feet. Often it may be advisable to repeat this twice, concentrating on the muscle groups that are more tense. The purpose for doing this is twofold. First, it will assist the rider at relaxing before a race. Second, it may make it easier to identify specific areas of the body that may be holding the most tension during competition, so that during the actual race the rider can simply tighten and loosen these muscles to help reduce some of the tension.

The next portion of the exercise focuses on mentally relaxing the rider. After the muscle groups have been relaxed, the rider should picture him- or herself resting at a place that further enhances relaxation, such as on a beach or in the mountains, or whatever setting the individual finds to be particularly relaxing. This assists in clearing the mind of negative thoughts and feelings.

Once physically and mentally relaxed, the rider should begin to picture or visualize riding the race in his or her mind. Research in all areas of athletics has proven that such visualization can be a tremendous asset to performance. The rider can picture him- or herself riding the race either through his or her own eyes or as if on a movie screen. For example, the pursuiter might picture him- or herself at the starting line feeling relaxed and calm, yet ready and focused on the race. After the race begins, the rider should picture him- or herself on each lap and think about what should be done in order to be successful. Visualization is an exercise that should be continually repeated until the rider is able to feel the way he or she wants to during the race, both physically and mentally. It can be very beneficial at helping the cyclist become aware of physical tension, clearing the mind of negative thoughts and providing a positive attitude toward the performance.

Conclusion

The development of a sophisticated psychological skills program to assist cyclists with mental preparation before and concentration during competition has become a necessity for improvements in competitive performance. The research and practical work that has been accomplished with the U.S. Cycling Team indicates that cyclists at the novice as well as the elite level can benefit from an organized educational program in sport psychology. The need for future research exists in all areas, including road and track cycling at all levels.

References

Nideffer, R.M. (1976). *The inner athlete: Mind plus muscle for winning.* New York: Thomas Crowell.

PART IV

Vehicle Design

Human-Powered Vehicles: Evolution and Future

David Gordon Wilson

Human-powered vehicles as defined herein will exclude pushcarts, where the person or persons providing the power are not carried by the vehicle. Thus, it is relatively certain that, despite the myths found in several ancient cultures of flying bird-men and despite the sketches of an almost-contemporary chain-driven bicycle attributed by some, under the fire of skeptics (McGurn, 1963), to a pupil of Leonardo da Vinci, the first human-powered vehicles were boats.

Early Human-Powered Boats

The earliest human-powered boats were undoubtedly logs on which people lay or sat astride and paddled with their hands or pieces of bark. The first boats of which there are records (rock carvings, ca. 3300 B.C.) were those of the Egyptians and were equipped with a mast and sail as well as with a line of rowers on each side (Capper, 1980). As the leadership in Mediterranean and European boat building passed to the Phoenicians, the Greeks, the Romans, and the Vikings, vessels in general continued to have both sails and oarsmen for three principal reasons: (a) the winds were uncertain, (b) sail technology was such that the vessels could not point close to the wind, and (c) a large number of rowers provided offensive capability to military ships and, on commercial vessels, discouraged piracy.

The technology of using men to propel large boats reached a high degree of sophistication. In Europe, quinqueremes had five banks of oarsmen on each side, with up to seven men on each oar, the total crew numbering perhaps 500 (Foley, 1981; Pounder, 1965). Figure 1 shows a large 17th-century galley having 55 oars or sweeps, with five men on each.

In the South Pacific, Polynesian peoples traveled huge distances in a variety of advanced vessels, including twin-hulled catamarans and rafts.

There were smaller canoes, of course, made by Native Americans and others, and Eskimo kayaks. Rowed boats developed in China, India, and Japan. All reached high levels of beauty and sophistication in design, construction, and, undoubtedly, operation.

However, in what seems in the clarity of hindsight to be a rather remarkable lack of enterprise, the human power in these various boats was almost

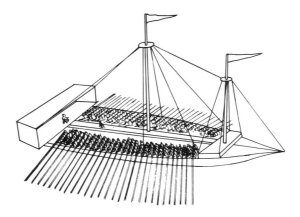

Figure 1 Early 17-century galley. *Note.* From *Bicycling Science* (p. 2) by F.R. Whitt and D.G. Wilson, 1982, Cambridge, MA: The MIT Press. Reprinted by permission.

all produced by the arms and back muscles. The legs, which even the ancients must have realized could produce more power than arms and back combined, were either inactive, as in canoes and kayaks, or used as props, as in rowing. It was not until the early 1850s that an unnamed London boatman, involved in the river races that had started there in 1715, polished his seatboard and sat on an oiled sheepskin. He could thereby slide back and forth to use the power of his legs as well as that of his arms and back. Within a year or two, wooden seats were equipped with rollers and rails and wheels, and the high speeds of today's sliding-seat "shells" were being approached.

From that decade until 1985, developments in human-powered boats were confined to refinements of shape, construction methods, and especially materials, but the basically excellent concept of using the leg muscles to drive oars or sweeps remained unchallenged. The remarkable achievement, in 1985, of high-speed human-powered travel on hydrofoils will be discussed in the last part of this article; the next discussion will focus on developments of land vehicles.

Bicycles, Tricycles, and Quadricycles

The earliest land vehicles propelled by riders rather than pushers or haulers seemed to have been novelties or experiments, involving very low speeds (Ritchie, 1975) and therefore creating little excitement.

But excitement is just what greeted the hobby-horse (Figure 2), invented by Karl von Drais in Germany in about 1814. Many texts confine von Drais's invention, which he called simply a *Fahrmaschine* or "travel machine," to one of making the front wheel steerable of a nonsteerable French "Celerifere." However, modern scholarship has shown that there were no such devices as nonsteerable hobby-horses (Roberts, 1982). It is difficult to imagine what utility they could have had. Von Drais was awarded a patent for his vehicle in 1815, when he was 30. It seems justifiable, therefore, that he should be credited with the rather profound discovery that man could balance on a single-track vehicle. Today it might seem obvious, but leading physicists and mathmeticians still argue about how a bicyclist balances. Because of his discovery, Von Drais might be appropriately considered the "father of the bicycle."

In addition to creativity, von Drais displayed two other traits that seem typical of those who revolutionize technology: He was a showman and a businessman. He was soon demonstrating that his machine could exceed the speed of both runners and horse-drawn carriages, even over journeys of 2 or 3 hr. This seems remarkable, considering that his *Fahrmaschine* was a heavy, wooden-wheeled device one straddled and pushed along with one's feet. The secret of its speed was probably that the roads were hilly, and on the downhills von Drais could take his feet off the ground and coast, going far faster than the horse-drawn coaches, which descended hills with their brakes on hard so as not to run down the horses.

Von Drais' vehicles, known as "Draisiennes," became the rage of Paris. He took them to the U.S.A. in 1821. He was imitated in London by a coachmaker named Denis Johnson, whose lighter and more elegant conveyance was soon known as a "dandy-horse," partly because Johnson set up a riding school for "young gentlemen."

Figure 2   The Draisienne. *Note.* From *Bicycles and Tricycles* by A. Sharp, 1896/1977, Cambridge, MA: The MIT Press. Reprinted by permission.

The Fallow Years

With so promising a start for human-powered vehicles, and with so many other technological marvels coming in a seemingly never-ending stream, it is surprising that the introduction of the Draisienne was followed by a lack of development for 40 years. The reason for this is unknown, but possibly can be attributed to the fact that the technical world became fascinated by railways, which were under intense development and spread to an extraordinary extent in the 1821–61 period and beyond. Perhaps people felt that there would be no need for the strange and uncomfortable two-wheelers, but this seems to be an unsatisfactory explanation, given the fertility of man's imagination.

There were some lone inventors making improvements. In Britain, Louis Gompertz fitted a swinging, ratcheting hand drive to the front wheel of a Draisienne in about 1821. In about 1839 a blacksmith named Kirkpatrick Macmillan, from near Dumfries, Scotland, made the first known attempt to harness leg muscles to turn the wheels directly. He added cranks to the rear wheels of a steerable velocipede, with connecting rods to swinging pedals (Figure 3). Because he made it possible for the rider to pedal and stay continuously out of contact with the ground, Macmillan might be called the originator of the true bicycle. He rode 225 km (140 mi) to Glasgow, a rather extraordinary feat given the state of the roads of those days and the hilly country, and received the first known traffic ticket, a fine of 5 shillings for knocking down a child among the throng that pressed around him. But Gompertz and Macmillan worked alone and lacked the companion skills of showmanship and business drive that allow an innovator to change the world.

It would be an exaggeration to claim that all development except that by Gompertz and Macmillan ceased. From 1815 to 1870 the term *velocipede* was used for any foot-propelled vehicle. A series of four-wheeled

Figure 3   Macmillan's rear-driven velocipede. *Note.* From *King of the Road* (p. 35) by A. Ritchie, 1975, London: Wildwood House. Reprinted by permission.

velocipedes—we would probably call them ''cycle-cars''—of increasing sophistication was made by Willard Sawyer (Ritchie, 1975), an accomplished coachmaker in Kent, U.K. (Figure 4). From about 1840 to 1870 he exported them around the world. They were used by a few enthusiasts, but no movement developed.

The Great Leap Forward

What may seem to us the obvious step of fitting cranks to the front wheel of a Draisienne was taken by Pierre Michaux, a carriage maker in Paris, in 1861 (Figure 5). He set the flame that, from about 1867 on, roared through France, the United States, and later Britain. The first true bicycle craze was underway. There are (disputed) claims that others preceded him—Artamanov in Russia in 1801 and P.M. Fischer in Schweinfurt, Germany, in 1850–55, for instance—but credit for the bicycling revolution belongs indisputably to Pierre Michaux and his son Ernest and to a controversial employee-turned-competitor, Pierre Lallement.

Why, and why then? There seems to have been no major technological development to catalyze their success. The two-wheeled pedaled velocipede could have been invented in 1820, although the weaker metals of that time would have led to a less graceful machine. Perhaps it was helped

Figure 4 A four-wheeled velocipede by Sawyer. *Note.* From *King of the Road* (p. 41) by A. Ritchie, 1975, London: Wildwood House. Reprinted by permission.

Figure 5 The Michaux pedaled velocipede. *Note.* From *Bicycles and Tricycles* (p. 148) by A. Sharp, 1896/1977, Cambridge, MA: The MIT Press. Reprinted by permission.

by Michaux craftsmanship, which was widely praised. Perhaps it was Michaux's management ability: He organized factories that could produce five machines a day, one of the first examples of high-volume production of a consumer product. Perhaps it was the Michaux family's flair for promoting the machines with demonstrations and races. But above all the velocipede was fun to ride, and thousands did so.

We might not think it so entrancing nowadays. The wooden wheels had rigid compression spokes and iron rims. This vehicle was, understandably, called the "boneshaker"; it was only in the late 1860s that rubber was nailed onto the rims to cushion the harsh ride, and ball bearings were first used to give easier running.

The Entry of the Aggressive British

The French temporarily lost their leadership in the velocipede market because of the Franco-Prussian War of 1870–71, when the factories were required to turn to production of armaments. In the U.S. the patent office was reportedly overwhelmed with applications for protection of ideas for improved velocipedes. Britain, however, was the most aggressive workshop of the world, and production started there more to fill the unsatiated French demand than to supply any domestic market. Technical leadership was repeatedly taken by James Starley. The suspension or tension wheel had already been designed in 1808 by the aeronautical pioneer Sir George Cayley (Pritchard, n.d.). Around 1870 Starley introduced the "lever-tension" wheel, with radial spokes and a lever for tensioning and torque transmission (Figure 6), and in 1876 he came up with the logical extension of this idea, the tangent-tension method of spoking (Figure 7). This has remained the standard spoking method to this day.

Figure 6   Starley's level-tension wheel. *Note.*   From *Bicycles and Tricycles* (p. 342) by A. Sharp, 1896/1977, Cambridge, MA: The MIT Press. Reprinted by permission.

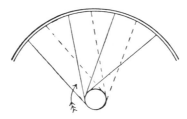

Figure 7   The tangent-tension wheel. *Note.*   From *Bicycles and Tricycles* (p. 342) by A. Sharp, 1896/1977, Cambridge, MA: The MIT Press. Reprinted by permission.

The Coming of the "Ordinary"

Boneshaker front wheels were made larger by degrees to give a longer distance per pedal revolution and therefore greater speed on favorable ground. Starley and others recognized the advantages of using a chain as a step-up transmission, but experimenters found that the available chains quickly froze up or fractured in the grit and gravel of contemporary roads. Therefore front wheels were made as large as comfortable pedaling would allow. A bicycle was bought to fit one's leg length, as trousers. A large "ordinary" would have a driving wheel 60 in. (about 1.5 m) in diameter (Figure 8). In the English-speaking world we still translate gear ratios into equivalent driving-wheel diameters, and this size corresponds to a middle gear of a typical modern bicycle. (The French use, perhaps more logically, *la developpement*, the wheel's circumference.)

The 1870s were years of dominance of what we now call the high-wheeler. Outwardly high-wheelers appear to have matured fast, and then to have changed little. However, significant technological improvements came apace: Ball bearings were developed for both wheels and for the steering head; hollow tubing was added to the rims and forks; and tire rubber was greatly improved. Racers weighing under 14 kg (30 lb) were produced, and a ridable James ordinary of only 5 kg (11 lb) was produced.

The ordinary was responsible for the third two-wheeler passion, which was concentrated among the young middle-class men of Europe and the U.S. and was fostered by military-style clubs with uniforms and even buglers. The ordinary conferred unimagined freedom on its devotees; it also engendered antipathy on the part of the majority who didn't, or couldn't, bicycle. Part of the antipathy was envy. The new freedom and style were restricted to young, principally single, men. Strict dress codes prevented all but the most iconoclastic of women from riding ordinaries. Family men, even if they were still athletic, hesitated to ride because of the frequent severe injuries to riders who fell. Unathletic or short men

Figure 8   An Ordinary. *Note.*   From *Bicycles and Tricycles* (p. 150) by A. Sharp, 1896/1977, Cambridge, MA: The MIT Press. Reprinted by permission.

were excluded automatically. These prospective riders took to tricycles which, for a time, were as numerous as the ordinaries.

The Tricycle Bubble

There were two technological responses to the need to serve the "extra-ordinary" market. James Starley played a prominent role in the first, and his nephew John Kemp Starley in the second.

The first was the development of practical machines of three or four wheels, in which the need to balance was gone and the rider could be seated in a comfortable, reasonably safe, and perhaps more dignified position. Such vehicles had been made at different times for at least a century, but the old heavy construction made propelling them a formidable task. In fact, the motive power was often provided by one or more servants, who in effect substituted for horses. Starley's Coventry Lever Tricycle, patented in 1876, with his new lightweight tangent-spoked wheels, could be used with comparative ease by women in conventional dress and by relatively staid males. Starley produced this vehicle in large numbers for several years. In a prophetic move, he soon abandoned lever propulsion for more conventional cranks with circular foot motion (Figure 9); he had found a chain that worked, at least in the possibly more protected conditions of a tricycle. The chain could give a "step-up" transmission, whereas the lever was restricted to the wheel speed and so produced only a very

Figure 9 Starley's Royal Salvo tricycle. *Note.* From *Bicycles and Tricycles* (p. 175) by A. Sharp, 1896/1977, Cambridge, MA: The MIT Press. Reprinted by permission.

Figure 10   A modern tricycle of the early 1880s. *Note.*   From *Bicycles and Tricycles* (p. 171) by A. Sharp, 1896/1977, Cambridge, MA: The MIT Press. Reprinted by permission.

low "gear." Starley continued tricycle development with vigor until his death, reinventing the "balance gear" or differential for his highly success-ful Royal Salvo machine, which had two equally sized rear driving wheels. Both he and Pierre Michaux died in 1881, having greatly influenced the western world.

By 1886 the modern tricycle had evolved, with the modern riding posi-tion in which one sits or stands almost over the cranks and splits the body weight among handlebars, pedals, and saddle (Figure 10). This form of the tricycle was also very similar to the emerging form of the modern bicycle.

The Birth of the Safety Bicycle

There were many attempts to lessen the danger of riding ordinaries. A simple but quite effective approach was the substitution of handlebars that went under the thighs, so that when an inevitable forward "cropper" occurred, the rider could hit the ground feet-, instead of head-, first (Figure 11). A more radical design was typified by the American Star, in which the large driving wheel was in the rear and the small steerer in the front.

But these developments were too late to save the ordinary from being overthrown by another design revolution: the rear-driven, chain-transmission "safety" bicycle. It had several claimants as originators, but credit for successful introduction must go to John Kemp Starley, who designed a series of Rover safeties from 1884. By 1886 something very close to the modern diamond-framed bicycle had evolved (Figure 12). In 1888 John Boyd Dunlop, a Scottish veterinarian in Belfast, reinvented the pneumatic tire (it was invented in 1845 by another Scot, R.W. Thomson, for horse-drawn vehicles). Dunlop's early tires (made to smooth the ride of his son's tricycle) were crude, but by May 1889 they were used by W. Hume to win all four Belfast races he entered. Success in racing gave a clear signal to a public confused by a multitude of diverse developments.

Figure 11   Whatton underleg safety handlebars. *Note.*   From "Cycling" by Viscount Bury and G. Lacy Miller, 1887, *Badminton Library*, p. 323.

Figure 12   Starley's safety bicycle of 1886. *Note.*   From *Bicycles and Tricycles* (p. 154) by A. Sharp, 1896/1977, Cambridge, MA: The MIT Press. Reprinted by permission.

Bicyclists saw that, as in the case of the safety versus the ordinary, a development had arrived that promised not only greater speed and/or less effort, but greater comfort and, especially, greater safety. Within 4 years, solid tires had virtually disappeared from new bicycles, and Dunlop was a millionaire in the pound sterling of the day.

The Freeze

The safety bicycle continued to evolve in the 1890s and to grow in popularity, playing a very significant role, for instance, in the emancipation of women. The bicycles were made lighter, brakes and gears were improved, and road and track records were continually being set and broken.

And then something of great technological and social significance occurred. A group of racing people met in Paris in 1900 to decide on rules governing races. Among other details, they decided that the form of racing bicycles should be similar to those prevailing at the time. Only minor variations would be allowed.

The effects were not dramatic at first. In fact, they are dramatic only in hindsight. Why did a machine that was evolving so vibrantly from 1865 to 1900 suffer an almost complete cessation of development thereafter? The answer given by someone widely regarded as the most learned expert on the technological history of the bicycle, the late Frank Rowland Whitt, was that the bicycle had reached near-perfection by 1900, and further radical improvements were impossible.

However, perhaps the effect of the restrictive racing rules can be considered the answer to the question of why development stopped. There were, in fact, many developments of different forms of human-powered vehicles in this century. So-called "recumbent bicycles," or simply "recumbents" or "recliners," are examples that are close to my heart. Apparently advantageous recumbents were developed, built, and demonstrated many times earlier in this century. One called the Velocar (Figure 13) was ridden by a nonchampionship racer in 1933 and beat the world champion over several distances. The International Cycling Union met in Paris to argue for several days over whether or not the challenger should be recognized. The decision was that the Velocar, despite having two wheels and being propelled by a human being, was not a bicycle. In a world where success in racing largely determines commercial success, the message was clear and the effect devastating.

Figure 13 The 1933 Velocar recumbent bicycle. *Note.* From *Bicycling Science*, (p. 26) by F.R. Whitt and D.G. Wilson, 1982, Cambridge, MA: The MIT Press. Reprinted by permission.

The New World of Kremer, Kyle, and the IHPVA

Human-powered aircraft were not, of course, governed by rules about bicycling. In the 1950s there were no rules, and there were no aircraft. There had been many attempts at continuous flight on human muscle power, the most successful being Villinger's "Mufli," which made a 235-m flight in Germany in the 1930s. In Britain, Henry Kremer, an industrialist who wished to encourage healthy enterprise, decided in 1959 to offer a prize for the first team that could fly a human-powered aircraft around a figure-of-eight course a mile long. Activity started all around the world at universities, among aircraft-company apprentices, and in groups of friends. Trial after trial ended in failure. Kremer raised the prize from an initial £5000 to £50,000. Eventually in 1977 a Californian team headed by Paul MacCready, former national soaring champion, won in the Gossamer Condor, piloted and pedaled by Bryan Allen. They took what seemed to be a radically new approach to the design of human-powered aircraft. They chose a cruising speed of 9 mph, under 4m/s, not much more than half that of their competitors. This meant that less cruise power was required, but the aircraft had to have a huge wingspan. They also designed an aircraft that could be crashed and repaired within hours. Their "learning curve" was therefore rapid.

Henry Kremer then offered a prize of £100,000 for the first human-powered flight across the English Channel, and the MacCready-Allen team won that prize on its first attempt, in June 1979, in the Gossamer Albatross (Figure 14). Subsequently Kremer offered a series of prizes for

Figure 14 The Gossamer Albatross. *Note.* Photo courtesy of Du Pont.

Figure 15   The MIT Monarch Kremer prize winner. *Note.*   Photo by Steve Finberg, MIT.

Figure 16   The Watson ''White Dwarf'' blimp. *Note.*   Photo by Bryan Allen.

higher-speed aircraft, and the MacCready team, in a more orthodox craft, won one of these. The first was taken by a team of MIT aeronautical students in the Monarch monoplane (Figure 15), and the third by a German group in the "Musculair" (Schoberl, 1986).

These developments are bringing human-powered heavier-than-air flight a little closer to everyday reality, but the chances of it being a popular sport seem small. However, a human-powered blimp (White Dwarf, Figure 16) commissioned by the comedian Gallagher, designed by Bill Watson, and flown "all over the sky" by Bryan Allen in 1985, has real possibilities of starting a new sport.

Kremer's first prize encouraged me to offer a smaller prize in 1967, in collaboration with Liberty Mutual Insurance and the British journal *Engineering*, for any developments in human-powered land transport[1]. There were 73 entries from six countries. The competition closed in 1969[2], and the first prize was awarded to a "faired" (enclosed, streamlined) recumbent bicycle. The competition led to an upsurge of interest in new forms of human-powered land transportation. In California, Fred Willkie made two recumbent bicycles to my rough sketches, and the publicity he attracted encouraged others to start experimenting.

The IHPVA and the End of the Freeze

Chester Kyle was one who was making streamlined bicycles and other variations with his students at the University of California at Long Beach. When he came up against a problem of nonrecognition of speed records, he and his friends simply took the Californian approach: They formed a new group that issued its own rules. They called it the International Human-Powered-Vehicle Association (IHPVA). The rules that they drew up for racing were that there were (almost) no rules: The vehicles simply had to be propelled by human power alone, with no energy storage. The IHPVA began holding local meets and an annual International Speed Championship. A prize was offered for the first HPV to exceed 50 mph, 22 m/s; that was quickly achieved. Then the aim was to go over the 55 mph (24.5 m/s) national speed limit and be ticketed by the California Highway Patrol. This too fell quickly.

The Du Pont company, which had done so much to assist the aircraft builders, then offered a prize of $15,000 for the first HPV to exceed 65 mph, 29 m/s. The prize brought about a similar intensity of effort on many continents as the Kremer prizes. It was won in May 1986 by "Gold Rush," a faired bicycle designed by Gardner Martin and ridden by Fred Markham. The value to society of broad efforts to win prizes may be far greater than that of the prize if new forms of attractive HPVs suitable for commuting and recreation evolve.

Victory at Sea

No large prizes have yet been offered for new developments in human-powered boats, but progress has nevertheless been remarkable. All teams that have demonstrated high speeds have abandoned oars and adopted pedaling as the input and a propeller as the thruster. The fastest speed to date has been produced by the Flying Fish, a pedaled hydrofoil (Figure 17) developed by Allan Abbott and Alec Brooks in California. (They acknowledge that some of the inspiration came from an MIT professor of ocean and mechanical engineering, Patrick Leehey, through the bachelor's thesis of Brad Brewster [1979].) Groups in Britain and Switzerland are determined to better the speed of the Flying Fish.

The Future

I would like to discuss possibilities in two areas: speed and utility, in vehicles supported by gases, liquids, and solids.

Aircraft

The potential for dramatic development seems to be absent. It should be possible to win one or two more Kremer high-speed prizes (which must better the previous speed by at least 5%), but with planes weighing less than half that of the pilot, with wing sections giving very high lift-drag ratios, and propellers having over 85% efficiency, the only area left for substantial improvement is energy storage, which is allowed in this series of prizes. There is also the possibility that a modified method of pedaling coupled with hand cranking, perhaps through elongated oval paths, will allow a human being to produce up to 10% more power. With some of the drag increasing as the square of the speed, the potential for a major speed increase is not strong.

Figure 17 Allan Abbott on the Abbott-Brooks hydrofoil "Flying Fish." *Note.* Photo by Alec Brooks.

Human-powered aircraft do not seem likely to have a utility role. They can be flown only in low-wind conditions. They must stray only a little way from a very large hangar because they cannot be held down outside in a breeze and because the wingspan is of the order of 30 m.

There are two possible exceptions to this rather negative projection. One is the astonishing inflatable aircraft designed by F. E. To in England. This can be carried to a site on a small car, inflated with a low-power blower, and flown with less danger of injury to the machine or the pilot than is the case for other heavier-than-air machines. The second is the human-powered blimp. This can be flown in higher wind conditions (up to 2 or 3 m/s) than can the craft that rely on human energy to provide lift, and they require only small power inputs. In the event of a sudden wind they can descend and be tied down. These two types of craft seem to have potential for recreation. It is difficult to see much utility role. The low noise level of the blimps might give them an advantage in some special surveillance tasks.

Ultramarathon flights, such as that planned by MIT students over the supposed route taken by Daedalus from Crete to Greece, will undoubtedly thrill and challenge us into the far future.

High-Speed Boats

Four alternative ways of avoiding the high wave drag of hull-borne boats exist. One is the traditional use of hulls of extreme fineness ratio: shells that have length-to-beam ratios of 30 to 50. This approach also maximizes the surface-volume ratio, so that skin friction becomes the companion limit to wave drag. The second is to use submerged buoyancy; most of the lift would be provided by a submarinelike hull of minimum-drag shape at a depth below that at which wave drag is significant, and to provide stability by small surface pontoons or other means. The third is to use the equivalent of water skis, which have intermediate proportions of wave and friction drag. The fourth, which seems to be the best approach to speed, is to carry the rider-plus-machine weight on hydrofoils. The same laws apply as for aircraft; however, the medium is almost a thousand times as dense.

This increased density has good and bad effects on the effort to go fast in or on water. Compared with a human-powered aircraft, the foils and the propeller can be tiny. They also have to be far more robust to withstand the less forgiving nature of water. But the problems should be easier. There is no reason, therefore, why similar speeds should not be reached. The Musculair 2 has reached 12.3 m/s, 27 mph—why should not boats? On almost its first attempt, the Flying Fish of Allan Abbott and Alec Brooks reached half this speed. We may expect a progression of speed increases similar to that which occurred with aircraft, particularly if the stimulus of a prize is offered. Foil-borne craft in air and water share the problem of not producing sufficient lift until they exceed a critical velocity, and lift must be provided by another means (wheels in the case of most aircraft). Hydrofoil boats must also be supported by wheels or hulls at low speed. The penalty of carrying a hull is very considerable for a human-powered boat. We expect that the fastest hydrofoils will use wheels for the launch phase, or, as for the first Flying Fish, downward-sloping slips.

Utility Boats

If one wishes to stop in the water one must revert to tradition and use buoyancy. If one wants to be maneuverable, a short hull is required. Thus wave drag will limit the top speed to something around 2 m/s. A beautiful design that illustrates the design compromises involved is Garry Hoyt's "Waterbug" (Figure 18). This can be used in summer and winter, to travel on smooth ponds and to crash through ocean waves. To maintain stability it is fitted with about 150 kg of lead ballast.

A lighter utility boat could be designed using the submerged-buoyancy approach, but the inability to use it in shallow waters and the peculiar characteristic it would have of popping out of the water when the rider dismounted would reduce its attractiveness.

A method of propulsion recently developed for boats uses one or more vertically oscillating hydrofoils[3]. Propulsion efficiency increases with the mass of water acted upon by the propeller. In boats, a large-diameter propeller limits the water depth in which one can travel. An oscillating foil can act on a mass that is ideally in a wide, shallow rectangle, ideal for boats[3].

Figure 18   The Hoyt-Harken "Waterbug." *Note.*   Photo by Garry Hoyt.

Land Vehicles

Record breakers.   Although there have been suggestions of using ice and skate blades for attempts on the land speed record, so far all high-speed HPVs have used wheels. Thus presently land HPVs have the great advantage over air and water machines in that the same vehicle can be used for the speed record and as a utility machine. This was convincingly demonstrated by the Easy Racer recumbent bicycle "Gold Rush" when it won the Du Pont Speed Prize in May 1986 by exceeding 65 mph, 29 m/s. The basic bicycle is very similar to that sold for commuting and recreation.

If speeds significantly higher than this once-incredible level are to be reached, radical changes that will remove the vehicle from the province of the commuter will probably be required. There are three directions to go, all more or less expensive.

The first is to induce laminar flow over as much of the fairing as possible. As NASA's Bruce Holmes convincingly explained recently to the IHPVA, the aerodynamic drag, which is over 90% of the resistance to the record-breaker, can be reduced to a small fraction of its turbulent level by changing the normally turbulent boundary layer to laminar. To do this, the fairing must be extremely smooth and must incorporate suction slots or a porous surface. The power required to remove the air necessary to maintain laminar flow will take 5 or 10% of the power saved in reducing drag. How the pumping is to be done in a lightweight HPV is open to debate. One possibility is to have the rider breathe in through an air-bag reservoir connected to the porous surface.

The second radical change may be required to make the first possible: the use of steel wheels on steel rails. Still photographs of a sleek rubber-tired vehicle passing at high speed through the 200-m measuring track do not convey the extraordinary vibration and oscillation that these light vehicles experience from the inputs of a never-smooth track, the vagaries of the wind, and the almost superhuman pedaling of the rider. The vibration represents energy loss in itself and would make the maintenance of laminar flow much more difficult than if the vehicle were traveling smoothly in a straight line. A light narrow-gauge rail line with continuous rails supported to give high standards of alignment would have large advantages. The rolling resistance of steel wheels on steel rails is far lower than the best pneumatic tires, and wheels of half the present size would probably be optimum, thus reducing the fairing surface area. No steering would be required, so that fairing wheel slits—a source of drag—could be narrower. The rider could concentrate on optimizing power production, perhaps using hands and feet, without having to "drive." Such a vehicle would not be very useful in itself, but it would be very fast, and would solve many problems that might lead to interesting systems of HPV travel in the future.

The third possibility of considerably increasing the current speed record is simply to take further the direction already followed by the record breakers: to increase altitude. To do so probably requires the rail system just discussed. There is obviously a vanishingly small number of high-altitude roadways in the world where there is a smooth surface for 3 or 4 km and a favorable slope just within the IHPVA-established limit (two thirds of 1%). As it is, competitors in other parts of the world believe that Americans have an unfair advantage, having access to so many possible sites. But a 4-km rail line set up in the mountains at 3,000 to 5,000 m would require enormous resources, and a full oxygen supply for the rider would presumably be necessary. The debate over rules will intensify: whether or not to formulate regulations that, if not passed, would allow prizes to be won only by the rich.

If development were to proceed in these three directions, the speeds that would be reached would be very high, and would depend as much on the length of the runup rail line as on the design of the vehicle itself and on the abilities of the rider.

Utility land vehicles. The configuration of the future utility HPV will depend on its intended purpose. A semirecumbent riding position on a three-wheeled or four-wheeled vehicle would be ideal for some quiet retirement communities and for recreational use in locations protected from motor vehicles. For use on streets with occasionally heavy traffic I believe that a bicycle configuration is essential so long as the acceleration, cruising speed, or hill-climbing speed of HPVs differ greatly from those of motor vehicles. There are already some good examples of open and

Figure 19 "Leitra" utility tricycle. *Note.* Drawing by Carl Georg Rasmussen from *Human Power*, **5**(1), p. 14. Reprinted by permission.

enclosed tricycles (Figure 19). With regard to bicycles, I am heavily biased in favor of the long-wheelbase semirecumbent configuration (Figure 20). It needs a fairing that has conflicting requirements: to reduce wind drag, to protect the rider from precipitation and temperature extremes, to increase rider protection in accidents, to allow all-around visibility, and to be light and take up little space. We and others have experimented with many configurations, but we are still a long way from anything that is an overall advantage in highway use.

HPVs of any type would seem to have a special disadvantage in hilly areas, like San Francisco and Seattle. But it is possible that the disadvantage could be turned around by providing power assistance for the steeper uphills and by allowing coasting on downhills and human power on the flat. Several proposals have been made; two are shown in Figure 21. It would be exciting to have the opportunity of designing a human-powered transportation system for a new town based on some of these concepts.

Whether or not HPVs become more widely used for commuting and recreation depends only to a small extent, however, on technological improvements. Far more important are the hidden subsidies to motor vehicles. If these were reduced or removed the stimulus to use HPVs for many short-distance trips would be very significant, and our urban highways would be transformed (Wilson, 1986).

Figure 20 The Avatar-2000 recumbent bicycle. *Note.* Photo courtesy of NASA.

a

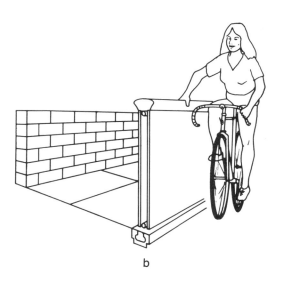

b

Figure 21 "CRUSWAY" transportation system based on HPVs (a), and moving handrail for assistance on hills (b). *Note.* CRUSWAY illustration courtesy of Syracuse University, and handrail illustration from *Bicycle Science* (p. 355–356) by F.R. Whitt and D.G. Wilson, 1982, Cambridge, MA: The MIT Press. Reprinted by permission.

Conclusions

The world of human-powered vehicles, still dominated by bicyclists, is healthy and exciting. The greatest advances will probably be on the water and would be stimulated by a prize similar to the Kremer and Du Pont prizes. The greatest need is for improved commuting highway vehicles. The costs of achieving significantly higher speeds on land, in the air, and on water are bound to increase greatly as relatively easy improvements in design and technique are incorporated.

Acknowledgments

Much of the material for this paper was extracted from "A Short History of Human-Powered Vehicles" in *American Scientist*, **74**, pp. 350–357, and "HPVs: A Blueprint for the Future," presented at the Third Scientific Symposium on Human-Powered Vehicles, 1986, IHPVA, Indianapolis, IN.

Notes

1. "Man has a physical and a psychological need to use his muscles." This was the opening statement on the cover of the July 21, 1967 issue of *Engineering*, London, UK, announcing the design competition.
2. "Winning entries: Design competition for man-powered land transport"—cover announcement of *Engineering*, April 11, 1969.
3. These foils are being developed by Wave Control Co. Roven, N-1920 Sorumsand, Norway.

References

Brewster, M.B. (1979). *The design and development of a man-powered hydrofoil.* Unpublished master's thesis, Massachusetts Institute of Technology, Cambridge, MA.

Capper, D.P. (1980). Sails and sailing ships. In *The New Encyclopaedia Britannica* (15th ed., vol. 16, pp. 157–158). Chicago, IL: Encyclopaedia Britannica, Inc.

Foley, V. (1981, April). Ancient oared warships. *Scientific American*, pp. 148–163.

Holmes, B. (1985). *Human Power*, **5**(1),

McGurn, J. (1963). The Leonardo debate. *Bicycle*, pp. 25–29.

Pounder, C.C. (1965, May). Marine engineering. *The Chartered Mechanical Engineer*, pp. 265–270.

Pritchard, J.L. (n.d.). *Sir George Cayley, the inventor of the aeroplane.* New York: Horizon.

Ritchie, A. (1975). *King of the road: An illustrated history of cycling*. London: Wildwood House.

Robert, D. (1982). Cycling mythology and unsung heroes. *The Boneshaker*, **11**(100).

Schobert, E. (1986). The Musculair 1 & 2 human-powered aircraft and the optimization. *Human Power*, **5**(2).

Sharp, A. (1977). *Bicycles and tricycles*. Cambridge, MA: The MIT Press. (Original work published 1896.)

Wilson, D.G. (1986, August). *A blueprint for an HPV revolution*. Paper presented at the Third International Human-Powered Vehicle Symposium, Vancouver, British Columbia, Canada.

The Mechanics and Aerodynamics of Cycling

Chester R. Kyle

In previous studies of bicycle performance, simple mathematical models along with experimental measurements of tire rolling resistance, aerodynamic drag, and human power output, have proven to be accurate predictors of actual time trial speed (Kyle & Burke, 1984; Kyle, Caiozzo, & Palombo, 1979). In this paper, any methods or equations that have not been described previously will be shown in the appendices.

Frequently, the answers to the questions posed below have been known for a long time; however with the recent introduction of new materials and components, the answers have sometimes become confused with what could be termed enthusiastic misconceptions. The enthusiasm for new ideas and equipment has sometimes obscured the underlying logic or principles. Probably the most recent controversy has been the effect of weight upon race times.

Is Bicycle and Component Weight Really Important?

Low weight in a bicycle has been almost a religion in cycling for nearly a century. Racers will spend hundreds of dollars to remove a single pound from their machine. The logic has been that light weight will give faster acceleration, less effort in climbing hills, and lower rolling resistance. In other words, it takes more energy to average the same speed with additional weight. These facts are still as valid as ever: No matter in what form, unnecessary weight is harmful to racing performance, provided the frame shape and stiffness can be maintained with a lighter machine.

Low weight in rotating components is even more important. To accelerate a rotating member such as a wheel, kinetic energy of rotation must be supplied, in addition to the kinetic energy of linear motion. For example, in a wheel, if the mass is mostly concentrated near the rim it would nearly double the energy required to accelerate an equal nonrotating mass. In other words, 1 lb added to a wheel is equivalent to nearly 2 lb on the frame.

An argument has recently been advanced that the flywheel effect of a heavy wheel can increase speed. There is only one way this could be so. By increasing weight, the oscillation in speed caused by each pedal stroke would be dampened. By having less speed variation, the average wind resistance would also be slightly less. Wind drag is proportional to the square of the speed, and large fluctuations in velocity would raise the average wind drag. There can be no other advantage, except that a heavy front disk wheel might be more stable in variable winds. However, other ways of compensating for this are probably available (such as changing the front end geometry), and added weight would still be a disadvantage.

To investigate this, a time-varying math model that included the change in speed due to pedal force as well as the effects of acceleration, wind resistance, rolling friction, and total mass, was used to predict the time in a 1,000-m time trial and a 4,000-m pursuit. The equations were solved by numerical computer integration. The net retarding force on a bicycle in the direction of motion at a given velocity is given by:

$$F = W \cdot (Crr + Sin(\arctan(s)) + A1 \cdot V) + 1/2 \cdot \varrho \cdot Cd \cdot A \cdot (V + V_w)^2 \tag{1}$$

English units will be used for calculations. V is the bicycle velocity in feet/second; Vw is the wind velocity with a plus sign being a head wind and minus being a tail wind; W is the total weight of the bicycle and rider in pounds; Crr is the tire rolling resistance coefficient assumed to be .0022; s is the slope of the course given as the rise divided by the horizontal distance with a plus sign being uphill and minus downhill; A1 is a coefficient related to the small variation of rolling resistance and bearing friction due to velocity (assumed to be .0000667); ϱ is the air density in pound/foot³; Cd is the drag coefficient; and A is the net frontal area of the bicycle and rider in feet². In this case, the air density was assumed to be 0.00233 slugs per cubic foot, the drag coefficient .9, and the frontal area 3.5 ft².

To calculate the time necessary for a cyclist to accelerate to a certain speed, Newton's equation may be used:

$$M \cdot dV/dt = T - F \tag{2}$$

M is the mass in pound-second²/foot, t is the time in seconds, and T is the thrust of the wheel upon the ground in pounds induced by the pedaling action of the rider. To calculate acceleration time it is more convenient if the above equation is multiplied by the velocity V. Then the thrust term is changed to the power generated, $T \cdot V = P$ in foot pounds/sec:

$$M \cdot V \cdot dV/dt = P - V \cdot F \tag{3}$$

For both Equations 2 and 3, if it is desired to solve for distance instead of time, the substitution is made $dV/dt = V \cdot dv/dx$ where x is the distance in feet. For a 180-lb rider, actual race acceleration times and distances for a 1,000-m race on a level course with no wind are closely matched if the rider delivers 1.7 horsepower during acceleration (935 ft-lb/second). In the 4,000-m pursuit, 1 horsepower closely matches the actual race acceleration times and distances. Equation 3 was numerically integrated for the time of acceleration shown in Table 1. The acceleration distances were also found but are not shown. The acceleration distance when subtracted from the total distance gave the distance covered at an assumed steady average speed, thus permitting the calculation of the total race time.

Once the rider is up to speed (37.5 mph for 1,000 m, 31 mph for 4,000 m), then another calculation procedure was used to find the average steady speed. The wheel thrust T is a variable that changes depending upon the crank angle. It may be approximated by a cosine function:

$$T = Mm \cdot [1 + \cos (2 \cdot (\theta + 90))]/R \qquad (4)$$

Mm is the maximum wheel torque in foot pounds (the average torque times 2), θ is the crank angle with vertical being 0 and clockwise being positive, and R is the gear ratio in feet. The gear ratio is given by:

$$R = Dw \cdot Nc/Nw \qquad (5)$$

Here Dw is the diameter of the rear wheel in feet, Nc is the number of teeth on the crank sprocket, and Nw is the number of teeth on the wheel sprocket. For convenience, a 90-in gear (7.5 ft) and a 27-in. rear wheel were used for all calculations. The average wheel torque $Mm/2$ was found knowing the speed and the total drag from Equation 1.

Combining Equations 1 and 3 and numerically integrating using 5° increments of crank travel, the variation in speed during a crank cycle could be found. By letting the program run, the equilibrium speed at any total mass M could also be calculated. From this the effect upon race time of added weight was computed. Figure 1 shows the variation of wheel

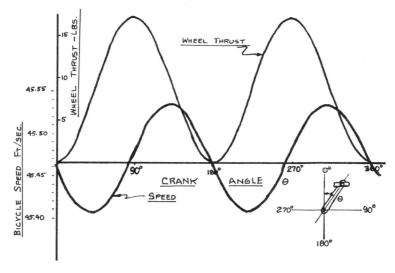

Figure 1 Bicycle speed variation due to variable pedal force.

thrust and bicycle speed at 31 mph due to this varying pedal force. The maximum wheel thrust is about 17 lb, and the speed variation is about 0.125 ft/s or 0.085 mph. With a higher weight, the speed variation is decreased in inverse proportion to the weight (for 185 lb vs. 180 lb, the variation is $(180/185) \cdot 0.125 = 0.122$). Consequently, the decrease in average wind resistance caused by damping the speed variation with added weight is very small and is far overbalanced by the harmful increase in rolling resistance caused by the extra weight.

In all cases the slowed acceleration, and the increased rolling friction caused by higher weight resulted in slower times. The predicted race and acceleration time (the time to accelerate to speed) is shown in Table 1. For reference, similar predictions by John Stout of Colorado State University are also shown (personal communication). His results show an even greater disadvantage to increased weight.

Because light disk wheels can be built with the same shape and rigidity as a heavy disk wheel, there is no advantage to a heavy disk wheel. Nor is there any reason for added component or frame weight on a racing bicycle unless handling and stability cannot be maintained.

An argument is often advanced for the use of rigid frames over slightly flexible frames, sometimes at the cost of added weight. It is often said that added flex means a loss in energy. Actually, all metals within the stress limits imposed by bicycle riding are nearly 100% elastic; that is, any energy put into deflection is conserved and returned almost entirely to the system just as with a completely elastic spring. This elastic energy during the pedaling cycle is fed back into the system in very complex ways that have not at present been completely analyzed. However, all of the energy is not lost; a good portion is used in lifting the body and frame weight or in helping to increase beneficial crank torque.

The difference in energy loss between a rigid versus a slightly flexible frame would no doubt be almost impossible to measure using current

Table 1 The Effect of Added Weight Upon Track Time Trial Races

Total weight rider plus cycle (lb)	1,000-m time(s)		4,000-m time(s)		Acceleration time	
	1	2	1	2	1,000-m (31 mph)	4,000-m (37.5 mph)
180	63.38	62.16	292.97	292.90	14.47	16.70
181	+0.024	+0.04	+0.05	+0.10	+0.09	+0.09
182	+0.05	+0.08	+0.10	+0.20	+0.17	+0.18
183	+0.07	+0.12	+0.15	+0.30	+0.25	+0.29
184	+0.10	+0.16	+0.20	+0.40	+0.34	+0.38
185	+0.12	+0.20	+0.25	+0.50	+0.42	+0.48
186	+0.15	+0.24	+0.30	+0.60	+0.50	+0.58

Note. 1 = Kyle's data. 2 = Stout's data.

experimental methods. And a flexible frame affords certain advantages, such as ride comfort and lighter weight, that are very important.

How Do Hills and Winds Affect Cycling a Circuit Course?

A cyclist who can travel at 20 mph continuously on level ground with no wind is placed upon a circuit course with equal slopes of 1 mi up and 1 mi down. To calculate the equilibrium speed in hills, Equation 1 was simplified for touring riders. The wind velocity was 0, the coefficient A1 was assumed to be 0, the rolling resistance coefficient Crr was .0035, and the frontal area was 4.5 ft². All other variables were the same as in Equations 1 to 5. At equilibrium speed, there is no acceleration so the equation becomes:

$$F = W \cdot [Crr + Sin(ArcTan(s))] + 1/2 \cdot \varrho \cdot Cd \cdot A \cdot V^2 \qquad (6)$$

$$P = F \cdot V \qquad (7)$$

Knowing the steady speed on level ground, 20 mph, the steady-state power could be calculated and assuming this power was constant both uphill and downhill, the equilibrium speed uphill and downhill could be found. This is reported in Table 2. These equilibrium speeds were used to find the course time. The time to negotiate the course is also shown in Table 2. The time is also given with 2 lb added to the bicycle. Obviously, any slope slows a bicycle down; the faster speeds downhill do not make up for the loss of time uphill. The main purpose of this illustration is to show that even small additions of weight can slow down a bicycle dramatically in hills or in rolling terrain. In road racing there is even more of an incentive to cut weight from a bicycle.

In all of the illustrations so far, the time differences have seemed small, but in distance, the leads are quite appreciable. For example, by carrying

Table 2 The Effect of a Hilly Circuit Course Upon Bicycle Speed 1 Mi Uphill and 1 Mi Downhill

Slope (%)	180 lb				182 lb			
	Speed uphill (mph)	Speed downhill (mph)	Time (min/s)	Average speed (mph)	Speed uphill (mph)	Speed downhill (mph)	Time (min/s)	Average speed (mph)
0	20.00	20.00	6:00.0	20.0	19.99	19.99	6:00.2	19.99
2	14.63	25.58	6:26.7	18.6	14.57	25.63	6:27.5	18.6
5	8.98	33.22	8:29.5	14.1	8.90	33.34	8:32.7	14.0
10	4.98	43.78	13:24.6	9.0	4.93	43.99	13:31.9	8.9

2 extra pounds up a 2% grade, a gap of 30 ft will separate two riders of equal ability at the finish of a 2-mi circuit course. For a 10% grade this lead distance is over 470 ft! This leaves very little mystery why heavy riders make poor hill climbers. Excess body fat is exactly the same as added bicycle weight. The effect of weight in hills is multiplied manyfold over the effect on level ground.

The effect of wind on circuit race times is not nearly so dramatic as the effect of hills. Using a rider who can average 20 mph on level ground on a 2-mi circuit course with a tailwind the 1st mile and a headwind the 2nd mile, and using the graphs in Kyle (1986), the circuit time can be calculated. The results are shown in Table 3. As can be seen, any wind will slow a cyclist down, but not nearly so much as do hills. Wind tunnel tests have shown that crosswinds, which weren't considered in the illustration, will increase the wind drag of a cyclist, so even in the crosswind sections of the course, average speeds will be lower. The speeds shown in Table 3 would be somewhat slower, depending upon the distance traveled in crosswinds.

Is Regenerative Braking Practical for Commuting Cyclists?

Every cyclist has, upon coming to a stop sign, either rolled through the stop or at least thought about it. The reason is obvious: Where their own energy is concerned, people are very conservative. A bicycle has no gas pedal; the energy for acceleration is provided entirely by human muscle and not gasoline. So why not conserve the kinetic energy wasted during braking and store it in a flywheel, or a battery, to be used later on in accelerating or hill climbing? This suggestion has been made over and over, and yet no practical system has ever been devised. Instead of spending a great deal of time designing systems that might conserve the energy of braking, a more useful approach might be to ask whether regenerative braking is worthwhile at all in cycling.

The first consideration is the efficiency of energy recovery in small systems like a bicycle. Losses in a small generator, battery, and motor system typically are from 60 to 70%. This means that only about a third of the

Table 3 The Effect of Wind on Bicycle Speed in a 2-Mi Circuit Course, Equal Distance With and Against the Wind

Wind speed (mph)	0	2	5	10
Speed with the wind	20.0	21.0	22.6	25.4
Speed against the wind	20.0	19.0	17.5	15.2
Time (min/s)	6:00.0	6:00.9	6:05.0	6:18.6
Average speed (mph)	20.0	19.95	19.73	19.02

energy put into the system can be recovered for later use. Although mechanical systems can be much more efficient than this, they also weigh much more and are far more complex, very expensive, and much harder to maintain. As previously shown, added weight on a bicycle is a burden that no cyclist will voluntarily tolerate. Let us assume that an overall efficiency of 50% is possible for the recovery, storage, and the power system, and that a practical lightweight device can be designed.

The next question is whether a significant amount of energy is available for recovery. Kinetic energy is proportional to the velocity squared, so that available energy increases rapidly with speed. Unfortunately, aerodynamic losses also increase as the velocity squared and these losses are continuous and not recoverable. This means that regenerative braking could only be useful if many stops are made and the average speed is high. In hills, the system would only be applied if the hill was too steep for coasting and the brakes were necessary. The regenerative mechanism would have to have the sensitivity of a brake to adjust the speed and stopping distance accurately. This in itself is a formidable problem.

Using Equations 8 and 9, a study of the energy balance in cycling at 20 mph can be made. Numerically integrating Equation 3 using 0.25 horsepower, the acceleration time and acceleration distance for each start was found for a level course with no wind. As a simplification in all calculations, A1 was set equal to 0, whereas the other variables were identical to those used in Equation 7. Assuming a constant deceleration during braking of 0.1 gravity, the time and distance for each stop could be found from the standard equations of constant acceleration as follows:

$$t = V_0/a \qquad (8)$$

where t is the deceleration time in seconds, V_0 is the initial velocity (20 mph) in feet/second, and a is the braking acceleration in feet/second^2.

$$x1 = (VO_2) / (2*a) \qquad (9)$$

Here $x1$ is the stopping distance in feet.

To find the energy balance during acceleration, the method of difference was used. The total kinetic energy was $(M \cdot V0^2)/2$, and the energy expended in overcoming rolling resistance was $W \cdot Crr$ times the distance covered during acceleration. The total energy supplied by the rider during acceleration was the average power times the time of acceleration. The difference between the total energy and the sum of the kinetic energy and rolling energy was the energy used in overcoming wind resistance.

During braking, the kinetic energy of motion provides the force necessary to overcome wind resistance and rolling resistance, and the excess is dissipated in heat during braking. No energy is supplied by the rider during braking; however, the energy wasted in overcoming wind resistance and rolling resistance must be subtracted from the total kinetic energy to find the net energy recoverable during braking. During steady motion, the energy balance may be calculated from the factors in Equation 3 and the kinetic energy of motion.

The results using these equations are shown in Table 4. The conditions used were a 5-mi commuting trip with a flying start; and the same trip with one start only, one start and one stop, two stops per mile and four stops per mile. A continuous output of 1/4 horsepower (187 W) was assumed for the cyclist, which is the energy requirement at a speed of about 20 mph for a typical touring rider. A 180-lb total system weight was used.

The available energy that was wasted in braking varied from 2% in the case of one start to 31% in the case of four stops per mile. Using a recovery efficiency of 50%, this means that only about 1/6 of the energy expended by the rider could be used for acceleration or hill climbing under the best case studied. Under almost every imaginable condition, the recovery would be less than this. The conclusion is unavoidable that regenerative braking is not an attractive project. Even if it were possible, the added weight, cost, maintenance, and limited utility would discourage almost everyone from using it. The fact that it is an intriguing technical problem should not blind designers to the fact that any effort and money spent on the concept would be ultimately wasted in the case of cycling.

Are Alternative Transmission Systems Attractive in Cycling?

The possibility of an alternative power transmission system that would be superior to the present chain and sprocket drive is similar to the problem of regenerative braking. Such a system has several requirements,

Table 4 The Energy Used in Commuting 5 Mi[a]

Condition	Wind resistance	Rolling resistance	Kinetic energy[b]	Total energy[a]	Average speed (mph)
Flying start	106,920	16,632	2,407	125,959	20.00
No stops	85%	13%	2%	100%	
One start	105,930	16,632	2,407	124,969	19.81
No stops	85%	13%	2%	100%	
One start	105,389	15,841	2,407	123,636	19.71
One stop	85%	13%	2%	100%	
2 stops per mile	90,116	15,706	26,477	132,361	17.27
(11 total)	68%	12%	20% (17%)	100%	
4 stops per mile	74,774	14,852	50,547	140,173	15.36
(21 total)	53%	11%	36% (31%)	100%	

[a]Energy is given in foot pounds. [b]The energies shown are the total supplied by the rider. During braking, stored kinetic energy is used to overcome wind and rolling resistance. Therefore, recoverable kinetic energy is less than that supplied by the rider (about 350 foot pounds is wasted per stop). The recoverable kinetic energy is shown in parentheses.

which seem obvious, but judging from the hundreds of times these criteria have been ignored, perhaps it would be wise to list them. Any successful variable speed system must be at least as efficient, reliable, inexpensive, light in weight, silent, simple, easy to maintain, and economic to repair as present chain drive systems. Any new design that ignores even one or two of these criteria is almost doomed to failure.

The present chain drive system has been under development about a century, and for efficiency and simplicity, it is very hard to beat. While carrying loads of less than 1 horsepower, a well-lubricated sprocket and chain drive system will deliver from 95 to 98% of the energy put into it. Most of the conventional power drive systems used in industry or transportation were designed to carry large loads with reasonable efficiency, but with the low loads of a bicycle, they can be highly inefficient. Small hydraulic drives seldom deliver more than 50% of the energy input, and small electric systems are no better. In fact, the low energy efficiency of most proposed drive systems will eliminate probably two thirds of them from consideration.

The rotary motion of a standard crank automatically conserves the kinetic energy of the legs as they speed up and slow down. Almost all of the frequently proposed linear pedal travel systems waste this kinetic energy because it takes muscular action to slow down the legs at the end of the pedal travel. Minimizing friction in linear travel systems is also difficult. If none of the other factors eliminate a proposed transmission, then high cost, complexity, noise, vibration, or questionable benefits will ruin the chance of success of almost all of them.

Hundreds of alternative schemes have failed over the past few decades. This fact does not seem to discourage continual attempts at improvement. However, a system superior to the crank, chain, and sprocket is certainly not easy to design. Probably the greatest chance of success would be not to concentrate upon changing the basic system but to try to modify the pedal power cycle to increase biomechanical efficiency. Different sprocket shapes or simple cam systems may have some benefits, but even this remains to be conclusively proven.

Can Wired-On Tires Ever Compete With Tubular Tires in Racing?

During the past 2 years, the rolling resistance of bicycle tires has been measured and reported in several publications (Kyle & Burke, 1984; Kyle & VanValkenburgh, 1985). The results of representative tests are shown in Table 5. Wired-on tires or "clinchers" have made dramatic advances in technology until they now are light, have low rolling resistance, and are relatively inexpensive compared to most tubular tires or "sew-ups." In fact, recent advertisements report that clinchers are superior to sew-ups in rolling resistance. This claim is somewhat misleading. As can be seen from Table 5, the rolling resistance of the best tubular tires is still somewhat superior to the best of the current clincher tires. The best clinchers

Table 5 The Rolling Resistance of Bicycle Tires[a]

Tire make	Size	Weight (g)	Tire pressure (psi)	Tread type	$Crr\%$[b] Surface type[c]		
					Linol.	Conc.	Asph.
Tubular tires ("sew-ups")							
Continental Olympic	27 in. × 18mm	133	120	Fine file	.19	.17	.22
Same tire			100		—	—	.22
Vittorio Cronometro	27 in. × 18mm	189	120	Fine file	.20	.23	.27
Continental Olympic	24 in. × 18mm	119	120	Smooth	.26	.23	.28
Continental Olympic	24 in. × 18mm	135	120	Coarse file	—	.27	.31
Vittorio Cronometro	24 in. × 18mm	176	120	Fine file	.26	.25	.30
Clement Colle Main	27 in. × 18mm	92	120	Smooth	.16	—	—
Clement Colle Main	24 in. × 18mm	107	120	Smooth	.21	—	—
Clement Colle Main	20 in. × 18mm	83	120	Smooth	.29	—	—
Clement Novo Seta Ext.	27 in. × 1 in.	—	100	—	.26	—	—
Soyo Super Sprint	27 in. × 18mm	—	100	Smooth	.26	—	—
Soyo Piste 130	27 in. × 18mm	—	100	Smooth	.26	—	—
Continental Cotton	27 in. × 1 in.	—	100	—	.30	—	—
Clement Criterium 250	27 in. × 1 in.	—	100	—	.32	—	—
Wolber Competition	27 in. × 1 in.	219	100	Narrow rib	—	—	.28
Wolber Performance	27 in. × 1 in.	219	100	Coarse file	—	—	.31
Saturae	27 in. × 1 in.	253	100	Coarse file	—	—	.40
Clement Futura	27 in. × 1 in.	317	100	Coarse file	—	—	.59
Clement CF 2001	27 in. × 1 in.	333	100	Narrow rib	—	—	.54

(Cont.)

Table 5 (Cont.)

Tire make	Size	Weight (g)	Tire pressure (psi)	Tread type	$Crr\%$[b] Surface type[c] Linol.	Conc.	Asph.
Wired-on tires ("clinchers")							
Avocet 20	700C	232	100	Smooth	.29	—	.36
Avocet 30	700C	203	100	Smooth	.29	—	.33
Michelin Hilite Comp	700C	213	100	Smooth	.29	—	.33
Turbo R	700C	219	100	Smooth	.26	—	.31
Turbo S Kevlar	700C	—	100	Smooth	.23	—	.27
Turbo S	700C	—	100	Fine file	.26	—	.29
Specialized Ultralite	700C	—	100	—	.26	—	—
IRC HP 90	27 in. × 1.25 in.	480	100	Rib	—	—	.31
SCCR 800	27 in. × 1.25 in.	468	100	Rib	—	—	.31
IRC Handy Tour	700C	191	100	Rib	—	—	.31
Panaracer High Extra	700C	339	100	Rib	—	—	.40

[a]Data from Kyle and Burke (1984) and Kyle and VanValkenburgh (1985). [b]To calculate the rolling friction against a bicycle, multiply the rolling resistance coefficient (Crr) by the total weight of the bicycle and rider, and divide by 100. Although Crr will vary depending upon the tire pressure and the roughness of the road surface, it does not vary significantly with speed. [c]Linol. = linoleum, Conc. = concrete, and Asph. = asphalt.

do have a lower rolling resistance than almost all sew-ups; however, high-quality tubular tires are still unequaled. The total wheel weight is less, they can carry a higher tire pressure, and the rolling resistance is less. Even the smallest difference in rolling resistance that is listed in Table 5 can mean a gap of several feet at the line in a 1-mi race (Kyle & Van-Valkenburgh, 1985). So using the best tire available for racing is critical.

In the future, it is hardly conceivable that the rim weight of a wired-on tire of standard design can be reduced to equal that of a tubular. Flanges are necessary to support the forces caused by air pressure, and these flanges amount to excess material on the rim not required by a tubular. As previously stated, weight is critical in racing. A tubular tire can carry more pressure than a wired-on, thus on smooth surfaces it will have a lower rolling resistance even though it may be equal to a wired-on at lower pressures. Also, any of the technology for the casing, tread, and tube material developed for high-quality wired-on tires can be easily duplicated by tubular tire manufacturers. The best tubulars are thus always likely to have equal or lower rolling resistance than the best wired-ons, even at identical pressures. Therefore, unless unforeseen design changes are made in the wired-on tire and rim, they will not be able to compete with high quality tubular tires in cycle racing.

This is not to say that they won't be useful in training, touring, or in club races. Wired-on tires are easier to repair, less expensive, and just as convenient to carry as tubulars, and they are superior in rolling resistance to almost all tubular tires. Because of this their continued dominance in bicycle tire sales is assured. Tubular tires will no doubt remain with a small but secure market as a specialty item used mostly for racing.

What Is the Effect of Aerodynamic Wheels and Components?

At racing speeds, wind resistance is over 90% of the retarding force against a bicycle; consequently, if this drag can be lowered even slightly, the speeds will increase. The fastest speed a standard racing bicycle can go, powered by the world's best cycle athlete, is about 45 mph for 200 m on a smooth indoor track. Completely enclosed streamlined bicycles, piloted by second-category athletes, have gone over 20 mph faster (65.48 mph). It has been conclusively proven that aerodynamic streamlining will also improve the speed of a standard racing bicycle as evidenced by the numerous records set using disk wheels. Nevertheless, except for the disk wheel, aerodynamic improvements are still not used by the majority of cycle racers. This will no doubt change rapidly in the future as new equipment becomes readily available.

To predict the effect of aerodynamic drag reduction upon race times, the method described in Kyle and Burke (1984) was used. The results of the computer simulation is shown in Table 6. As a check upon the method, John Stout (personal communication, 1984, 1985) used another computer model to perform the same calculations. The results of the two methods

Table 6   The Effect of Aerodynamic Drag Reduction Upon Time Trial Race Times

Drag reduction at 30 mph		1,000 m 37.5 mph 1:03.5		4,000 m 31 mph 4:50	
Pounds	Grams	1	2	1	2
0.02	9	−0.06 sec	−0.43 sec	−0.28 sec	−0.24 sec
0.04	18	−0.11	−0.088	−0.56	−0.50
0.10	45	−0.26	−0.22	−1.26	−1.26
0.20	91	−0.53	−0.45	−2.52	−2.53
0.40	181	−1.06	−0.90	−5.06	−5.10
1.00	454	−2.71	−2.28	−13.04	−13.11

Note.   1 = Kyle's data. 2 = Stout's data.

agree very well. The models predict that even a drag reduction of 10-g drag at 30 mph will result in a lead distance of 2 ft in the 4,000-m pursuit.

If aerodynamic equipment is used compared to completely standard traditional equipment, time improvements of as much as 13 s are possible in the 4,000-m pursuit. Of course in international competition, some aerodynamic equipment is usually used on racing bicycles, so a more realistic figure would be from 2 to 5 s faster.

What Type of Disk Wheel Is Superior?

One of the most effective ways of reducing aerodynamic drag is the use of disk wheels. The drag of several commercially available disk wheels, as well as several prototypes, was measured in the low speed wind tunnel at the University of California at Irvine. Also some spoked wheels were measured for reference. The results of the tests are shown in Table 7.

The wheels were measured both statically and rotating at a rate equivalent to the wind speed. Some of the wheels were also measured drafting behind a wheel and bicycle frame. Compared to a standard 36-spoked, 27-in. wheel with flat rim, and a 1-in. tire, a disk wheel can achieve over 150-g drag reduction, which would result in several seconds saved in a 4,000-m pursuit. The data in Table 7 show that although the rear wheel is drafting behind the frame, giving it about 25% lower drag than the front wheel, the drag reduction of the rear wheel is about the same as the front wheel.

Regarding shape, there doesn't seem to be much difference in drag between the two most common types, the flat wheel and the lens-shaped wheel. The flat wheels, being lighter than most of the lens-shaped wheels, are therefore the most advantageous. The Kevlar tension membrane wheel is the lightest of all and has a semilens shape. This wheel is not commercially available. Its weight is only slightly higher than a standard wheel, and it is extremely strong. Wheels of this design will probably dominate the racing market in the future.

Table 7   The Aerodynamic Drag of Disk Wheels

Wheel	Wheel weight (g)	Wheel size (in.)	Wheel drag (g, at 30 mph)		Wheel drag—drafting behind bike frame	
			Fixed	Rotating	Fixed	Rotating
Ambrosio Ener DM – Lens	2,787	27	110	171	60	98
Aerosports Flat	1,146	27	113	123	75	101
Cinelli Lens	1,894	27	122	142	–	–
Sugino Flat	1,393	27	108	129	–	–
Aerosports Kevlar – Lens	782	27	103	136	–	–
FIR ARD Flat	1,902	27	117	159	67	96
Raleigh #1 Flat	1,174	27	110	158	81	111
Raleigh #2 Flat	1,688	27	145	183	91	149
Wolber Disk #1 Fl.	1,550	27	–	–	–	–
Wolber Disk #2 Fl.	1,125	27	–	–	–	–
36 Round Spokes Standard Rim	710	27	211	315	–	–
28 Aero Spokes Aero Rim	687	27	149	194	91	146
18 Round Spokes Aero Rim	714	27	146	206	100	154
Aerosports Flat	975	26	99	109	–	–
Raleigh #3 Flat	993	24	95	112	60	93
Aerosports Kevlar – Lens	674	24	92	134	71	96
16 Aero Spokes Aero Rim	477	24	138	137	78	103
Aerosports, Aero Rim, 18 Aero Spo.	525	24	136	127	–	–

Can a Practical Safety Helmet Also Reduce Aerodynamic Drag?

Another quite simple and inexpensive way to reduce aerodynamic drag is to use improved clothing and helmets. The recent rule requiring safety helmets in U.S. racing has raised the question, Can an aerodynamic helmet pass safety regulations and still give a substantial drag reduction compared to other types of safety helmets? The aerodynamic drag of several helmets was measured in the low-speed wind tunnels at California State University at Long Beach and the University of California at Irvine. A mannequin was placed in cycling position in the wind tunnel, and the total drag of the mannequin was measured wearing various helmets.

The results are listed in Table 8. Three of the helmets tested have aerodynamic shapes and will also pass safety regulations. These are the Giro Advantage, the new Bell Aero Helmet, and the Monarch Aerodyne. All of these, however, fail to meet the UCI maximum length requirement of 30 cm. Later model helmets are indeed under 30 cm; however, they were

Table 8   The Aerodynamic Drag of Bicycle Helmets at Wind Speed of 30 mph

Helmet make	Relative drag (g)
Czech Aero Helmet[a]	0
Bald head or rubber cap over hair[a]	0
1984 USA Aero (38 cm long)[a]	−54
1986 USA Aero (30 cm long)[a]	−28
Giro Advantage	+29
Bell Aero	+36
Monarch Aerodyne	+50
Bell Prime	+113
Bell Tourlite, no visor	+116
Brancale[a]	+117
MSR	+118
Bell Windjammer	+129
Short hair[a]	+132
Bell Biker	+132
Bell Tourlite with visor	+142
Bailen	+143
Skid Lid[a]	+162
Kucharik Standard (leather strap)[a]	+181
Kucharik Super (leather strap)[a]	+185
Pro Tech[a]	+203
Long hair[a]	+244
Bell VI Pro	+280

[a]Will not pass ANSI standards.

not available for testing at the time. The wind tunnel tests show that it is quite easy to design a helmet that gives a substantial aerodynamic drag reduction and still provides adequate head safety. Helmets with a smoothly contoured shell and either no vents or well-placed vents can cut drag by over 100 g compared to more conventional helmets. This will give a dramatic advantage to time-trial cycle racers.

Which Components Give the Greatest Aerodynamic Advantage?

Table 9 summarizes the effects of aerodynamic streamlining on the standard racing bicycle. The data in Table 9 are based upon wind tunnel tests and the math models given in Kyle and Burke (1984). With each equipment item is shown the incremental improvement possible when that item

Table 9 The Benefits of Aerodynamic Equipment in a 25-Mi Time Trial

Item	Approximate cost ($)	Drag reduction at 30 mph (g)	Time savings for 25 mi (s)	Cost/s saved ($)
Aero bike frame	400–1,000	130	42	9.52–23.80
Spoked aero wheels	350	120	39	8.97
Aero handlebars	350	90	29	12.06
Front disk wheel[a]	350–1,500	42	14	25.00–107.14
Rear disk wheel	350–1,500	40	14	25.00–107.14
Aero helmet[b]	70	40–130	14	5.00
Aero clothing[c]	120	40–120	14	8.57
Aero water bottle	30	40	14	2.14
24-in. front wheel	175	30	—[d]	—
Pedals	80	25	9	8.88
Cranks and sprocket	120	17	6	20.00
Total			195	

[a]If two disk wheels are used directly, then the time savings would be about 67 s for the two together compared to standard wheels. The cost would be about $10.45–$44.77/s saved. [b]The drag reduction shown depends upon what type of helmet was replaced by the Aero helmet. The minimum reduction was used for the calculation. [c]This is comparing Lycra Spandex skin suits and Lycra shoe covers to standard cotton or wool clothing. The variation is due to the type of material used and to the suit design. The minimum was used for the calculation. [d]Although 24-in. wheels have a lower wind resistance than 27-in. wheels, the 24-in. tire has more rolling resistance. The two nearly cancel each other. Still, the 24-in. wheel weighs less and accelerates faster, therefore there would still be some advantage to using a small wheel in front, especially on a hilly course. In a team time trial, the smaller wheel allows the team to draft more closely, thus reducing the wind resistance of the group. Thus, there is a substantial advantage to the smaller wheel in team events.

is used with the previous components or if it replaces one of the listed components. The times are additive. The times are for U.S. or English national class 25-mi time trialists. The equations show that slower time trialists should improve their times slightly more than those shown.

Acknowledgments

The work cited in the present paper has been underway since 1982 at California State University at Long Beach. The author wishes to acknowledge the support provided by research grants from the U.S. Cycling Federation, the U.S. Olympic Committee Biomechanics Laboratory, and Bell Helmets.

References

Kyle, C.R., & Burke, E.R. (1984, September). Improving the racing bicycle. *Mechanical Engineering*, pp. 34–45.

Kyle, C.R., Caiozzo, V.J., & Palombo, M. (1979). Predicting human-powered vehicle performance using ergometry and aerodynamic drag measurements. In *Proceedings of International Meeting on Human Powered Transportation* (pp. 200–224). New York: Metropolitan Association of Urban Designers and Environmental Planners.

Kyle, C.R. (1986). Mechanical factors affecting the speed of a bicycle. In E.R. Burke (Ed.), *Science of cycling* (pp. 123–136). Champaign, IL: Human Kinetics.

Kyle, C.R., & VanValkenburgh, P. (1985, May). Rolling resistance. *Bicycling*, pp. 141–152.

Goals, Rules, and Technological Innovation

Paul B. MacCready

The technology of cycling can include not only the vehicle but also the rider who powers and guides the vehicle, the rider's training, the use of the vehicle for recreation or competition, and the underlying research, development, and manufacturing. This paper will focus on the vehicle, while still considering the users and suppliers. The aim is to explore factors that stimulate cycling, especially through technological innovation. (The implicit assumption is that the growth of cycling is a worthy cause.) The exploration includes considering what cycling is, how rules determine technology and how they can either invigorate or stultify innovation, and how several other sports have handled compromises of rules. What all this means with respect to cycling will be considered, and some recommendations and conclusions will be suggested.

Motivation is, of course, the primary drive for technological innovation and arises from both psychological and economic factors. For cycling, motivation includes the ego drives of competitors, the enthusiasms of researchers, the economic goals of manufacturers, recreation enjoyment for the sporting participant, convenience for commuters, and the innate characteristic of humans to brag about equipment.

What Is Cycling?

Human power can be used for moving a person on land or water, with or without a vehicle. Cycling is a special case of a vehicle having wheels and moving over the ground. Consideration of human-powered locomotion from a larger framework helps to define and illuminate the cycling portion.

A person swims in water but can move faster with the aid of swim fins, webbed gloves, and certain winglike devices operated by the legs. More complex devices eventually constitute vehicles. Some rare boats are propelled by legs, but most involve arm-operated paddles or oars (e.g., paddleboards, surfboards, kayaks, racing shells, rowboats, and to be complete, even 300-man oared boats from several thousand years ago).

As for land, there are skis and snowshoes for snow, and skates for ice, whereas for ordinary surfaces there are bare feet, "human-powered shoes" in great variety, stilts, pogo sticks, skateboards, scooters, and cycles with one, two, three, or four wheels (mostly leg-driven, but some, such as wheelchairs, using arms). One can even add somersaulting and walking on one's hands and also note the application of human power to mountain climbing.

Human-powered flight requires a vehicle. The vehicles at present are all large, lightweight, propeller-driven devices.

To complete the picture, note that animals other than man provide power for vehicles, usually to move man or some load of interest to man. Sometimes muscle power is augmented, as with electric or gasoline motors. Small fossil-fuel motors can generate 10 and even 100 times as much power as a person and can permit a vehicle to have better performance and be heavy, rugged, and safe. Battery power is more limited but still packs much more wallop than muscles and has the added potential of regeneration from braking or charging from on-board photovoltaic cells. Sometimes wind or wave motion is harnessed to help propel a vehicle that also uses human power.

Finally, we need to note that gravity, through nonhorizontal terrain, plays a significant role in cycling. Climbing uphill takes extra power at the rate of weight times ascent speed. Moving slowly on foot, the extra power is considerable; moving fast on a bicycle, the ascent speed can be large and the extra power requirement huge.

Thus there is a whole spectrum of power sources for apparatus and vehicles that transport people, from relying 100% on human muscles to 0%. Here we focus on bicycles powered solely by muscle, while recognizing that some interesting technological innovations may arise from a bit of augmentation by electricity, fossil fuel, or wind. If the augmentation dominates, then we end up with a car or motorcycle, which may be practical but eliminates the exercise benefits and challenges of cycling.

Man is inefficient as a runner. With efficient mechanisms (bicycle, ice skates), he can move about twice as fast as running, to a speed where air drag starts to dominate. Then, with a streamline fairing, the speed can be doubled again. The inefficiency in running is due to the loss of potential energy with each step as the center of gravity is raised and lowered without effective energy storage and recapture and poor recapture of the kinetic energy of moving limbs.

The bicycle is an extremely efficient mechanical device for deriving power from the rider. The constant center-of-gravity position eliminates the potential energy loss in each cycle, while the pedal-chain-wheel-inertia system avoids the kinetic energy loss. The bicycle, with its large diameter, low-drag wheels, is also extremely efficient as a device for moving over a smooth, hard surface. No shoes, scooter, skateboard, roller skates, or pogo stick offers the combined effectiveness of a bicycle in power extraction and motion efficiency. Vehicles with other than two wheels have special features: The unicycle emphasizes fun with great demands in skill; three- and four-wheel cycles emphasize stability for less agile cyclists and in some cases a great load-carrying capability that is used commercially, especially in other countries.

The bicycle readily reaches a high enough speed that the standard vehicle is fun to ride, useful for sport, touring, commuting, and exciting competitions. It is a wonderful device to lure people into healthy exercise.

In races, however, the speeds are such that aerodynamic drag becomes a dominant factor. Thus vehicle design looms large, and the troublesome challenge for rule makers is to provide definitions and limits for vehicles so that winning cyclists are fairly selected.

Design Evolution and the IHPVA: Analogy to Natural Evolution

Given enough time for development, entities evolve, within the constraints of physical law, to fit a desirable opportunity. A close analogy exists between the way goals (rules, motivation) stimulate or inhibit technical developments and the way the characteristics of a particular ecological niche in nature (the local limits, opportunities, competition) serve to design the creatures that fill the niche.

Evolution of creatures, devices, or ideas works on the simple basis that things that leave descendants are those that work well enough to survive the competitive pressures and leave descendants. There is no right or wrong and no perfection, just the criterion of relative success. Whether the law of the jungle or the law of manufacturers' economic competition is involved, what succeeds succeeds. In nature, the ecological niche establishes the rules; any solution can enter the fray and will be scored versus competitors. In man's technology, with developments taking place thousands or millions of times faster than in nature, the economics of large scale manufacturing is a strong forcing function and this market depends on standardized demand and hence on the existence of rules and advertising.

Almost a century ago, after several decades of design innovations, the conventional "safety bicycle" emerged with its two equal-size tangent-tension spoke wheels, pneumatic tires, and chain-driven rear wheel. The standard bicycle of today differs from this ancestor only in detail; except for the gear shift, the changes would scarcely be detectable to the casual observer. One reason the 1986 and 1886 bicycles are similar is that the 1886 version was so good, being efficient, safe, easy to ride, easy to store, and simple and inexpensive to build. But another reason is that bicycle competitions, which tend to set technological standards even if only a small percentage of cyclists compete, dictated that the vehicle be standardized (therefore not be improved) so no rider would have an unfair advantage. Like a species of animal, the multitude of these satisfactory bicycles fitted well their broadly based and economically driven "ecological niche" and the design evolved only very slowly and in minor ways as the decades went by.

One modern view of natural evolution has a new species sometimes evolving out of a stable, established species via a major, rapid, adaptive change labeled *punctuated equilibrium*. In a suggested scenario, a small group of animals somehow must operate in isolation from the main group, in a circumstance where different ecological pressures are found to be especially favorable to certain inheritable genetic aberrations or traits. The genes (the carriers of the creature's design to the next generation) of the odd superior individual in the large population get submerged in a massive gene pool and have little effect. But in a new, small, isolated ecological niche, the superior individual's superiority can be relatively more important for survival, the individual's genes will be less diluted in the small population, and in relatively few generations a new species can evolve. Eventually the new species may even spill over into the large original ecological niche, prove competitively superior there, and completely supplant the original species.

In 1975, the International Human-Powered Vehicle Association (IHPVA; P.O. Box 51255, Indianapolis, IN 46251) was formed to stimulate the development of fast human-powered vehicles without the inhibiting effects of rules. The sole criterion of success was "going fast," with no concern about the mechanism or configuration. The resulting evolution of new designs was rapid, as a small number of inventors (initially in Southern California) found what worked in this new isolated "ecological niche." Fantastic speeds are now being achieved (65 mph, 105 kmh); equilibrium was "punctuated."

After a few years of strictly speed competitions, IHPVA added competitions for "practical" vehicles. The definition of "practical" is still in a state of flux, as are the criteria for judging the vehicles, but the overall aim is clear: a human-powered vehicle that is safe, fast, versatile, comfortable, economical, and attractive to both commuters and long-distance riders. A new "species" can only evolve from this competition if a design emerges that is so satisfactory it becomes widely manufactured; no such design has yet been demonstrated.

For half a century there have occasionally been isolated pioneers showing that streamlined fairings permit high speeds or that unusual configurations show promise for meeting a specific customer's desires, but such aberrations had negligible impact on conventional bicycles. Serious developments of mainstream touring, sporting, and racing bicycles were economically driven and tended to be ones that could be comfortably assimilated into the mainstream, such as the 10-speed derailleur and improved brakes. The major trends that kept cycling healthy over the last few decades have been popularization of variations on the theme of the conventional two-wheel bicycles with standard seating position. The economy and versatility of the 10-speed gearshift brought many customers into the field. BMX bikes for competition and rough use around town have created a substantial new market, and mountain bikes are a recent success story.

IHPVA has popularized an enthusiasm for generating significant change and, with its competitions, media interactions, newsletters, and technical symposia, has stimulated inventors, cyclists, manufacturers, and universities to explore technologies for the future. The international publicity accorded early IHPVA records no doubt helped stimulate the aerodynamic innovations for standard bicycles that began in 1976. By 1978, aerodynamics, tubing, clothing, and helmets were commonly contributing to higher speeds. Dr. Chester R. Kyle, cofounder of IHPVA, has been a significant contributor to the technology that in 1984 produced the U.S. Olympic bicycles.

Rules and Their Effects

In 1938, the Union Cyclist Internationale (UCI) established rules against recumbents and streamlined fairings in racing. After the 1976 developments cited above, in 1978 the UCI loosened the rules on the prohibition of aerodynamic features. In 1984, an aerodynamic rule milestone (or millstone, depending on your point of view) was achieved when Moser was permitted to set an official 1-hr record at Mexico City with a bike that had been tailored in a wind tunnel and featured solid wheels, and subsequently similar Olympic bikes were accepted. The door for innovations via aerodynamic modification has certainly been opened a significant amount, but at the cost of some controversy about the past decisions and questions about where this all leads and what rules will best serve the purposes of cycling.

There is also the question of the criteria for competition. In a team sport, such as soccer, the winner is a team, not an individual. In a 100-m freestyle swimming race, the winner is clearly the individual. For a faired bicycle/ tricycle speed event or a human-powered airplane challenge, the vehicle is a major part, and the prize or honor is usually shared by the cyclist and the vehicle developer. In the Tour de France, an individual wins but is aided by his team. In international sailplane competitions, radio communications permit the several competitors from one country to coordinate thermal hunting and give an improved chance to each of them and a still larger chance to a particular one. Such coordinating communications complicate the issue of whether the winner is an individual or a team. This coordination is done by some countries with well-disciplined teams; with other countries where discipline is less characteristic and where the competition is clearly considered as selecting an individual winner, the radio is not used for collusion purposes (and a competitor may even use it to mislead the competition while also gleaning from it whatever useful information he or she can).

It seems logical to adopt the general principle that the official winner(s) of a competition is the individual or group whose efforts were dominant in determining the winning. For solo events where no apparatus is required (e.g., swimming and running) or where the apparatus offers no special advantage (e.g., tennis, bowling, chess), the principle is straightforward to apply: The winner is the winner. For team events, the team is clearly the winner. In every case, a coach/trainer may have made a significant contribution, even masterminding a football triumph, but the competitor(s) gets the official reward. Where the apparatus makes a unique contribution to winning, the designer/developer (or sometimes the sponsor) gets some or most of the plaudits.

Categories promote competition by matching competitors reasonably. The hare races the tortoise only in myth. Categories based on size or weight or age or sex are easily defined. Categories based on experience or ability are generally harder to define, and there is continuing controversy about amateur versus professional. Categorization is brought to a high level in BMX racing: age groups, subdivided into novice, intermediate, and expert classes based on the number of top finishes in a lower class.

Where the rules must also consider apparatus, categorization can get troublesome (except where the competition is about apparatus, as with the IHPVA speed event). Sailboat races between Hobie 16s or between Star Class boats should be fair, but questions do arise. One competitor may have better sails or a wider choice of sails. The rules committee has to decide what is permitted. For the Star Class, small improvements in design have been authorized that help keep the class technically up-to-date and that allow manufacturers to sell new models without wiping out the class.

Sailplane competitions have provided a strong stimulus for that sport since the first glider competitions in 1920 in Germany. Through the 1920s and 1930s and then after World War II, both contests and record attempts produced developments and performances that could not even have been imagined by the first pioneers. As the gliders became more efficient, the pilots learned how to locate and exploit upcurrents, first to stay aloft longer, then to fly further. The need for speed as well as efficiency drove the designs to higher wing loadings and to advanced structural concepts to provide safety even in the severe weather wherein the best lift was found. Regulations arose for safety reasons, in the form of certification for both the vehicles and the pilots. Before about 1950, contests considered duration, distance, and altitude; thereafter, the focus was on distance, which in effect combines all three. As distances got greater with improving vehicles, instrumentation, piloting strategy, and meteorological understanding, speed events were added, especially closed-course speeds that kept the sailplanes from venturing inconveniently far from the contest airport. There were no one-design competitions because there were so few vehicles of one type until the Schweizer 1-26 became ubiquitous. Competition categories did arise in the 1950s. There has always been the open class. Now there has been added a "standard" class (15-m span, no flaps) and a "15-m class" (like open class, but span limited to 15 m). Also there are now some initial competitions with self-launched (auxiliary-powered) sailplanes. In addition to the stimulus of sailplane competition, there are awards for achieving certain distances, durations, or altitudes (the Gold C, Diamond, etc.).

Sailplaning is just a hobby, but the forces for innovation have been so strong that the technological advances have been huge. Modern open-class sailplanes, with 22-m wingspans, glide as flat at 60:1 and, using thermals, complete triangle courses of hundreds of kilometers at average speeds exceeding 130km/h. The vehicles can cost more than $50,000, even before the instrumentation (including a flight-optimization computer) and radios and navigation gear and oxygen equipment are added.

The growth of hang gliding was rapid throughout the 1970s. The first contests were more the equivalent of picnics or get-togethers, but they served to fire the imaginations of everyone present. The only scoring was for spot landings and later bomb drops with bags of flour. The real goal was safe and pleasant flights with hang gliders having beautiful, individualistic appearances. By the mid-1970s the sport had matured to where the manufacturers combined voluntarily and established the certification of safe vehicles, while clubs supported a national organization to certify pilots. The safety record improved. Contests began focusing on aerial maneuvers, duration, and distance. Vehicle performance improved markedly. A small number of contest participants kept pushing manufacturers to better performance limits, but the larger number of sport pilots pushed manufacturers on a different course focused on control and comfort. In the U.S., the field has been getting smaller since its heyday in the late 1970s. Liability problems contributed to the decline, and also many pilots diverted into powered ultralight aircraft, sailplaning, and regular lightplanes. For hang gliding, the main benefit from rules was the improvement in safety.

The Heart of the Dilemma in Cycling

The simmering pot of aerodynamic improvements boiled over in 1984 when UCI made a controversial decision and accepted a record made with a disk wheel. The rules permitted design changes for structural reasons but not aerodynamic reasons. (General rule 49 stated ''...the use of protective shields, wind brakes, bodywork or other devices on any part of the bicycle . . . for the purpose of reducing wind resistance shall be prohibited.'') By omitting spokes and making the outer shell structural, the disk wheel was made legitimate. Its significant aerodynamic benefits were achieved, allegedly within the constraints of the rules. A spoked wheel covered with nonstructural lids, essentially identical in structural function and aerodynamic function, would be illegal. Who knows what the regulatory body would decide in the future about a spoked wheel with sturdy lids adding significantly to the structure. Designers and manufacturers now need to invest resources based on guesses about the rule interpretations of the future. The same goes for streamlined handlebars: supposedly built with an airfoil cross section for structural reasons, actually made that way for aerodynamic reasons (and apparently with little concern about the danger from the sharp trailing edge in an accident).

If you asked 100 cycling officials, competitors, and manufacturers the question, ''Are disk wheels and streamlined handlebars made because of structural benefits?'' you would get 100 ''no's.'' If you asked, ''Are they made because of their aerodynamic drag benefits?'' you would get 100 ''yeses.'' If you asked whether the disk wheels and streamlined handlebars fit either the intent or the letter of the UCI rules, there would be some differences of opinion; the rules are somewhat ambiguous, and so various interpretations are possible. If you asked whether they are good for the sport, there would also be differences.

The year when a structural change was made for obvious aerodynamic reasons, yet accepted as within the rules, was 1984. A philosopher, examining the implication of the decision that in effect ignores the contradiction in ''Aerodynamics is structure,'' would probably note the connection with another ''1984'': George Orwell's classic book. Orwell introduced us to ''doublethink,'' with Big Brother coaxing/coercing us to see no contradiction in phrases such as ''War is peace'' and ''Ignorance is strength.''

Increasing speeds, records, new heros, and new technology all help vitalize a field, lure participants, and fuel manufacturing. The new aerodynamic bicycles and clothing and helmets provide such benefits, but there is a question about where all this leads. Track meets, marathons, and jogging are all part of a field that has grown healthily, *without* controversy about equipment. Tennis is another sport where equipment is not expensive, and skill, not technology, determines the winner. Does cycling need aerodynamic improvements? A big stimulus to U.S. cycling in 1986 was Greg Le Mond's Tour de France victory. Would this stimulus have been altered by disk wheels on all participants rather than spoke wheels? I doubt it. Annual record breaking could be assured if the rules would feed in a little more use of aerodynamic fairings each year, but I suspect the negatives of such an approach would outweigh the benefits.

Resolving the Dilemma

To resolve the dilemma for the rest of this century requires input of people involved in all phases of cycling, especially those with the perspectives of philosophers and the mythical wisdom of Solomon. In the definition of a racing bicycle, there is no simple solution and no pleasing everyone, but the problem must be resolved. I find it disturbing to have observed designers paying much more attention to how to push the edges of the existing rules and how to exploit ambiguity than to how to straighten out the rules.

Now the dividing line between cycling competitions as human skill/stamina events and as technology events must be clarified. Pandora's Box has been opened and mischief will proliferate unless wisdom is applied. My prejudice is that future competitions that purport to determine the top athlete should use bicycles with limitations that clearly minimize advantages from aerodynamics (using bicycles and helmets that emphasize safety). Developments would focus especially on mechanisms (elliptical sprockets, cams, gears, etc.) and on training techniques. Other open competitions could be like those IHPVA already features, where aerodynamic innovation is given free rein. I cannot see the viability of a middle ground where aerodynamics is partially admitted, where the "intent" of a developer must be considered, where design rather than function is specified, where drag reduction is permitted by one means but not by another, where participants in the field are coaxed into practicing or accepting "doublethink." Because I am not closely connected to the cycling field, I do not have a high regard for my own prejudices in this area. I look forward to seeing how others who are more intimately involved handle the challenge for the next decade: how to define, unequivocally, the legitimate bicycle that advances cycling.

An obvious solution is to have the most prestigious cycling competitions be ones where equipment gives the rider no special advantage. One method is to provide identical bicycles to the contestants, or at least to require random switching of bicycles between contestants in multirace events. A special liability problem is introduced, however, if the rider is not responsible for his or her own equipment. Another method is to emphasize an event such as a hill climb, a low-speed event where bicycle differences confer very little advantage. The most generally applicable method would be to certify bicycles that all have a minimum drag at racing speeds.

The minimum drag technique could produce vehicles featuring safety and economy and take the pressure off pushing the limits of structure. With a high minimum weight, high minimum rolling (tire) drag, and a minimum aerodynamic drag (obtained any way the designer wants), speeds would be lower but records would continue to be set because of improved training.

Weight is easily determined. Total drag is difficult but not impossible to ascertain. Tire drag is at least rather independent of speed, and at high speed it is much less than aerodynamic drag but can vary with tire pressure, temperature, and surface. Aerodynamic drag can only be ascertained in a meaningful way if a "standardized rider shape" is mounted on the vehicle as the vehicle moves at the specified speed, say coasting down a slope or mounted in a tunnel. I am aware of the difficulties inherent in such calibration. I am not especially optimistic about obtaining a satisfactory resolution of the challenge, but anything seems better than the present situation of permitting aerodynamic improvements on a rather arbitrary basis. The concept deserves creative investigation before rejection, and, if rejected, the alternatives must be appreciated.

Goals, Rules, and Innovations

My observations and conclusions pertaining to these three topics may be listed as follows:

1. Publicized competitions foster innovation, even where the rules inhibit *major* innovation, because opportunity always exists for some innovation, and new and improved technology is of considerable interest to most riders and hence to manufacturers.
2. Paradoxes in the present cycling rules about structure versus aerodynamics must be resolved. The legitimate racing bicycle must be clearly and permanently defined, even if the definition represents a significant departure from today's aerodynamic bicycle. Competitors, inventors, manufacturers, spectators, and officials deserve such a clarification of what is a bicycle and of whether cycle racing is to be a test of competitors' skills or of vehicles.
3. In all sports involving equipment there is justification for some "open" events (consistent with safety), no matter how many "constrained" events there are.
4. For showing individual stamina and skill, high-speed races could be conducted on moderately slow, very safe bicycles (heavy ones with draggy aerodynamics and draggy fat tires) if a standard drag specification can be agreed on and measured. It is reasonable to suggest that some races and measurements be initiated to explore the concept, but I doubt that the present bicycle race culture would respond

with enthusiasm. Hill climbs and the related racing of mountain bikes over complex terrain are well accepted. Although the rider cannot establish a record applicable to other locations, there is the stimulus of local records and winning.

5. The IHPVA land vehicle races should continue, with at least the open class for absolute speed through 200-m traps and also a long open-category race of approximately 1 hr, in which vehicles must cope with maneuvering and winds. If a velodrome is available, a 4-km time trial is also desirable, as well as a 1-hr event.

6. In order to stimulate the development and appreciation of practical vehicles, such as could be used in commuting, competitions are held at the annual IHPVA event. However, the specific definition of "practical" is not agreed upon, and in any case the judging cannot be absolutely quantitative. Speed is readily measured but is only one contributor to a total score that incudes convenience, maneuverability, and safety. The imperfection of rules should not be considered a valid reason for avoiding the practical vehicle event.

7. In open categories, especially as exemplified by the IHPVA races, a useful philosophy is to have rules lag technical developments and so not inhibit the developments. Thus, although the IHPVA rules prohibit stored energy from sources outside the rider, a rider might be permitted to store energy (as in a battery) during one part of the event for use in a later part. Also, the vehicle could be permitted to exploit real-time wind power via a sail wing or on-board windmill. If energy storage or wind augmentation produced a race winner, great. If the advantage was so large that the new technique would be essential for future winners, then a new open category could be set up permitting it, and another "semi-open" category could be devised prohibiting it, or a single dominant category could be selected. Innovation is served by this attitude.

8. Technical symposia are effective at stimulating invention. They promote the exchange of ideas while establishing an enthusiasm for new creations.

9. The standard bicycle is an elegant design, with admirable dynamics, simplicity, and ruggedness. The touring bicycles of the year 2000 or even 2050, and perhaps even the racing bicycles, will probably be rather similar to the present vehicles. I suspect these will continue to win out in the marketplace over recumbents or even more divergent designs.

10. The future success of bicycles as commuting devices will depend less on technological improvements of vehicles than on social acceptance, traffic competition, foolproof locks, effective lighting and reflectors, and helmet laws. Safety is a dominant and ultimately limiting factor.

11. Auxiliary energy can assist commuting and touring. Just 2 or 3 lb of batteries can give you the equivalent of 1,000 ft of altitude to apply as you want: accelerating after stops or maintaining traffic speed up a hill. On a sunny day, 4 sq ft of solar cells can assist you with 0.05 HP continuously or can recharge a battery. Two or three pounds of rubber

bands can store the energy of a stop from 20 mph to be used in the subsequent speedup. Two or three pounds of gasoline can power the vehicle for hours or even days. However, you have to consider why you have a bicycle. If you really want a motorcycle or car, get one.

12. Formal rewards constitute a strong driving force for achievement, whether the rewards are dollars or ego fulfillment from fame or self-satisfaction from winning. A money prize for a technological development typically stimulates development efforts costing many times the prize amount. The Kremer prizes for human-powered flight triggered two decades of worldwide developments that probably represented an investment 30 times greater than the prize money. Formal prizes provide a beneficial focus for both inventors and competitors.

13. The preoccupation in our advanced countries on technology and competition deserves a lot of thought and discussion. Health, happiness, longevity, and appreciating and fitting in with nature rather than modifying or destroying it—these need consideration as we work on technological innovation. Goals, motivation, and rewards versus innovation may be imprecise subjects for exploration but, in my opinion, should be given high priority. Cycling, a positive subject with few negatives, can serve as a benign catalyst for such philosophizing.

14. Rules and categories inhibit innovation by limiting options, and stimulate innovation by motivating many riders to participate in the field and hence media interest and manufacturers to support and develop the field. There is no one answer to the conflicts inherent in simultaneously inhibiting and stimulating innovation. Persons setting up demonstrations, races, and records will have to accept complexity in rules and categories while striving for simplicity. Officials should be cautiously flexible. Some decisions will prove to be less successful than others; the decision makers will find that they cannot please everyone. Their rewards will be in knowing that they are helping with a sport of great value both to man the scientist and engineer and man the athlete and creature of nature.

Contributors

M. P. Argentieri
The Emergency Care Research
Institute
5200 Butler Pike
Plymouth Meeting, PA 19462

M. A. Boitano
USNH—Box 141
FPO, Seattle, WA 98778

Edmund R. Burke, PhD
Spenco Medical Corporation
P.O. Box 2501
Waco, TX 76702-2501

Phillip S. Clifford, PhD
Anesthesia Research
VA Medical Center
Milwaukee, WI 53295

Leo P.V.M. Clijsen
Interfaculty of Physical
Education
Free University of Amsterdam
Department of Exercise
Physiology and Health
Mgr. V.D. Venstraat Space 49
5482 El, Schijndel
The Netherlands

J. Richard Coast, PhD
Human Performance
Laboratory
Department of Health and
Physical Education
Texas A&M University
College Station, TX 77843

Francesco Conconi
Centro di Studi Biomedici
Applicati allo Sport
Via Luigi Borsari, 46
44100 Ferrara
Italy

David L. Costill, PhD
Human Performance Laboratory
Ball State University
Muncie, IN 47306

Peter R. Francis, PhD
San Diego State University
San Diego, CA 92182

Randolph G. Ice
Human Performance Center
12200 East Washington
Boulevard
Suite O
Whittier, CA 90606

Andrew A. Jacobs
The Winning Edge
6724 Troost, Suite 407
Kansas City, MO 64131

Chester R. Kyle, PhD
California State University
1250 Bellflower Boulevard
Longbeach, CA 90840

Norman F. LaVoie
School of Physical Education
Lakehead University
Thunder Bay, Ontario P7B 5EI
Canada

Jon G. McLennan
293 Willow Street
Bishop, CA 93514

Paul B. MacCready
AeroVironment, Inc.
825 Myrtle Avenue
Monronia, CA 91016

Jan Melichna
Department of Psychology
Univerzita Karlova
Ovocny trh 5
Czechoslavakia

Mary M. Newsom
Department of Educational
Services
United States Olympic
Committee
1750 East Boulder Street
Colorado Springs, CO 80909

Ed Price
Department of Physiology and
Biochemistry
Palmer College of Chiropractic
— West
Sunnyvale, CA 94087

Andrew L. Pruitt, MS, ATC
Western Orthopaedic Sports
Medicine and Rehabilitation
1824 Williams Street
Denver, CO 80218

Frank S. Pyke
Centre for Sports Studies
Canberra College of Advanced
Education
P.O. Box 1
Belconnen ACT 2616
Australia

John G. Seifert
Exercise Physiology Laboratory
The Quaker Oats Company
617 W. Main Street
Berrington, IL 60010

David P. Swain, PhD
Division of Health, Physical
Educaton and Recreation
Marshall University
Huntington, WV 25701

Peter J. Van Handel, PhD
USOTC — Division of Sports
Medicine
1750 East Boulder
Colorado Springs, CO 80909

Paul S. Visich
Borgess Medical Center
Institute for Cardiovascular
Health
1521 Gull Road
Kalamazoo, MI 49001

David Gordon Wilson
Massachusetts Institute of
Technology
Mechanical Engineering,
Room 3-455
Cambridge, MA 01239